1 View over Cheddar Gorge. 2 The National Trust Village of Allerford. 3 Cruising the Kennet and Avon Canal. 4 Walking the Coleridge Way. 5 The country's only apple distillery, the Somerset Cider Brandy Company.

LOCAL LIFE

Small towns and villages such as Frome, Axminster and Nunney are typically great places to experience local Somerset life, whether you're just there for a potter or for one of the monthly farmers' markets – or, better still, a pint in the pub.

MALCOLM MCHUGH/A

LORETTA DAMSKA/S

TRAVELLINGLIGHT/ISTOCK

BILLY STOCK/S

Bradt

Somerset

*Whether it's nosing around a hamstone church, wildlife
watching on the Levels, enjoying a tipple of cider,
or going for long walks across Exmoor,
Somerset does Slow better than anywhere.*

CRAIG JOINER PHOTOGRAPHY/A

NIGEL JARVIS/S

ADAM BURTON/AWL

GUY EDWARDES PHOTOGRAPHY/A

1 Glastonbury's colourful High Street. 2 Dunster is one of the best-preserved medieval villages in England. 3 The golden-toned hamstone village of Montacute. 4 King John's Hunting Lodge, Axbridge. 5 The village of Nunney is dominated by its castle. 6 The Flemish-style Market House, Castle Cary. 7 Selworthy – a taste of quintessential rural England. 8 Hauser & Wirth, Bruton.

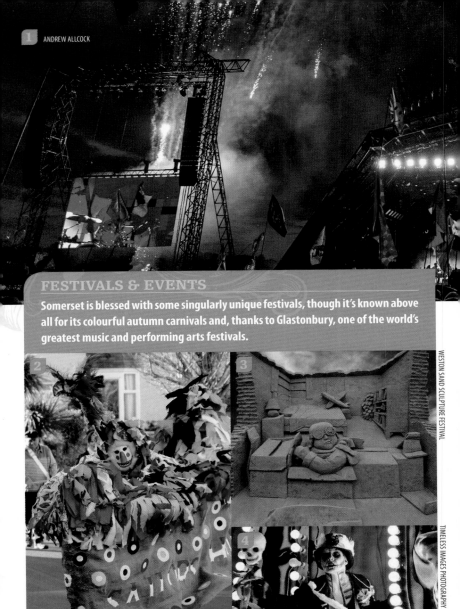

FESTIVALS & EVENTS

Somerset is blessed with some singularly unique festivals, though it's known above all for its colourful autumn carnivals and, thanks to Glastonbury, one of the world's greatest music and performing arts festivals.

1 The legendary Pyramid Stage, Glastonbury. 2 Minehead's weird and wonderful Hobby Horse Festival. 3 Weston-super-Mare's Sand Sculpture Festival attracts master sculptors from around the world. 4 Bridgwater Carnival claims to be the largest illuminated carnival in Europe. 5 Exmoor National Park is perfect for star-gazing.

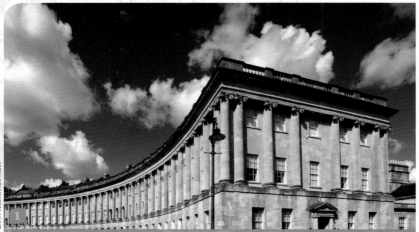

BATH

From its world-famous Roman Baths to a wealth of glorious Georgian architecture, the UK's only UNESCO World Heritage City is unmissable – and close by are some exciting trails, including the brilliant Two Tunnels walk.

1 The Royal Crescent. 2 Thermae Bath Spa offers glorious city views. 3 The Roman Baths. 4 Exhibits at the Herschel Museum of Astronomy.

AUTHOR

Norm Longley was brought up in Somerset, attending schools in Yeovil and the Quantocks, and after a 15-year hiatus – albeit still returning on a regular basis to see family and friends and the occasional Yeovil Town game – moved back in 2009, settling in the village of Chilcompton, roughly equidistant between Bath and Wells. With his family he often spends weekends roaming the

Somerset countryside in search of exciting and/or novel things to do – or at the very least, hunting down good food and drink. He has been a guidebook writer for around 20 years and has written for *The Guardian* and *Independent*.

AUTHOR'S STORY

I have lived in Somerset, on and off, for most of my life, originally moving here at the age of seven and attending school in the wonderful Quantock Hills. As a family we rarely ventured beyond the county's borders, which was certainly no bad thing, my earliest memories being of outings to Weston-super-Mare and fossicking on Kilve Beach. Walks weren't particularly high on the agenda, at least not until scouting expeditions to more exotic (or so they seemed) outposts, such as Black Down on the Mendips and Dunkery Beacon on Exmoor. An extended period of time living away from Somerset – in Serbia, London and Cambridge among other places – did nothing to dampen my enthusiasm for the county. In fact, these absences only served to remind me of just some of the things I'd missed: lush meadows and apple-rich orchards, rolling green hills, and the marshy wetlands with their stunning birdlife.

Still, absence makes the heart grow fonder, so they say, and it wasn't before time – in 2009 – that I returned permanently to Somerset, eventually settling in Chilcompton, which is very much my home base now. And when the opportunity arose to write a book on my home county, naturally I jumped at the chance. Hence, with family frequently in tow, I tried to leave no stone, or indeed corner, unturned: I've hiked hidden valleys, cycled abandoned railway lines, observed common cranes on the Levels, camped in the rain on Exmoor – and, of course, sampled lots of cider. We've loved every minute of it – I hope you do too.

First edition published August 2019
Bradt Travel Guides Ltd
31a High Street, Chesham, Buckinghamshire, HP5 1BW, England
www.bradtguides.com
Print edition published in the USA by The Globe Pequot Press Inc,
PO Box 480, Guilford, Connecticut 06437-0480

Project Manager: Anna Moores
Cover research: Yoshimi Kanazawa
Colour section research: Marta Bescos

ISBN: 978 1 78477 617 6

British Library Cataloguing in Publication Data
A catalogue record for this book is available from the British Library

Photographs
© individual photographers credited beside images & also those from picture libraries
credited as follows: Alamy.com (A); Avalon Marshes Landscape Team, Somerset Wildlife Trust
(AMLT, SWT); Awl-images.com (AWL); Bath & North East Somerset council (BNESC); Exmoor
National Park Authority (ENPA); istockphoto.com (iStock); Shutterstock.com (S);
@somersetciderbrandy (SCBC); Superstock.com (SS); Visit Exmoor (VE)

Front cover The Somerset Levels, taken from Glastonbury Tor (Ahmad Alsharhan/
Alamy Stock Photo)
Back cover Catherine Hill, Frome (Nigel Jarvis/S)
Title page The Circus, Bath (Mark Sunderland/AWL)

Maps David McCutcheon FBCart.S
Typeset by Ian Spick, Bradt Travel Guides and Pepi Bluck, Perfect Picture

Production managed by Jellyfish Print Solutions; printed in the UK
Digital conversion by www.dataworks.co.in

ACKNOWLEDGMENTS

First of all, huge thanks to the people of Somerset – far too many to mention here – who have been so generous with their time, and without whom there would of course be no book at all.

Thank you to Emma Gibbs for doing such a sterling job editing, while I also reserve enormous gratitude to the team at Bradt, especially Anna Moores and Rachel Fielding, who have helped see this project through – their patience has been nothing short of extraordinary. Thanks, too, to Tim Locke for support and guidance, especially with walks and mapping.

Above all, love and thanks to Christian, Anna, Luka and Paddy, not only for accompanying me on innumerable excursions and lengthy walks, but also for their support during those times when the well had almost run dry.

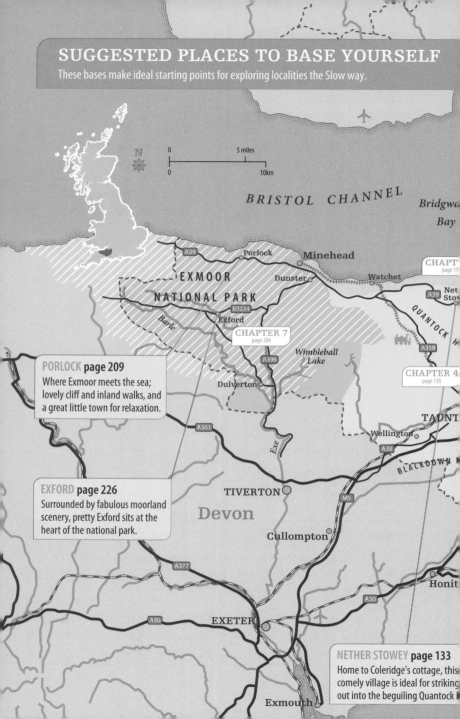

SUGGESTED PLACES TO BASE YOURSELF

These bases make ideal starting points for exploring localities the Slow way.

0   5 miles

0   10km

N

BRISTOL CHANNEL

Bridgwa
Bay

A39   Porlock   **Minehead**

Dunster   Watchet

EXMOOR

NATIONAL PARK

B3224

Barle

Exford

CHAPTER 7
page 204

Wimbleball
Lake

A396

Dulverton

CHAPT
page 15

Net
Sto

A39

QUANTOC

A358

CHAPTER 4
page 130

TAUNT

Wellington

A38

BLACKDOWN

PORLOCK page 209

Where Exmoor meets the sea;
lovely cliff and inland walks, and
a great little town for relaxation.

A361

Exe

EXFORD page 226

Surrounded by fabulous moorland
scenery, pretty Exford sits at the
heart of the national park.

TIVERTON

Devon

M5

Cullompton

A377

Honit

A30

A30

EXETER

NETHER STOWEY page 133

Home to Coleridge's cottage, this
comely village is ideal for striking
out into the beguiling Quantock

Exmouth

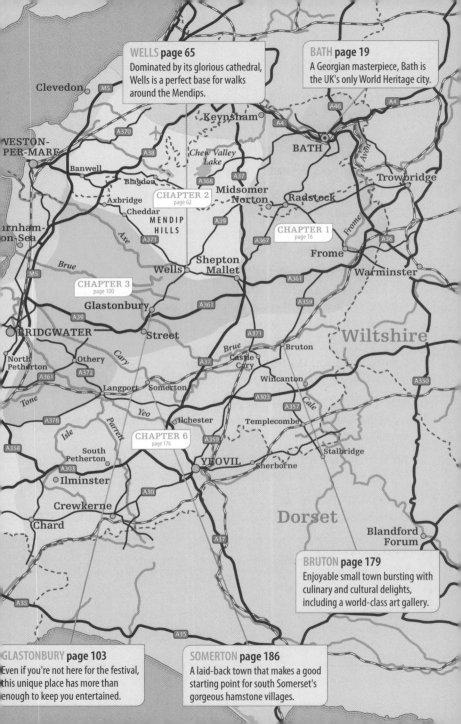

WELLS page 65
Dominated by its glorious cathedral, Wells is a perfect base for walks around the Mendips.

BATH page 19
A Georgian masterpiece, Bath is the UK's only World Heritage city.

CHAPTER 2
page 62

CHAPTER 1
page 16

CHAPTER 3
page 100

CHAPTER 6
page 176

BRUTON page 179
Enjoyable small town bursting with culinary and cultural delights, including a world-class art gallery.

GLASTONBURY page 103
Even if you're not here for the festival, this unique place has more than enough to keep you entertained.

SOMERTON page 186
A laid-back town that makes a good starting point for south Somerset's gorgeous hamstone villages.

Clevedon
WESTON-SUPER-MARE
Banwell
Blagdon
Axbridge
Cheddar
Burnham-on-Sea
Wells
Glastonbury
BRIDGWATER
Street
North Petherton
Othery
Langport
Somerton
South Petherton
Ilminster
Crewkerne
Chard

Keynsham
Chew Valley Lake
Midsomer Norton
Radstock
MENDIP HILLS
Shepton Mallet
Bruton
Castle Cary
Wincanton
Ilchester
Templecombe
YEOVIL
Stalbridge
Sherborne
Blandford Forum

BATH
Trowbridge
Frome
Warminster

Wiltshire
Dorset

Axe
Brue
Cary
Brue
Tone
Isle
Parrett
Yeo
Cale
Frome
Avon

M5
A370
A38
A368
A37
A39
A371
A361
A39
A361
A371
A37
A359
A303
A357
A359
A30
A37
A35
A358
A303
A361
A372
A378
A46
A4
A36
A350
A367

CONTENTS

FOLLOW US

Tag us in your posts and share your adventures using this guide with us – we'd love to hear from you.

f BradtTravelGuides   @BradtGuides & @normlongley
@bradtguides   bradtguides
bradtguides

SOMERSET

The inhabitants of this county are plain, honest, and hospitable, but unpolished, and reserved in conversation. They entertain a kind of indifference for the rest of the world, owing, probably, to the good opinion they entertain of their own portion of it.
John Strachey, 1737

Slow Somerset – has a nice ring to it, doesn't it? But what does that mean? Carlo Petrini, founder of the Slow Food Movement, once suggested that Slow was 'about learning to give time to each and every thing' – and for me, that certainly includes travel. In fact, in many parts of Somerset it's impossible to do anything other than take it Slow – whether that's because you're stuck behind a tractor trundling along one of the narrow, meandering country lanes, or because you're caught in lengthy conversation over a pint of cider with a couple of locals down the village pub. Patience is a necessity, as well as a virtue, here. Somerset has so much to offer the Slow traveller: coastal paths and bracing moorland walks, ancient ruins and castellated hamstone churches, wild wetland reserves with brilliant birdwatching, local farmers' markets, and, as you'd expect, endless possibilities for cider tasting.

Somerset frequently confounds expectations – it certainly confounded mine during the course of writing this book, and I've lived here on and off for most of my life. A county of immense rural beauty, pretty villages and stunning landscapes, Somerset take its name from the old English word Sumorsaete, meaning 'land of the summer people' or 'people dwelling in a summer pasture', supposedly because this is the time when the natives would celebrate the coming of warmer days with festivals and gatherings having hunkered down all winter. It is also, of course, the land of cider and cheese, so one thing's for sure: you'll not go thirsty or hungry in this part of the world. England's seventh largest – and for many its most quintessentially English – county, Somerset extends from the hills of Exmoor in the west to Bruton Forest in the east, from the Mendip Hills in the north to the Blackdowns in the south.

From the high coastal cliffs of Kilve and bracing scrubland of **Exmoor**, to the intimate wooded coombes of the **Quantocks** and the bleak mystery of the **Levels**, Somerset packs in more scenic variety than any other county I know. So when people ask me what my favourite place is, I can honestly say that I don't know. It changes frequently. While few places in Somerset can rival the Levels for my affections, I love walking across the wind-blown moorland of Black Down on the Mendips, or the silent expanse of Berrow Beach, while, on a clear, crisp day, nothing beats standing atop Dunkery Beacon in Exmoor looking northwards towards Pembrokeshire and the Brecon Beacons in Wales. And it's these same landscapes that have for centuries fired the imagination of writers

THE SLOW MINDSET

Hilary Bradt, Founder, Bradt Travel Guides

We shall not cease from exploration
And the end of all our exploring
Will be to arrive where we started
And know the place for the first time.
T S Eliot, 'Little Gidding', *Four Quartets*

This series evolved, slowly, from a Bradt editorial meeting when we started to explore ideas for guides to our favourite country – Great Britain. We wanted to get away from the usual 'top sights' formula and encourage our authors to bring out the nuances and local differences that make up a sense of place – such things as food, building styles, nature, geology, or local people and what makes them tick. Our aim was to create a series that celebrates the present, focusing on sustainable tourism, rather than taking a nostalgic wallow in the past.

So without our realising it at the time, we had defined 'Slow travel', or at least our concept of it. For the beauty of the Slow movement is that there is no fixed definition;

we adapt the philosophy to fit our individual needs and aspirations. Thus Carl Honoré, author of *In Praise of Slow*, writes: 'The Slow Movement is a cultural revolution against the notion that faster is always better. It's not about doing everything at a snail's pace, it's about seeking to do everything at the right speed. Savouring the hours and minutes rather than just counting them. Doing everything as well as possible, instead of as fast as possible. It's about quality over quantity in everything from work to food to parenting.' And travel.

So take time to explore. Don't rush it, get to know an area – and the people who live there – and you'll be as delighted as we are by what you find.

and poets, from R D Blackmore's *Lorna Doone*, set in 17th-century Exmoor, to Coleridge and Wordsworth, who both made the Quantocks their home for a short period of time.

The county has found favour with other distinguished personalities too. The influence of celebrated architect Edwin Lutyens, for example, runs right through the village of **Mells**, though he is also much lauded for his work at **Hestercombe Gardens**, alongside the renowned horticulturist Gertrude Jekyll – who was also responsible for showpiece gardens at Tintinhull and Barrington Court among others. My favourite garden, though, is the Margery Fish-designed **East Lambrook Manor Gardens**, which eschews formality in favour of colourful chaos. Tied in with many of these gardens are great properties, none more so than the sumptuous Elizabethan masterpiece that is **Montacute House**.

During the 15th and early 16th centuries, Somerset was one of the wealthiest areas in England, having grown rich on the wool trade, and this former prosperity is reflected in the quality of its churches, which are among the county's most thrilling and distinctive architectural landmarks: St James's in Cameley, St Mary's in Ilminster, and All Saints' in Martock are all superb specimens in this regard. Many of these take their inspiration from the peerless Wells Cathedral, one of England's great ecclesiastical glories – though the haunting, mist-swathed ruins of **Glastonbury Abbey** run it close.

For those seeking further cultural sustenance, well, beautiful **Bath** has it in spades, thanks to its world-famous Roman Baths and its legacy of extraordinary Georgian architecture, among much else, though it's hard to beat a day exploring **Wells's** small-town charms (for the record, it's actually England's smallest city) or **Bruton**, arguably Somerset's current cultural and gastronomic hotspot. The county's picturesque high points are many: among my favourites are Chew Valley, Burrington Combe, Clevedon Pier, Cadbury Castle and the distinctive hamstone villages of south Somerset – though no doubt you'll have your own.

A TASTE OF SOMERSET

Great wages and little work seem to be the general system of this place. The Somersetshire people are of large size and strong and very much given to eating and drinking.
Reverand William Holland, Over Stowey, 1799

The taste of Somerset is undoubtedly that of two things: cider and cheese. Despite competing claims from the likes of Herefordshire and Devon, Somerset is cider king, no question. Indeed cider has been produced in Somerset since the 11th century, making it one of the country's original cider-making counties; as well as being a jolly tasty alcoholic beverage, it was said to possess numerous health-inducing properties – maybe it still does. In any case, it was my good fortune (when I wasn't driving, that is) to be able to visit a number of the county's 30 or so cider producers during my travels for this guide. This also resulted in some entertaining encounters with a number of larger-than-life personalities, like Roger Wilkins of the eponymous scrumpy farm (page 110) and Julian Temperley, owner of the Somerset Cider Brandy Company (page 199) – two of Somerset's most idiosyncratic cider producers; it's worth noting though that smaller enterprises, such as Ham Hill Cider in Haselbury Plucknett (see box, page 196), are just as rewarding. Either way, a visit to Somerset is simply not complete without an excursion to a cider maker.

Playing a close second fiddle to cider is cheese, but not just any old cheese: this is the land of Cheddar. Sold in varying stages of maturity, cheddar is actually a generic name, hence it can be – and is – produced anywhere in the world, though it did originate in Somerset's eponymous gorge in the 12th century. It's still produced here, and still stored in its famous caves. Widely acknowledged to be two of Somerset's finest cheddar makers – and definitely worth a special visit – are Montgomery's in North Cadbury and the Westcombe Dairy in Evercreech. But there's more to Somerset cheese than just cheddar; a few others worth sampling are Somerset brie from the Lubborn Creamery (in Cricket St Thomas), Buffalo Blue from the Exmoor Blue Cheese Company (in Bishops Lydeard), all of which you can find in local farm shops, and Somerset ricotta from the aforementioned Westcombe Dairy.

To cider and cheese you can add any number of other uniquely Somerset products: Mendip lamb, Porlock Bay oysters (see box, page 212), Yeo Valley yoghurt, orchard fruits – including whortleberries from Exmoor – and, rather deliciously, smoked eels; for the last, you need go no further than the brilliant Brown and Forrest Smokery near Langport (page 127), which smokes just about anything that can be smoked.

An enjoyable way to experience Somerset's bountiful array of foodstuffs is to visit one of the monthly farmers' markets, where you

SOMERSET FARMERS' MARKETS

Axbridge first Saturday of the month (09.00–13.00; The Square)
Burnham-on-Sea last Friday of the month (09.00–13.00; High St)
Crewkerne third Saturday of the month (09.00–13.00; Henhayes Centre)
Frome second Saturday of the month (09.00–13.00; Cheese & Grain music & entertainment centre)
Glastonbury fourth Saturday of the month (09.00–14.00; Market Cross)
Keynsham second Saturday of the month (09.00–13.00; Market Walk)
Midsomer Norton first Saturday of the month (09.00–13.00; Hollies Gardens)
SFM@Frome Independent first Sunday of the month (10.00–13.00; throughout the town centre)

can browse, sample and of course buy fantastically fresh, seasonal produce; see the box above for a complete list of these markets. Failing that, you'll no doubt stumble across one of the county's many farm shops, which, if they don't sell produce from their own farmland estate (and many do), will, at the very least, be well stocked with locally sourced treats; many have an on-site café, too. Talking of which, there are some wonderful community cafés, few more enjoyable than the Strawberry Line Café in Yatton (see box, page 77), which employs adults with learning difficulties. Otherwise you can find tea shops in abundance, though especially in Exmoor.

More generally, eating out in Somerset is now a real joy, which almost certainly wasn't the case even just a few years ago. In this regard you'll find some truly wonderful country inns; a few places worth making a special effort to get to are the Lord Poullet Arms in Hinton St George (page 203), the White Hart in Somerton (page 187), and The Sheppey in Lower Godney on the Somerset Levels (page 112). But if it's straightforward Somerset ale you're after – from larger local breweries such as Bath Ales and Butcombe Brewing to artisanal outfits like the Quantock Brewery and the Wild Beer Co – then you might care to try one or two of my favourite pubs, such as the Queen Vic in Priddy (page 98) or the Railway Inn in Sandford (page 83) – though for sheer quirkiness you can't beat the Hunter's Lodge Inn near Wells (page 98). You'll no doubt stumble across your own favourite. Wine is something not normally associated with Somerset, but the industry is flourishing here, something that I can happily vouch for. Among the half a dozen or so small-scale wineries currently flying the flag for the county, two of my favourites are Wraxall near Shepton Mallet (page 61), and Smith & Evans near Langport (page 120); you'll find their wines in many of the farm shops, plus the occasional restaurant.

GETTING TO & AROUND SOMERSET

By its very nature, Slow travel favours public transport and leg power. At the beginning of each chapter I have given some suggestions for getting to and around each area, including car-free options wherever possible, and also ideas for walking and cycling – there's certainly no shortage of those two possibilities here in Somerset. Inevitably, it's not feasible to get to every place described in this book by public transport – and this is especially true of some of the less touristed sights, which by their very nature lie well off the beaten track – hence getting to them may well necessitate a car journey. This is no bad thing in Somerset, as many of the routes are fantastically scenic, and whether it's traversing the Levels,

SOMERSET WILDLIFE TRUST

Somerset is one of the most exciting and diverse counties in England in terms of biodiversity, and this is manifest in some truly outstanding wildlife-rich sites in landscapes as diverse as the Mendip Hills and the Somerset Levels. Doing a sterling job in helping to preserve this precious natural heritage is the Somerset Wildlife Trust (SWT). Formed in 1964 and now Somerset's leading environmental charity, the volunteer-run trust is responsible for somewhere in the region of 80 nature reserves, most of which are open daily and free to visit. Alongside flagship reserves like Catcott (page 114) and Westhay Moor (page 111), are many lesser-known ones such as Edford Meadow, renowned for its orchids and wildflowers, and Draycott Sleights (page 74), a great

spot for observing blue butterflies. One of the trust's most successful projects to date has been the restoration of former industrial peat diggings into prime wetland habitats in order to provide internationally important wintering habitats and spring breeding grounds for wetland birds, including many vulnerable species. Another major initiative is their Living Landscape Scheme, which aims to restore and reconnect wildlife habitats to the surrounding landscape.

The SWT run a superb series of events and talks all year round, which range from dawn chorus, butterfly or wildflower walks, to litter picks and coastal forages; there's a minimal charge in most cases, and they're a fantastic way to get kids involved in the wonderful outdoors.

a ride across the top of Exmoor or journeying through quiet country lanes, you'll likely find yourself constantly distracted.

PUBLIC TRANSPORT

General travel information for the county is available at ⊘ visitsomerset. co.uk, while ⊘ traveline.info is useful for journey planning. The main rail operators servicing the area are **Great Western Railway** (⊘ gwr. com), with regular mainline trains from London Paddington to Bath, Weston-super-Mare and Taunton (and more sporadic services to Castle Cary), as well as stations on the Weymouth to Bristol line (including to Castle Cary, Bruton, Frome and Bath); and **South Western Railway** (⊘ southwesternrailway.com), with services from London Waterloo to Yeovil Junction.

Local **buses** are fairly comprehensive, with numerous services fanning out from the likes of Bath, Yeovil, Taunton and Bridgwater, although services are inevitably limited in the more rural areas and may only operate on certain days. Don't expect much by way of Sunday services, anywhere in the county. There's more detailed travel information at the beginning of each chapter.

WALKING

Somerset is wonderful walking country, as I have discovered repeatedly during the course of writing this book. From the breezy heights of Exmoor and the Mendips to the rounded, green hills of Blackdown and the reclaimed wetlands of the Somerset Levels, rambling opportunities are endless – and endlessly varied. The views can be sensational: Dunkery Beacon on Exmoor, Hurlstone Point on the coast, Black Down in the Mendips, Brean Down, Glastonbury Tor, Cadbury Castle – these are just a few of the county's many magnificent vantage points.

Numerous long-distance footpaths bisect the county, the best known of which is the **South West Coast Path,** which begins in Minehead and leaves Somerset at County Gate near Malsmead, before winding its way around the Cornish coast and finishing up in Poole in Dorset, a total of 630 miles. Less strenuous treks include the 51-mile-long **Coleridge Way**, from Nether Stowey in the Quantocks to Lynmouth in Devon (though still in Exmoor); the **Macmillan Way West**, from Castle Cary to Barnstaple; and the **Mendip Way**, a 50-mile jaunt through the hills, starting in Frome and finishing near Brean Down. Of course, these are just the named trails, and, as such, does not necessarily render them the most rewarding treks. In most, but not all, chapters I have suggested a walk (sometimes several), the majority of which are decent leg stretchers. The ♀ icon on the regional maps indicates the location of each walk. Armed with a decent map (see below), you can of course always devise a walk of your own.

Walking maps & guides

Walkers and cyclists should get hold of the **maps** produced by the always dependable Ordnance Survey (⊘ ordnancesurvey.co.uk), either the pink-covered 1:50,000 Landranger series or the far more detailed orange-covered 1:25,000 Explorer series. The OL9 double-sided map covers all of Exmoor, while others covering the areas in this book are maps 128 *Taunton & Blackdown Hills*, 129 *Yeovil & Sherborne*, 140 *Quantock Hills & Bridgwater*, 141 *Cheddar Gorge & Mendip Hills West*, and 142 *Shepton Mallet & Mendip Hills East*.

If you're contemplating walking some (or indeed all) of the South West Coast Path, the best available guide is Cicerone's *The South West Coast Path*. Other walking guides to Somerset available include the AA's *50 Walks in Somerset*, and Jarrold's *Somerset from Bath to the Quantocks*, though both of these are now a little dated.

CYCLING

Somerset has an abundance of shared-use walking and cycling routes, many of which have appropriated the county's numerous defunct railway lines and canal towpaths. Three such paths – and ones that we as a family are very partial to – are the **Colliers Way**, the brilliantly conceived **Two Tunnels Greenway** (the longest cycle tunnel in the country) and the **Strawberry Line**. These routes are invariably incorporated within long-distance national cycle routes managed by Sustrans (⊘ sustrans.org.uk) – for example, the Collier's Way is part of Route 24.

Elsewhere, the county offers more than sufficient diversity to keep every kind of cyclist happy, from the tough, hilly climbs around Cheddar Gorge and the Mendips (a good friend of mine swears by night-time cycling here), to less exerting, but no less enjoyable, rides across the Somerset Levels or through the quiet country lanes of south Somerset. Mountain biking, too, is becoming ever more popular, with Exmoor and the Mendips in particular offering ideal terrain, including plenty of single-track trails, for hardcore enthusiasts. Bike hire is readily available in those areas where cycling is a prominent activity, such as the Mendips and Exmoor.

For information on maps, see opposite.

HOW THIS BOOK IS ARRANGED

MAPS

The map at the front of this book shows the area covered in each of the seven chapters. In turn, each chapter begins with a sketch map of the area, highlighting the places mentioned in the text. The numbers on the maps correspond to the descriptions in the text, helping you to find your way around. The ♀ on these maps indicates that there is a walk in the area. There are also sketch maps of these featured walks.

ACCOMMODATION

At the back of this guide (page 234), I've listed some accommodation ideas for each area, a mixture of camping, self-catering, B&B and hotels. Each was chosen because it has a special quality, be that location, character or service, or indeed all three of these. The hotels and B&B options are indicated by ♠ and self-catering ones by ⌂ under the heading for the area in which they are located. Campsites are indicated by ▲. Prices change regularly so are not mentioned, but I have tried to suggest whether a place is an upmarket option or more suited to the budget conscious.

FOOD & DRINK

I've included a cross section of my favourite food and drink options, including farm shops, food producers, cafés, pubs and restaurants. They were selected because they serve local produce or follow sustainable principles, or are just exceptionally good or atmospheric.

ATTRACTIONS

For attractions and activities, I have listed contact details and opening hours but it is worth checking websites for any changes. I have not listed admission fees as these change regularly. If a description does not say admission is free, you should expect to be charged.

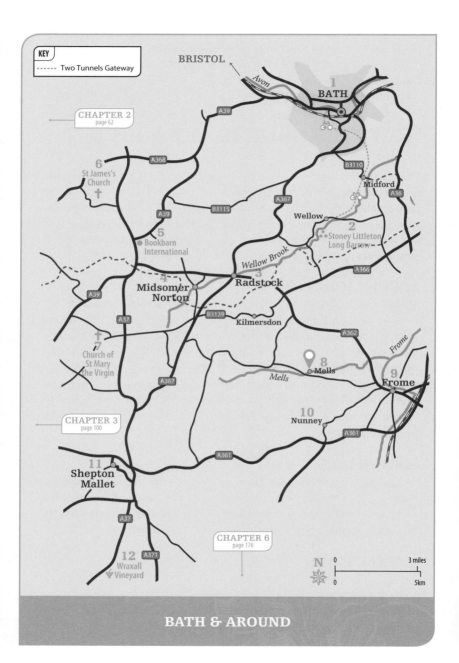

BRISTOL

Avon

1
BATH

CHAPTER 2
page 62

A39

A39

6
St James's
Church

A368

B3110

Midford

A36

B3115

A367

Wellow

2
Stoney Littleton
Long Barrow

5
Bookbarn
International

Wellow Brook

3

A366

4
Midsomer
Norton

Radstock

A39

A37

B3139

Kilmersdon

A362

Frome

7
Church of
St Mary
the Virgin

8
Mells

Mells

9
Frome

A367

CHAPTER 3
page 100

10
Nunney

A361

11
Shepton
Mallet

A361

CHAPTER 6
page 176

A37

N

0   3 miles

0   5km

12
Wraxall
Vineyard

A371

BATH & AROUND

1
BATH & AROUND

Although not an obvious Slow destination – it is a city after all – it was clear from the outset that **Bath** had a prominent role to play in this book. True, it can feel as if swamped by tourists at times, but I defy anyone not to be enraptured by its dazzling Georgian architecture and stupendous vistas. There are possibilities, too, for more exertive pleasures, such as the perennially popular Skyline Walk or the brilliantly conceived Two Tunnels Greenway. Heading due south from Bath, you hit coal-mining country, or at least what once was. To this end, there are many inducements to linger: the marvellous museum in **Radstock**, an otherwise nondescript town that wouldn't ordinarily feature on most people's radars, and a superbly restored section of the **Somerset and Dorset Joint Railway**, operating out of neighbouring **Midsomer Norton**. Also tipping its hat to the coal industry, and one of my favourite walks-cum-cycle rides anywhere in Somerset, is the **Colliers Way**, borne out of the remnants of the old Somersetshire Coal Canal and railway. Aside from being my home turf, I've always enjoyed a bit of hard-hitting industrial heritage, so this much underrated part of the county was a real joy for me to explore. But there are gentler outposts in these parts too: the villages of **Mells** and **Nunney** are blessed with outstandingly rich histories, the former littered with the works of celebrated architect Edwin Lutyens, the latter boasting a magnificent moated castle, one of just three in Somerset. Elsewhere, historic churches at Cameley and Emborough offer further cultural sustenance.

The only other centres of any discernible size covered in this chapter are **Frome** and **Shepton Mallet**, the former bursting with great energy and ideas, the latter a somewhat more unfashionable destination but not without merit. And while this chapter may be on the margins of cider country – more of those particular pleasures later on in the book – by way of compensation, there are also one or two commendable wineries where you can happily quaff an afternoon away.

GETTING THERE & AROUND

Bath has excellent road links, not least the M4, which skirts the city en route to Wales, and the A4, which links the city with Bristol. Most other places in this chapter are reasonably well served by bus, either from Bath, or between each other, though having your own wheels will of course make life that little bit easier.

TRAINS

Great Western Railway (⊘ gwr.com) operates train services from London Paddington to **Bath Spa** (taking just 90 minutes), which continue on to Bristol. GWR also operate the painfully slow, albeit intermittently picturesque, line between Bristol and Weymouth in Dorset, calling at Bath, Frome, Bruton, Castle Cary and Yeovil Pen Mill among other stations. Bath is also on the Cardiff–Portsmouth line, run by South Western Railway (⊘ southwesternrailway.com). Frome is also served by infrequent trains from London Paddington (taking 2 hours).

BUSES

Bus possibilities in this part of Somerset are decent. As you'd expect, Bath is the hub, with a comprehensive network of buses – mostly operated by First Bus (⊘ firstgroup.com/bath) – fanning out from the centre to outlying areas, including west to Bristol and, most useful for this chapter, south to Radstock and Frome.

CYCLING

This part of the county boasts some terrific cycling, and in particular some fabulous long-distance routes. While Bath's topography isn't particularly conducive to cycling, unless punishing gradients are your thing, there is the **Kennet and Avon Canal** towpath (which runs through the city), as well as the **Bristol and Bath Railway Path** (Sustrans Route 4; ⊘ bristolbathrailwaypath.org.uk), the UK's first off-road cycle route,

---

ℹ TOURIST INFORMATION

Bath Bridgewater Hse, 2 Terrace Walk ⊘ 01225 422212 ⊘ visitbath.co.uk
Frome Discover Frome, Black Swan Arts Centre, 2 Bridge St ⊘ 01373 465757
⊘ discoverfrome.co.uk
Shepton Mallet 70 High St ⊘ 01749 345258 ⊘ visitsheptonmallet.co.uk

which tracks a section of the old Midland Railway line for some 13 miles between the two cities; the stretch as you enter Bath (from the west) is particularly scenic, edging an attractive bend in the River Avon. Elsewhere, there's the immensely enjoyable 12-mile-long **Two Tunnels Greenway**, and the **Colliers Way** (Sustrans Route 24), which is roughly double the length of the Greenway.

WALKING

Bath's Skyline Walk (see box, page 38) is a genuine highlight, but beyond the city there are possibilities galore for stretching your legs. The aforementioned Two Tunnels Greenway and Colliers Way are as popular with walkers as they are with cyclists. There's also the 18-mile-long **East Mendip Way**, which forms part of the overall Mendip Way (covered in *Chapter 2*), which begins in Wells and passes through Shepton Mallet en route to its conclusion in Frome.

1 BATH

🏠 **Bath Priory** (page 234), **Pulteney House** (page 234)

Bath's setting, nestled within a deep hollow in a hill, is as dramatic as it is beautiful. And while I can't deny just a hint of bias when assaying the merits of what has effectively become my home city, it's fair to suggest that Bath has few peers. For all its many fine attributes – including some wonderfully idiosyncratic museums, its reinvented spa and of course the Roman Baths – the city's real glory is its outstanding confection of architectural forms, for which it has to thank the likes of Richard 'Beau' Nash, Ralph Allen, John Wood the Elder and John Wood the Younger who, between them, transformed the entire fabric of the city during the 18th century. Monumental ensembles such as The Circus, the Royal Crescent, Pulteney Bridge and Pulteney Street stand cheek-by-jowl with Neoclassical Palladian terraces and squares, and elegantly landscaped parks. In addition, there are some delicious pockets of greenery to escape to, as well as a brace of invigorating walks within touching distance, including the Bath Skyline, one of my favourite outings.

GETTING AROUND

Bath's compact centre lends itself perfectly to walking, even if it does contain its fair share of hills – in fact, this is just one aspect that makes

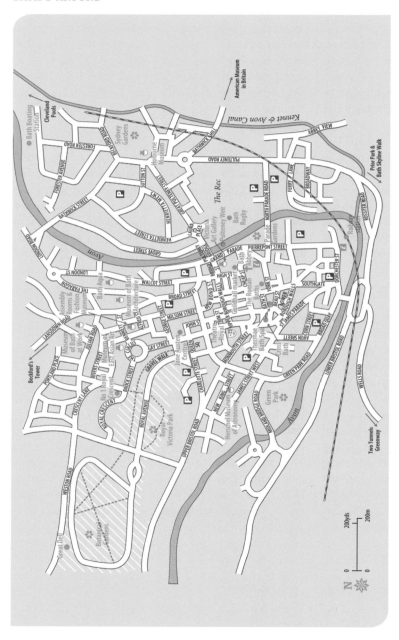

it such a joy to stroll around. Public transport, therefore, is generally not required unless, that is, you wish to visit one of the further- flung sites such as the American Museum or Beckford's Tower – though you could of course always cycle. If driving, there are three park and ride sites around Bath, all within a ten-minute journey of the centre: Odd Down, south of town on the road to Radstock; Newbridge, just off the A4 Bristol Road to the east; and Lansdown, northeast of the centre.

BIKE HIRE

Bath Bike Hire Bath Narrowboats, Sydney Wharf, Bathwick Hill, BA2 4EL ✆ 01225 447276 ⌂ bathnarrowboats.co.uk. Located by the Kennet and Avon Canal, a 15-minute walk from the centre, this excellent outfit has one standard charge (£15) whether it's an hour or a day.
Next Bike ⌂ nextbike.co.uk. Self-service bike hire at 14 stations across Bath, available 24/7. Registration is required first, either online, by phone or via an app. A lock is provided.

BATH ABBEY

✆ 01225 422462 ⌂ bathabbey.org ⊙ daily, but closed Sun until 13.00

Lording it over the surrounding streets and squares, Bath Abbey was raised in 1499 atop the ruins of a Norman cathedral, whose extant remains are still visible here and there. The most striking aspect of the soaring west front are two relief stone ladders on the turrets flanking the central window, with angels ascending (as well as one or two heading the other way). This rather lovely ensemble, which also features a grouping of angels worshipping at the feet of Christ, was conceived by the abbey's founder, Bishop Oliver King, following a dream he allegedly had.

Although largely devoid of ornamentation, the interior is no less impressive for it, from the eye-catching fan-vaulted ceiling (restored by Sir George Gilbert Scott in 1874) to the massive, stained-glass west and east windows, the latter blown out during the 1942 Blitz. But it's the less obvious detail that makes the greater impression here. For example, the abbey's 1,500 or so memorials – reputedly more than any other place of worship in England save for Westminster Abbey – which mostly take the form of wall tablets and ledger stones. Indeed you could spend all day poring over the inscriptions, which represent folk from all walks of life: for example, the one on Granaldo Pigott's stone, who was by all accounts sincere to his friends, affable to his inferiors', and another (whose name I couldn't quite establish) who 'fell out of his bed in a moment of social pleasure'. The mind boggles.

BATH: A POTTED HISTORY

Legend has it that Bath was founded by Prince Bladud, who, in order to cure a diagnosis of leprosy, spent a period of time in the nearby Avon Valley wallowing in the same hot mud that had apparently cured his swineherd of lesions. Healed, Bladud (reputedly the father of King Lear, of Shakespeare fame) took the throne, whereupon he founded the city of Bath (Caerbardum) in recognition of the springs' healing powers. No doubt this story has been embellished, but what isn't disputed is that the Celts dedicated the local waters to the goddess Sul, before the Romans pitched up and renamed the settlement Aquae Sulis (Waters of Sulis), at the same time establishing a sophisticated complex of bathhouses. During the Middle Ages, the city emerged as a key wool-trading centre before steady decline set in, a decline that was spectacularly reversed in the 18th century as the baths were revived and the city acquired its grandiose architectural set pieces – Bath's golden age had well and truly arrived.

The 18th century was also a time of significant cultural efflorescence for the city: having acquired its first theatre, alongside the Assembly Rooms and the Grand Pump Room, Bath was second only to London as a centre for entertainment and creativity. The middle and upper classes arrived in their droves, and leading personalities such as Thomas Gainsborough, who cemented his reputation as a world-class portraitist during his 16 years in the city, and Jane Austen – perhaps the name most synonymous with Bath – were drawn to the city. The 19th century wasn't so kind to Bath, as it was usurped by more fashionable resorts such as Brighton, although the opening of the Kennet and Avon Canal in 1810, alongside Brunel's extension of the Great Western Railway in 1840, did much to alleviate the city's economic struggles. In April 1942 Bath was heavily bombed as part of the so-called Baedeker Blitz, a Nazi campaign to destroy Britain's most treasured historic sites as identified in the eponymous German travel guides, though – the Assembly Rooms aside – its Georgian heart was largely spared. In 1987 Bath was designated a UNESCO World Heritage Site, and it remains the only city in its entirety in the UK to be thus inscribed.

A major restoration project, called Bath Footprint, is currently underway (and not due for completion until 2021) to repair (among other things) the abbey floor, sections of which are slowly subsiding. Over time, huge voids have been created underfoot as a result of thousands of decomposing bodies (possibly 6,000); the Victorians encountered a similar problem a century or so earlier, but simply filled up these spaces by churning up the graves and chucking all the bodies back together again. Another important aspect of the project involves water being diverted from the neighbouring Roman Baths to the abbey as a means of heating the building (the drain currently bypasses the abbey en route to the River Avon) – a clever eco-friendly initiative. If you're prepared to pay a bit extra, and still have some energy to expend, it's worth climbing the 212 steps to the top of the Clock Tower for superlative views of the city spread out below and the hills beyond. Better still, pop along to one of the free Tuesday lunchtime organ recitals.

THE ROMAN BATHS

Stall St ✆ 01225 477785 ⬧ romanbaths.co.uk ◷ 09.00–18.00 daily, mid-Jun–Aug until 22.00

Sitting atop one of the city's three hot springs, the Roman Baths reached their apotheosis around AD4, after which time they gradually fell into disrepair. Despite periodic forays into the site, resulting in the occasional discovery, it wasn't until the Victorians got wind of what was below in the late 1870s (flooding in the basements of nearby houses gave the game away) that excavations began in earnest. Once topped by a 65ft-high, barrel-vaulted roof – the **Great Bath** you see today is as much Victorian as it is Roman; these relatively modern accretions include tall circular pillars (that shadow the stumpy remains of the square Roman ones) rising up to a surprisingly low terrace complete with weather-beaten statues of Roman emperors and governors. The water itself, vaporous and topped with a thin layer of algae, looks disagreeable enough lest anyone think it might be a good idea to test it out, although people did bathe here until as recently as 1978. The only interlopers these days are freshwater snails (*Physella acuta*), thought to have come from North America (hence their presence is a bit of a mystery), who apparently thrive on the water's unique bacterial properties and typically cluster around the lip of the pool.

"Once topped by a 65ft-high, barrel-vaulted roof – the Great Bath you see today is as much Victorian as it is Roman."

For all the Great Bath's grandeur, the true heart of the site is the neighbouring, and much smaller, **Sacred Spring** (aka King's Bath), from whence some 242,000 gallons of water spouts each day at a sizzling 46°C. An overflow carries off surplus water into a nearby drain and then forth to the River Avon about 400yds distant – testament to the Romans' superior engineering skills. The Sacred Spring comprised part of the Temple of Sulis Minerva, whose pediment (or at least the partial remains of) is the museum's single most impressive exhibit. Centred on

DAMN YOU!

One display here in the baths that often gets overlooked in the rush to see the meatier exhibits is a set of Roman curse tablets. Bathhouse thefts – perhaps the taking of a cloak or a purse – weren't uncommon back in the day, and in such cases the victim would inscribe one of these tablets, essentially lead or pewter sheets, with a message, which would then be cast into the spring for the goddess Minerva to wreak her revenge upon the perpetrator. Some messages were particularly vengeful, for example one reads 'may he who carried off Vilbia from me become as liquid as water'. One tablet is inscribed in what is believed to be the only known surviving Celtic text written in Latin in the UK, while another betrays the earliest known reference to Christianity in the UK. As such, these tablets – around 130 were discovered here at the Baths – represent truly outstanding documents pertaining to the lives of ordinary folk, so much so that they've been inscribed on the UNESCO UK Memory of the World Register list.

a gorgon's head, this superbly crafted stonework bears several illusory carvings (for example an owl, a dolphin, a globe), the meanings of which have vexed scholars for centuries. Elsewhere, look out for the gilt bronze head of Sulis Minerva that once adorned the same temple – supposedly one of just three to exist in the UK – and an extremely rare haruspex (a soothsayer) stone. The adjoining **Pump Room** has changed little since its Georgian heyday, and afternoon tea here is a real treat, though it doesn't come cheap; there is also occasional live music.

To get the most out of your visit, I'd suggest coming first thing in the morning or late afternoon when the crowds are generally thinner – allow the best part of two hours to take it all in. The baths, though, wreally come into their own on summer evenings, when they are lit by flaming torches.

THERMAE BATH SPA

Hot Bath St 01225 331234 thermaebathspa.com

It was a long time coming, but the reopening of spectacular-looking Thermae Bath Spa was ultimately worth the wait. Possibly in operation as far back as the 12th century, the baths' fortunes had frequently fluctuated before the rot set in, literally, in 1978 when they were rendered obsolete. Attempts to get the spa up and running again in the late 1990s and early 2000s were repeatedly thwarted by interminable wranglings and delays, until it was finally pronounced open in 2006. Forming the centrepiece of the modern complex is the Nicholas Grimshaw-designed **New Royal Bath**, a handsome cuboid mass of honey-coloured stone and glass. The spa draws its water from three springheads: the King's Spring (which also fills the Roman Baths), the Cross Spring and the Hetling Spring.

The spa comprises three main bathing areas. On the bottom floor is the free-form Minerva Bath, though most bathers make an immediate beeline for the stunning rooftop pool, which is particularly enticing on a cold day; the views, especially at sundown, are sensational. Sandwiched in between these two, the old steam rooms have recently been replaced by a multi-sensory wellness suite comprising five rooms (among them an infrared sauna, ice chamber and Roman steam room), which you can freely saunter between. If you fancy going the whole hog, there are treatments galore available: an invigorating hot-stones massage, perhaps? As advance bookings are not possible (and the baths are, of course, incredibly popular), you'd do well to plan your visit carefully; generally speaking the best time to go is on a weekday, either early morning or late afternoon.

Bookending the western end of Grade I-listed Bath Street – and part of the Thermae Baths Spa complex – is the oval, open-air **Cross Bath**, conceived by Thomas Baldwin and John Palmer in 1798, and fed by its own eponymous spring. Like Thermae Bath Spa, it has enjoyed a similarly spectacular restoration and is used for both public use and private hire.

FROM PARADE GARDENS TO GREAT PULTENEY STREET

Set against the backdrop of the peculiar-looking Empire Hotel (now comprising luxury apartments), **Parade Gardens**, on Grand Parade, is a popular lunchtime worker's retreat, bounded on one side by a stone balustrade and on the other by the River Avon. Laid out with formal lawns, there's much to take in as you amble around: fragmentary remains of an old Monk's Mill; statues of Bladud (with one of his pigs) and Mozart; and a pet cemetery. Best of all though are the head-on views of the frothing **Pulteney Weir**, and, beyond this, Pulteney Bridge (page 26). Note that a small fee is payable to enter the gardens during the summer months. On the opposite side of the river is the rather antiquated, but much loved – and on match days tremendously atmospheric – **Recreation Ground** (aka the Rec), home of Bath Rugby since 1894. The stadium has long been earmarked for redevelopment, as has that whole side of the waterfront, though few are holding their breath.

The **Victoria Art Gallery** (Bridge St ✆ 01225 477233 ⊘ victoriagal.org. uk) is a minor delight with some big-hitters on display too, including a couple of pieces by Thomas Gainsborough and one of very few paintings in the UK by Paul Klee, the wildly colourful *Small Harbour Scene*. There are also one or two lovely evocations of wartime Bath, notably *London Street, Bath* by Walter Sickert, who spent his last years in the city, as well as a clutch of enchanting rural scenes, in particular *The Watersplash* by English realist Henry Thangue. For me though, the gallery's prize acquisition is *Calvary*, a characteristically dramatic, large-scale biblical scene by Mihály Munkácsy (1844–1900), arguably Hungary's finest painter; donated to the gallery by one Mrs English in 1919; that it should be here at all is quite something.

"Pulteney Bridge is unique for being one of just five bridges in the world to have shops lining both sides."

A few paces down from the gallery, turning right as you exit, is the **Guildhall market** (⊘ bathguildhallmarket.co.uk), where stallholders have been plying their trade for nigh on 800 years. An atmospheric, though little-frequented bazaar, it's home to an enjoyable potpourri of traders selling everything from jewellery and leather goods to cheese, coffee and confectionery. It's well worth a nose around.

Spanning the River Avon just a stone's throw from the Guildhall is Robert Adam's **Pulteney Bridge**, unique for being one of just five bridges in the world to have shops lining both sides – indeed you wouldn't even know that you were crossing a bridge at all. In case you were wondering, the other four are the Krämerbrücke in Erfurt (Germany), the Pont des Marchands in Narbonne, the Ponte Vecchio in Florence and the Ponte Rialto in Venice, the last of which provided the inspiration for Adam's version here.

Leading away from the bridge, **Great Pulteney Street**, at roughly 300yds in length, ranks alongside the Circus, Queen Square and the Royal Crescent as one of Bath's most important architectural set pieces, though many, including me, rate this their favourite. A grand thoroughfare designed by the prolific Thomas Baldwin, Great Pulteney Street was originally conceived as part of a larger residential quarter, though this never materialised owing to a shortfall in funds, hence the series of strangely truncated side streets along its length – for example, Sunderland Street, about halfway down, has but one address. Elsewhere, keep your eyes peeled for a couple of original Victorian postboxes.

HOLBURNE MUSEUM & CLEVELAND POOLS

Great Pulteney Street spears east towards the area known as Bathwick, location of a couple of standout sights. First up is the **Holburne Museum** (Great Pulteney St ✆ 01225 388569 ✆ holburne.org), a sumptuous three-storeyed mansion fronted by a Corinthian portico and triple-arched loggia. The building variously functioned as a hotel, therapeutic centre and college before settling into its present role as the city's first public art gallery, in 1916. It's a wonderfully disparate collection, at the heart of which is a stash of goodies acquired by William Holburne himself. These are located within the glass and ceramic extension, which courted no little controversy when it was built in 2011, its dissenters objecting to the use of such contemporary building materials (as opposed to Bath stone, heaven forbid). However, not only does it look fabulous, but it has also freed up heaps more space to display many of the museum's hitherto unseen exhibits.

Holburne, who fought at the Battle of Trafalgar aged just 11, was an inveterate collector, hence this trove of vases, spoons, gems, plaquettes, miniatures and so on – here too are three paintings by Pieter Brueghel the Younger, supposedly the largest grouping of works by the artist in the country. The museum's star exhibit, however, resides in the gallery of British paintings, namely Thomas Gainsborough's vast *The Byam Family*. A first-rate example of the artist's genre of the landscape portrait, it features a rather self-satisfied-looking George Byam and his wife Louisa out for an afternoon stroll with their daughter Selina, who was a later addition to the picture.

As an aside, Jane Austen fans may care to pop across the road to 4 Sydney Place where a plaque denotes this as the author's first home in Bath. Indeed, Austen would frequently take walks in **Sydney Gardens**, which back on to the Holburne. Laid out as commercial pleasure grounds at the end of the 18th century, it's a function they still fulfil today despite being sliced in two by the Great Western Railway (which, I hasten to add, runs below the garden and not through it). The main path running through the centre of the gardens leads down to the **Kennet and Avon Canal**, from where you can walk all the way to Reading, if so inclined.

Tucked away on Hampton Row, a quiet residential crescent of stone-built cottages near the Kennet and Avon Canal, **Cleveland Pools** (clevelandpools.org.uk) is the country's oldest open-air pool, albeit one that currently stands semi-derelict. But thanks to the dedication of the Cleveland Pools Trust, big plans are afoot for the restoration of the entire complex, including the pools themselves – the main, 25m pool is currently one large, weed-infested pond – and the curved building, which comprises a cottage flanked by half a dozen cubicles on either side. However, there is the small matter of finance, so whether or not this ambitious project sees the light of day is largely dependent upon the Heritage Lottery Fund. Founded in 1815, the then river-fed pools were a popular summer retreat with the Victorians, before their decline and eventual closure in 1984. The site was then let out, somewhat bizarrely, as a trout farm and aviary. The Trust took over in 2005, since which time the baths have stood forlornly awaiting their fate – the target for completion is 2021 so watch this space. In the meantime, the pools can be visited on guided tours starting from Abbey Green, though you must book your place (and pay a fee) at the tourist information office (page 18).

MUSEUM OF BATH AT WORK

Julian Rd 01225 318348 bath-at-work.org.uk Apr–Oct, daily; Nov–Mar, Sat & Sun

It's often overlooked that, beyond its graceful Georgian crescents and golden stone façades, Bath is a working city just like any other. And it's the city's rich industrial legacy that is the subject of the enlightening Museum of Bath at Work. The core of the exhibition commemorates the many business enterprises of one J B Bowler: mechanical engineer, brass founder and fizzy drinks manufacturer, to name but three of his roles. Following the closure of the business in 1969, the fixtures and fittings were purchased by local businessman Russell Frears, although it took another decade or so before he settled upon these unconventional premises, the only extant Real Tennis court in the country, dating from 1777 and a rare example of a free-standing Georgian building. Using old photos, the rooms – the foundry, brass finishing room, bottling plant and so on – have been reconstructed much as they were back in the day. Here too is the cheerfully cluttered workshop of Keevil & Sons, one of Bath's foremost 18th-century cabinet-makers, and a mock-up quarry.

MUSEUM OF BATH ARCHITECTURE

The Paragon ✆ 01225 333895 🖱 museumofbatharchitecture.org.uk ⏰ mid-Mar–Nov, 13.00–17.00 Mon–Fri, 10.00–17.00 Sat & Sun

Occupying a similarly idiosyncratic building five minutes' walk away along the wide curving sweep of the Paragon is the Museum of Bath Architecture. This beautifully proportioned chapel was one of dozens commissioned by Selina Hastings – Countess of Huntingdon and a fervent champion of the Methodist movement – in some of England's more fashionable towns during the mid 18th century. The exhibition documents the city's transformation from a workaday provincial town into one of Europe's greatest examples of urban planning, including the work of the men behind it, such as John Wood the Elder, whose set of drawing instruments – acquired at auction in 2016 – is unquestionably the most prestigious item on display. Elsewhere there are examples of some typical

"If you've got kids, direct them towards the Lego station, leaving you to enjoy the displays in quiet contemplation."

Palladian structural features, such as pediments, tiled hipped roofs and sash windows, alongside various aspects of interior ornamentation: marbelling, stencilling, plastering, woodcarving and the like. Rounding things off, there's an impressive 1:500 model of the city in all its scaled-down splendour. If you've got kids, direct them towards the Lego station, leaving you to enjoy the displays in quiet contemplation. The chapel also makes for a marvellous venue, as I can testify having taken in a wonderful concert of Balkan music here one evening.

THE ASSEMBLY ROOMS
& THE FASHION MUSEUM

Bath's **Assembly Rooms** (Bennett St ✆ 01225 477173; National Trust) is among the city's most beloved buildings, albeit one that was almost totally rebuilt following catastrophic bomb damage during the Blitz in 1942. Completed in 1771, the Assembly Rooms were designed by John Wood the Younger for the express purpose of hosting dances, card games, afternoon tea and the like for the emerging leisure classes here in Bath – it's no exaggeration to suggest that it was the country's finest Georgian rendezvous at that time. Now owned by the National Trust, the Assembly Rooms comprise a quartet of sumptuous rooms: the Card Room (now home to a café); the Tea Room, featuring an elegant double-columned balcony; the stately Ball Room; and the Octagon Room, which holds the largest of the building's extraordinary collection of Whitefriars crystal chandeliers – apparently the White House tried to purchase these in the 1950s – unsurprisingly they were given short shrift. Visitors are free to nose around, but by far the best way to enjoy these wonderful surrounds is to attend an event, as we were fortunate enough to do one spring evening during the always brilliant Bath Festival, the occasion a concert by the sublime Welsh harpist Catrin Finch and the charismatic kora player Seikou Keita.

Faithfully restored following World War II, the Assembly Rooms reopened in 1963, which is when the then Museum of Costume, hitherto located in Eridge Castle, Kent, moved into the basement. Founded by Doris Langley Moore, an inveterate fashion collector and designer in her own right, it was recast in 2007 as the **Fashion Museum** (✆ 01225 477789 ⊘ fashionmuseum.co.uk), cementing its reputation as one of the foremost museums of its kind anywhere in the world. The permanent exhibition is an illuminating trawl through the ages, from Shakespeare-era leather gloves and men's Tudor shirts to Georgian robes and garments worn by the likes of Vivien Leigh and Elizabeth Taylor, many items having been bequeathed by Langley Moore herself. The Dress of the Year is a much-anticipated annual highlight, while the museum's temporary exhibitions are invariably prestigious affairs. You don't necessarily have to be a fan of fashion to enjoy this, but it helps.

"The Octagon Room holds the largest of the building's extraordinary collection of Whitefriars crystal chandeliers."

MUSEUM OF EAST ASIAN ART

12 Bennett St ✆ 01225 464640 ⊘ meaa.org.uk ◷ from noon Tue–Sat & Sun

Occupying a handsome corner building just across the road from the Assembly Rooms, the delightful Museum of East Asian Art is the private collection of Brian McElney, who cultivated his interest in the subject while practising as a lawyer in Hong Kong in the 1970s and 80s. This led to the opening of the museum in 1993, the only one in the UK dedicated solely to southeast Asian art. Now well into his eighties but as indefatigable as ever, Brian maintains an occasional presence around the place. Spread thematically over three floors, it's a wonderful assemblage of predominantly ceramic, jade and bronze artefacts, some dating

JANE AUSTEN & BATH

The one name above all others most synonymous with Bath is Jane Austen, who moved to the city in 1801 with her parents and her sister, Cassandra. It's been well documented that Austen had a somewhat uneasy relationship with Bath, as letters to her sister are apt to suggest. However, what is certainly true is that the time she spent here informed much of her work, principally *Northanger Abbey*, much of which was actually written on visits to Bath prior to moving here – the book's heroine, Catherine Morland, was 'all eager delight, her eyes here, there and everywhere, as they approached its fine and striking environs' – and *Persuasion*, which was written at a time when she appeared to have tired of city life, although the death of her father in 1805 almost certainly contributed to her increasing sense of unhappiness.

You can learn more about the author's time in Bath in the **Jane Austen Centre** at 40 Gay Street (☏ 01225 443000 ☍ janeaustencentre.co.uk), a few paces down from number 25, where she briefly lived with her mother and sister in 1805 (now an anonymous dental practice). In truth, there's little here to truly excite Austen devotees – for example, there are none of her personal effects – though a couple of exhibits are worth poring over. One is the only known waxwork of Austen; unveiled in 2014, its creator Melissa Dring largely based the waxwork on a watercolour painted by Austen's sister, Cassandra, though the authenticity of that has been questioned. Here too is a letter from Mark Carney, Governor of the Bank of England, together with a special issue £10 note of the new polymer variety featuring Jane Austen on the reverse – she usurped Charles Darwin who appeared on the old cotton paper note. The note was launched in 2017, 200 years after her death, though the image has attracted opprobrium in some quarters with accusations that she has been unnecessarily, and inaccurately, prettified.

back to Neolithic times, but otherwise spanning the Chinese Imperial dynasties as well as Japan and Korea. Among the many sumptuous items that caught my eye was a jade boy holding a black cat from the Chinese Song Dynasty (AD960–1279), and a gold and gilt bronze water dropper in the shape of a pumpkin. Look out, too, for a rare collection of armorial porcelain, including a soup tureen bearing the coat-of-arms of the Pratt family, John Jeffreys Pratt having served as an MP for Bath in the late 18th century.

FROM THE CIRCUS TO THE ROYAL CRESCENT

The first circular terrace in modern Europe, the **Circus** was the idea of John Wood the Elder, whose interest in prehistoric stone circles provided him with the inspiration for this architectural showstopper. In the event, Wood popped his clogs shortly after laying the foundation stone in 1754, leaving his son to finish the job off. Hemmed in by three curved segments of Grade I-listed townhouses, the central grassy square, now populated by massive plane trees, was once, believe it or not, a reservoir serving the needs of the surrounding houses. The street's most famous resident was Thomas Gainsborough who moved into number 17 in 1759.

A magnificent sweeping arc of 30 terraced townhouses, the nearby **Royal Crescent** is John Wood the Younger's masterpiece, trumping even the grandiose set pieces designed by his father. The Crescent was unquestionably *the* address back in the late 18th century, and 250 years on, it remains no less desirable, or any less expensive of course. Save for the posh Royal Crescent Hotel (numbers 15–17), all the houses here are exclusively residential, unlike those in Queen Square or the Circus.

As you'd expect, the Crescent has had its fair share of notable residents over the years: Isaac Pitman, who established the system of shorthand, lived at numbers 12 and 17; the soprano Elizabeth Linley lived at number 11, and social reformer Elizabeth Montagu lived at number 16. One of the Crescent's more bizarre episodes occurred in 1972 when the then owner of number 22, Amabel Wellesley-Colley, took it upon herself to paint her door (and for good measure her shutters) primrose yellow – contrary to the prevailing white colour – much to the displeasure of the local council. A lengthy legal battle ensued, which, incredibly, reached the Department of the Environment, though in the event Wellesley-Colley successfully defied the authorities and the door has remained the same colour ever since – and predictably has become something of a tourist attraction in itself. The gently sloping lawn fronting the Crescent is for the exclusive use of its residents, and as such is divided from the public parkland area by a ha-ha (a steeply dropping ditch).

"The Crescent was unquestionably the *address back in the late 18th century, and 250 years on, it remains no less desirable."*

For an insight into how one of these houses would have once looked, pay a visit to **No. 1 Royal Crescent** (✆ 01225 428126 ⌨ no1royalcrescent. org.uk), which, since 2006, has also incorporated Number 1a (the former service wing), from which it was separated in 1968. Originally home to Irish landowner Henry Sandford (thereafter the house functioned as a seminary and lodgings), it's an enjoyable romp through the Tardis-like interior, with very informative attendants on hand in each of the dozen or so rooms. The standout room, for me at any rate, was the Withdrawing Room, crammed full of Chippendale and Hepplewhite and featuring a fine harpsichord by Jacob Kirkman of Alsace, though Sandford's similarly well-furnished bedroom on the floor above perhaps holds greater appeal for its elevated views of the Crescent.

A lush green sprawl beginning below the Royal Crescent and extending almost all the way down to the Upper Bristol Road, **Royal Victoria Park** is by some distance the city's largest open space, at a whopping 57 acres. Opened on the occasion of Princess (later Queen) Victoria's visit in 1830, the park was one of the earliest examples of a municipal park anywhere in the country. There's stacks to see and do here, including botanic gardens, tennis and minigolf, while the children's adventure play area near the bottom is one of the best you'll come across.

QUEEN SQUARE & AROUND

A short walk down from the Circus, Queen Square was John Wood the Elder's first public commission and effectively signalled the start of the development of the upper part of town, which also included the Circus and the Royal Crescent. Despite the incessant din of traffic, the central community garden – at its prettiest in spring, when the cherry blossom is out – is a little lunchtime haven for neighbouring office workers, and for folk participating in games of *boules* on one of the large gravel *pistes*.

HERSCHEL MUSEUM OF ASTRONOMY

19 New King St ✐ 01225 446865 ⬦ herschelmuseum.org.uk ⊖ 13.00–17.00 Mon–Fri, 10.00–17.00 Sat & Sun

I'll lay my cards on the table and state that the Herschel Museum of Astronomy is my favourite museum in Bath, which I wasn't really expecting. A handsome, five-floored Georgian townhouse (albeit a grade or two below those on the Royal Crescent and the Circus), 19 New King Street was home to William Herschel and his sister Caroline between 1777 and 1782. Taken over by the William Herschel Society in 1978, it was later inaugurated as a museum, since which time it has been dedicated to celebrating the great deeds of the eponymous musician and astronomer.

The exhibits are exceptional – there's stuff here that's more than a match for anything on display in the Greenwich Royal Observatory in

WILLIAM HERSCHEL: ASTRONOMER EXTRAORDINAIRE

Of all the many celebrated personalities to have made their mark on Bath, few are as compelling as William Herschel. Born in 1738 in Hanover, Germany, Herschel left the country for Britain when he was 19, settling in Yorkshire before arriving in Bath and taking up a position as the director of the Bath Orchestra – as the son of a bandmaster in the Hanoverian Guards, this was his initial calling. But it was as a self-taught astronomer that Herschel gained world renown, and in particular it was his discovery of *Georgium Sidus*, or Uranus, on 13 March 1781 – a discovery that brought the known number of planets in the solar system to seven – that set him apart from his contemporaries. It also earned him the title of Court Astronomer to King George III, an appointment that necessitated the Herschels' relocation from Bath to Datchet, a move neither William nor his sister Caroline was enamoured with.

During his lifetime Herschel constructed more than 400 telescopes – Sir Patrick Moore called him 'the best telescope maker of his time and possibly the greatest observer who ever lived', and who are we to argue with

him? In fact, Herschel's Great Forty-Foot Telescope – located within the grounds of Observatory House, the Herschels' last home in Slough – was, at the time, the largest ever made. The house has long since gone, while two remaining pieces of the telescope – the mirror and a section of tube – are kept within the Science Museum and the Royal Observatory respectively.

Among Herschel's other significant achievements was the discovery of the sixth and seven moons of Saturn, and the discovery of infrared; it's also been suggested that he might have discovered rings around Uranus. Most observers concur that Herschel owed much of his success to his sister Caroline (no mean astronomer herself), who collaborated with her brother on numerous projects – a fact acknowledged by the Royal Astronomical Society, who elected her an honorary member in 1835, the first woman to be inducted into the society. William died in 1822, aged 84, and is buried in Slough, while Caroline eventually returned to Germany where she died in 1848.

London (where, incidentally, you can find more Herschel memorabilia): George Adam's brass drum orrery (a model of the solar system) dating from 1782, a collection of exquisite celestial pocket globes, and part of the space camera used on the 1986 Voyager mission that encountered Uranus. Centre stage though are Herschel's personal effects: the infrared glass prism he used in experiments on thermal radiation, a selection of handmade mirrors, and a travel diary (complete with sketches) he took with him on a trip to Scotland. Caroline's visitors' book, meanwhile, recalls the many illustrious guests they received at Observatory House in Slough, Byron and Haydn among them. Pride of place, however, goes to the full-size brass and rosewood replica of the 7ft telescope Herschel used to discover Uranus. Another room offers rare insight into Herschel's musical prowess. Once you're done inside, head out to the small but beautifully landscaped garden, site of Herschel's great discovery (see box, opposite).

BECKFORD'S TOWER

Lansdown Rd ℘ 01225 422212 ⌂ beckfordstower.org.uk ⊙ mid-Mar–Oct, Sat & Sun

Around 1½ miles north of the city centre, and another of Bath's under-visited sites is Beckford's Tower, named after the eponymous novelist, traveller and collector. A shabby-looking gatehouse – albeit one adorned with some fabulous Italian-Romanesque carvings – announces an agreeably dishevelled Victorian cemetery, all weed-choked pathways and wonky headstones. Beckford's second major building project after the fantastical Gothic folly that was Fonthill Abbey in Wiltshire (which eventually collapsed), the 154ft-high Lansdown Tower – to give it its official name – was designed by Henry Goodridge and completed in 1827. Of Neoclassical design, with a brightly coloured, mock-medieval interior, the tower had fluctuating fortunes following Beckford's death – among other things there was a fire in 1931 – leaving the place in a rather sorry state, until 1993 when the Bath Preservation Trust got its hands on it.

Today, the Tower houses a small but worthy **museum**, which sheds fascinating light on this colourful and compulsive character. While much of Beckford's collection was dispersed following his death, a number of items have been retained by the Trust. Held within the former Small Library and the much grander Etruscan Library are paintings, porcelain and oriental antiquities; standout exhibits include an oversized book of watercolours dating from 1844, and a gorgeous oak coffer and stand believed to be one of a set of four specially commissioned by Beckford.

Having cast your eye over that lot, climb the fine circular staircase (154 steps) that ascends to the restored Belvedere, itself topped with a gilded cast-iron octagonal lantern roof. Although the Belvedere is enclosed, the views of the surrounding countryside – Bath itself is barely visible, just as Beckford had intended – are superb. If you don't fancy the uphill hike to get here, take the Lansdown **Park and Ride bus** number 31 to Lansdown Cemetery.

WILLIAM BECKFORD: REGENCY ECCENTRIC

I am determined to enjoy my dreams, my Phantasies and all my singularity, however irksome and discordant to the worldlings around… in spite of them, I will be happy.

William Beckford was a fascinating character, though one often overlooked among the clamour to acknowledge Bath's more celebrated personalities. This is somewhat odd given his status as one of the nation's wealthiest men and one of the most influential collectors of the time. Born in London in 1760, Beckford was already a millionaire by the age of nine, inheriting his father's vast fortune – one made on the back of the slave trade – although this gilded childhood was by all accounts an unhappy one. An insatiable collector – he had no interest in the family business, only spending the proceeds – Beckford accumulated an astonishing number of artefacts from all ages and cultures, in addition to commissioning many more, some from the most renowned craftsmen in Europe – he held a particular fascination for Medievalism and Orientalism. His writings, too, were highly regarded, earning him comparisons with Byron (whom he had once entertained at Fonthill Abbey), though his oriental Gothic fantasy, *Vathek*, written at the age of just 21, was his only true and lasting work.

One event, however, was to define his life. In 1784, the then married Beckford was caught *in flagrante* with 16-year-old William Courtenay (aka 'Kitty') – whom he had met some years earlier – at Powderham Castle in Devon, the Courtenays' ancestral home.

PRIOR PARK LANDSCAPE GARDEN

Ralph Allen Dr ✆ 01225 833977 ◷ Feb–Oct; free guided tours 11.30, Tue & Thu

Situated within a narrow, steep-sided valley, Prior Park Landscape Garden was commissioned by Ralph Allen in 1742 and laid out by the poet Alexander Pope, though Capability Brown is alleged to have had a hand in proceedings at some point. The entirely naturalistic landscape comprises woodland, meadows and pastureland, with cows mooching about. Lording it over the entire site is the elegant, curved sweep of Allen's former mansion – now Prior Park College – below which lies a serpentine lake, from whence water cascades to a wilderness area below. Walking round, Priory Path breaks off right and up through woodland to a summit covered in yellow meadow anthills, which offers superlative citywide views. Down at the bottom, pause a while (and have a drink) at the Tea Shed, keeping an eye out for herons and coots – and if you're lucky, a kingfisher – before pressing on around the perimeter towards the iconic **Palladian Bridge**. Perched atop a dam, and one of three

It didn't take long for the London press to get wind of the incident, which put paid to any hopes Beckford may have had of a peerage, at the same time ensuring that his social standing took a mighty tumble. He was exiled on the continent with his wife Margaret, though she died two years later and Beckford returned to England in 1789, becoming a recluse as a result of his earlier sexual misconduct. He continued, though, to travel intermittently to the continent on extended buying trips.

Moving to Bath from Fonthill in 1822, Beckford originally had designs on purchasing Prior Park, but (by now heavily in debt) instead had to settle for two flats on Lansdown Crescent. He also acquired the strip of land between here and the then newly built Lansdown Tower, and it was between the two that he would ride each day, invariably stopping en route to admire the views. But by this stage, with his reputation well and truly in tatters, there was little left for him to do but enjoy his personal fiefdom alone. Beckford is buried in the cemetery adjoining the tower, though at the time of his death in 1844 this wasn't consecrated, so he was originally interred at Bath Abbey Cemetery; his tomb, a large granite sarcophagus nestled on its own little grassy island (you can't miss it), is as ostentatious as the man himself. As a mark of how sought-after Beckford's collection is, many of his possessions are now held by some of the world's most prestigious museums, among them the V&A, the National Gallery and the Wallace Collection in London, and the Metropolitan Museum of Art in New York City.

such structures in the country (and just four in the world), the bridge is riddled with stone-carved graffiti, and while most is of historic vintage (the oldest known one dates from 1799, locate it if you can), it has, unfortunately, acquired some modern variants. From here the path slowly winds its way back to the top, passing an icehouse along the way.

Depending upon the season, you may see snowdrops, daffodils, primroses and wild garlic, so a repeat visit is always worth considering. Returning in summer, the contrast to a previous winter visit was stark: stripped-back trees had given way to lush foliage and the meadows were carpeted with wildflowers. Note that access

"Lording it over the entire site is the elegant, curved sweep of Allen's former mansion."

is tricky, both to the site and once inside, owing to the steep, occasionally uneven, terrain. You could always combine a visit here with the Skyline Walk (see box, page 38), which skirts the gardens. Otherwise, it's a 25-minute **walk** uphill from city centre, or **bus** 2 stops outside.

BATH SKYLINE WALK

For the best perspective on Bath's dramatic setting, have a crack at the six-mile-long Skyline Walk, which takes in the heights of **Claverton Down** and **Bathampton Down** over to the east. Walking it clockwise, you start on Bathwick Hill (not far from the Holburne Museum) and continue in a circular fashion, taking in woodland, valleys and meadows along the way. Be prepared though: it is steep in parts, and after heavy rain can get sticky underfoot. You'll come across the occasional architectural oddity too, in particular **Sham Castle**, an 18th-century folly by Ralph Allen. If you really want to make a full day of it, or just fancy a pit stop, both the American Museum and Prior Park Gardens lie en route. There's a downloadable map on the National Trust website (nationaltrust.org.uk), while OS Explorer map 155 is a useful aid, though neither of these are essential as it's all very well signposted.

AMERICAN MUSEUM IN BRITAIN

Claverton Manor, Claverton ✆ 01225 460503 🖥 americanmuseum.org ⊙ mid-Mar–Oct & end Nov–mid-Dec

Occupying the grounds of Claverton Manor since 1961, the American Museum rates as one of my three favourite Bath destinations, in large part because of its gardens, which have recently undergone quite a transformation. Designed by Washington-based landscape architects Oehme, Van Sweden, the **New American Garden** was only laid out in late 2018 and looks fantastic: beautifully manicured lawns bisected by gravel walkways and beds fielding the largest collection of native US trees, plants and shrubs anywhere in the country. Keep your eye out for the natural amphitheatre, a small but perfectly formed grass circle surrounded by steep banks. Just below here, the Mount Vernon Garden is a faithful recreation of the gardens in George Washington's home, which themselves were heavily influenced by British landscape design. The views over the Limpley Stoke Valley are among the finest Bath has to offer – and there's no shortage of competition in that department.

The manor itself, a distinguished Georgian building dating from 1820, showcases the only collection of American decorative and folk art outside the United States, and rather wonderful it is too. It begins with an illuminating trawl through key moments in American history and the people that have shaped these events. To this end it's refreshing to see extensive coverage given to Native Americans, and the many objects here (pottery, moccasins, war bonnets and a fine Sioux buckskin dress for example) clearly demonstrate the remarkable cultural diversity of the various ethnic groups. Another room is devoted to Santo art, the practice of carving and painting wooden sculptures of saints, which was popular throughout New Mexico. Even more impressive are the Period Rooms, transferred here from various parts of the States and which illustrate the material cultures of a specific era: Conkey's Tavern, the Perley Parlor and the Shaker Workroom for example, though I particularly enjoyed the 17th-century Puritan Room from Massachusetts, which effectively functioned as an all-in-one living space, sleeping area and kitchen – the oak and maple wood fixtures and fittings look fantastic.

For many though, the museum's real treasure is its quilts and textiles collection, widely acknowledged to be the finest outside the States. Spanning the early 18th to mid 20th centuries, these technically brilliant, boldly patterned works of art (the museum has some 250 samples, around 50 of which are on display at any one time) range from exuberant Hawaiian arrangements to the simpler, though no less striking, designs favoured by the Amish community; doubtless you'll have your own favourite. As an interesting aside, it was here at Claverton Manor that Winston Churchill gave his first political speech, in 1897. To get here take **bus** U1 or U2 to the university, from where it's a ten-minute walk.

☕ FOOD & DRINK

Colombian Company 6 Abbey Gate St, BA1 1NP ✆ 07534 391992 ⟁ thecolombiancompany.com. You really can't move for decent coffee shops in Bath these days, but for me this place, run by a welcoming Colombian husband/Spanish wife team, currently sits top of the pile. The coffee, with beans sourced from a single Colombian farmer, is brewed various ways (Aeropress, Chemex, French press), and best enjoyed with a wedge of blackberry and lemon cake; the interior looks fab too, with its colourful decorations and a counter culled from a slice of tree.

Colonna & Smalls 6 Chapel Row, BA1 1HN ✆ 07766 808067 ⟁ colonnaandsmalls.co.uk. The marvellous aroma is the first thing that greets you inside this cultured coffee house, whose knowledgeable baristas rustle up some of the city's tastiest coffee. With three espressos and three (single origin) filters on the go on any given day, this is one for bean geeks.

Franco Manca 12 Brunel Sq, BA1 1SX ✆ 01225 962168 ⟁ francomanca.co.uk. Quartered within one of the old railway arches down by the station – hence the constant rumble of trains above – this perennially popular chain pizzeria doles out delicious sourdough pizzas made fresh to order at very affordable prices.

THE TWO TUNNELS GREENWAY & COLLIERS WAY

After years of blood, sweat and quite a few tears, the 12½-mile-long **Two Tunnels Greenway** (www.twotunnels.org.uk) was inaugurated to great fanfare in 2013. A joint partnership between the local authority and Sustrans, this shared-use path (part of National Cycling Route 244) runs part of the length of the old Somerset and Dorset Joint Railway (page 44), and whether you're a walker, runner or cyclist, it's a fantastic outing. The project was conceived in a pub (where better?) when a few locals got chatting about the possibilities for reopening the tunnels, closed in 1966 as part of Beeching's swingeing cuts. This then morphed into the Two Tunnels Community Group who, working alongside the aforementioned agencies, got the ball rolling with work finally beginning in 2010.

I've done the Two Tunnels a few times now, and it's always great fun – if nothing else, the sheer novelty factor is sure to engage younger family members. A good place to start is the car park at the Hope and Anchor pub in **Midford**, where the old station platform is still visible, raised above the old trackbed along which the path now runs. From here it's about half a mile to **Combe Down Tunnel**, which, at 1,829yds long (just over a mile), is the country's longest walking and cycling tunnel – apart from slight curves at each end, it's dead straight, though to spice things up a bit, piped chamber music is played at various intervals and there's the occasional art installation for some visual stimulation. Exiting Combe Down Tunnel brings you out on to the old Tucking Mill viaduct, before the second, much shorter **Devonshire Tunnel** (513yds) beckons. Exiting this one, you can drop down into Bear Flat, from where it's a short walk (or cycle) down into the city centre. Otherwise, you can continue along the path to the western suburb of Twerton or return the way you came; if doing the latter, you can reward yourself with some well-earned refreshment at the Hope and Anchor. The tunnel is always open, but the lights are only on between 05.00 and 23.00. If you are coming by public transport, the nearest train stations are Bath Spa and Oldfield Park, while the Bath to Frome bus (number 267) stops in Midford.

The Two Tunnels Greenway links up with the **Colliers Way** (colliersway.co.uk) a 23-mile-long shared-use path that is also part of the National Cycling Network (Route 24). Starting at the spectacular Dundas Aqueduct five miles south of Bath, the Colliers Way proceeds south to Frome, for much of the way tracking the old Somerset and Dorset Joint Railway, which itself was built over the Somerset Coal Canal, hence the name – there are certainly enough reminders of the area's industrial past, particularly around Radstock and Kilmersdon. Unlike the Two Tunnels it's not completely traffic-free, though what road there is is mostly quiet country lanes.

Hall and Woodhouse 1 Old King St, BA1 2JW 01225 469259 hall-woodhousebath. co.uk. On first glance, this cavernous place – an old auction house building – appears to be little more than an oversized Wetherspoons, but don't be put off. Take a closer look and you'll find an easy-going and very welcoming restaurant-cum-bar that's popular with all-comers, including young families. There are several comfy seating sections to choose from, though we tend to make a beeline for the living room area, complete with low, wooden coffee tables, squishy leather sofas, games and books.

Noya's Kitchen 7 St James's Parade, BA1 1UL ℰ 01225 684439 ♢ noyaskitchen.co.uk ☺ Tue–Sat. Under the sure hand of Noya Pawlyn, who fled Vietnam at the age of seven, visitors are served a five-course set menu, that may feature beautifully crafted morsels like pork dumplings, chicken sticks with lemongrass, or coconut fish stew. Lunches are a simpler, though no less delicious, affair, and you can BYO in the evenings too. This is Bath dining at its most exciting.

The Salamander 3 John St, BA1 2JL ℰ 01225 428889 ♢ salamanderbath.co.uk. Forget the slew of modern, trendy pubs and bars currently doing the rounds in Bath and head to this good old-fashioned hostelry, which attracts a merry band of punters here to sup on Bath Ales beers, not to mention a few Belgian offerings. Gets lively on rugby match days.

Yak Yeti Yak 12 Pierrepont St, BA1 1LA ℰ 01225 442299 ♢ yakyetiyak.co.uk. This place has been a staple on the Bath restaurant scene for aeons and remains as popular as ever. Delicious Nepalese cuisine is the order of the day – for example, Sherpa noodle soup with chicken, or slow-cooked lamb with bamboo shoots, though vegetarian dishes are given equal weighting. You've a choice of conventional seating or, much more fun, there's cushioned floor seating.

SOUTH OF BATH

From Bath, the A367 meanders south through undulating countryside to the county's one-time coal-mining heartland. Although by no means traditional tourist territory, it's one of the most interesting and distinctive corners of the county, with vestiges of the area's industrial past in plentiful supply, most conspicuously in Radstock and Midsomer Norton, unlovely as they may otherwise be. The villages of Mells and Nunney, together with historic churches at Cameley and Emborough, are more refined cultural propositions. Heading further south still, with the Mendips (covered in the next chapter) looming to the west and the county of Wiltshire to the east, neither Frome nor Shepton Mallet are immediately Slow targets, but both have enough about them to merit an extended visit.

2 STONEY LITTLETON LONG BARROW

Wellow BA2 8NR ℰ 0370 333 1181 ☺ open access; English Heritage

Just outside the village of Wellow, five miles south of Bath, Stoney Littleton Long Barrow is one of the finest examples of a Neolithic burial chamber anywhere in the country, and thus ranks as one of Somerset's most important ancient monuments. Long barrows, elongated stone monuments to the dead, are among the country's oldest surviving architectural traditions, and as such represent the earliest forms of ritual inhumation; the one here at Stoney Littleton dates roughly from 3500BC.

Stoney Littleton is easily accessible by car, and well signposted; heading south out of Wellow, take a left turn down Littleton Lane, which wends its way to a small parking area – usefully, in the summer months there's a kiosk opposite selling drinks and ice creams. From the car park, it's a steady uphill walk through a couple of sheep-filled fields to a limestone outcrop and the barrow itself, a shallow grassy mound surrounded by a restored dry-stone wall.

A spooky-looking entrance (note the ammonite fossil cast on the doorjamb) beckons in curious visitors. Indeed, the most exciting aspect of the tomb is the opportunity to venture inside the 43ft-long passage, which is no more than 3ft high (ducking required) and comprises seven small chambers: three pairs of side chambers and an end one – more or less standard form for a long barrow. Although there's nothing to see inside, it's good fun all the same. It's believed that the tomb was first opened in 1760, although it wasn't properly excavated until some 60 years later when a local farmer stumbled upon a handful of human remains, some burnt; most of these have long since disappeared, but a few are currently held within the City Museum in Bristol.

A wonderfully secluded spot, with satisfying views down through Wellow Brook, you're quite likely to have the place all to yourself. Walkers can take in the barrow as part of the Colliers Way (see box, page 40), which is a far more rewarding way of reaching the site. Afterwards, you could do worse than pop into the cosy Fox and Badger pub in Wellow for a pint. To get to Wellow, take **bus** 757 from Bath to Peasedown, from where it's a 2½-mile walk east.

3 RADSTOCK

Radstock is an oddly muddled place, its centre, such as it is, a traffic-choked double roundabout at the bottom of Radstock Hill (the main road in from Bath), from where a tangle of roads fan out towards nondescript residential areas. While it wouldn't be unkind to submit

CASHING IN ON COAL

While it may have been the case that coal was mined in Somerset by the Romans – the first documented evidence of mining in the area appears to date from the 14th century – it wasn't until 1763 that coal mining was established on an industrial scale. The **North Somerset Coalfield** extended from Pensford and Nailsea, south and west of Bristol respectively, down to Radstock and the Nettlebridge Valley further south. While nothing on the scale of the great Welsh coalfields, north Somerset was nevertheless a significant area of production, with 79 collieries in operation at its peak at the turn of the 20th century. Alongside the mines came improved transport links, notably the Bath extension of the Somerset and Dorset Railway, and the Somersetshire Coal Canal, whose two branches afforded the coalfield access east towards London via the Kennet and Avon Canal – though one branch subsequently became a tramway.

There were few families in this part of Somerset who didn't have at least one member working the mines – this often included children, who were paid two pence for a six-day week opening ventilation shafts or pulling coal wagons along the tracks. Conditions were of course appalling and disasters were commonplace, though none were more tragic than the Wellsway Colliery Disaster of 1839, which resulted in the deaths of 12 miners, and the Norton Hill Pit Disaster of 1908, in which ten miners perished.

Numerous factors contributed to the industry's gradual decline, not least increased competition and cheaper substitute fuels. By the end of the 1930s there were just 14 collieries left in the Somerset coalfield. As coal seams became increasingly uneconomical – the narrow seams that were a feature of many pits hereabouts made coal extraction both difficult and unproductive – and the political climate shifted, further closures were inevitable, and so it was, in 1973, that the last two pits in the coalfield, Writhlington and Kilmersdon, were wound up, bringing an end to over 200 years of industrial-scale mining in north Somerset.

While the landscape is much changed since those days, there are still many reminders: the volcano-shaped spoil tip of the former Old Mills Colliery just outside Midsomer Norton; the derelict Somerset and Dorset Railway line that now forms part of the Colliers Way cycle route (see box, page 40); remnants of the old Somersetshire Coal Canal (lengths of which have been restored to water); and ranks of terraced mining cottages, which are particularly prevalent in Midsomer Norton, Radstock and many other surrounding villages.

that Radstock lacks much by way of identity or charm, its industrial past is very much worth delving into.

This rich heritage is evocatively recalled in the **Radstock Museum** (✆ 01761 437722 ☌ radstockmuseum.co.uk ☉ Feb–Nov, 14.00–17.00 Tue–Fri & Sun, 11.00–17.00 Sat), as good a local museum as you'll find anywhere. Unmissable, thanks to the enormous winding wheel outside, the museum occupies the town's beautifully restored Victorian market hall, whose most notable feature is its refurbished clock which, curiously, is visible both inside and out. The museum's main exhibition, entitled Somerset Coalfield Life, proudly documents the roles played by various groups throughout the mining community – sports clubs, brass bands, trade unions and so on – while a mock-up mine amply illustrates the perils involved working the seam. For added pizzazz, in 2018 a new Virtual Reality simulation was inaugurated, whereby visitors 'descend' to the depths for a tour around an old mine, complete with pit ponies and miners going about their business. The kids were keen to give this fully three-dimensional trip a try (as, in fairness, was I) and they weren't disappointed; it's cleverly done and great fun.

"A mocked-up shop acknowledges the contribution made to the community by the local Co-operative Society."

Alongside the mines, other trades and industries flourished in the area, many of which are represented here: printing, bookbinding, cobbling and blacksmithing, for example. Meanwhile, a mocked-up shop acknowledges the contribution made to the community by the local Co-operative Society, which was set up in 1868 and whose present incarnation (the ingeniously titled Radco) is located just across the road. In a nod to the now-defunct Somerset and Dorset Railway (which is well covered in the exhibition), the sweet little café is bedecked with railway memorabilia. It's worth pointing out that the museum has a lively Twitter feed (@RadstockMuseum), which is also the best source of information for the many wide-ranging events and talks held here.

On an altogether different note, Radstock has a little-known link with Lord Admiral Nelson – well, his grandson at least: the Reverend Horatio Nelson-Ward was the town rector between 1853 and his death in 1888, and a display here in the museum offers insight into his contribution to the town.

4 MIDSOMER NORTON

Like Radstock, Midsomer Norton has, on the surface at least, little to commend it, but it's a buzzy place all the same, especially on the first Saturday of each month when the farmers' market pitches up in the centre of town. It's also home to the delightful **Somerset and Dorset**

Trust Railway (✆ 01761 411221 ✆ sdjr.co.uk; ☉ 13.00–16.00 Mon, 10.00–16.00 Sun; see website for train running times), located at **Midsomer Norton South station** a few hundred yards from the centre of town, at the top of Silver Street.

The S&DR came into being in 1862 following the amalgamation of the Somerset Central Railway and the Dorset Central Railway (whose main line ran from Bath to Bournemouth), though this station, which opened in 1874, lay on the Evercreech Junction to Bath branch line. The main line was used heavily by both passengers and freight, popular with the holidaying masses heading to the south coast (there was even a service between Manchester and Bournemouth, the 'Pines Express'), and a key transportation hub for the local pits, in particular nearby Norton Hill colliery. It was a busy old place for sure.

As part of the massive restructuring programme of the railways resulting from the Beeching Axe in the 1960s, the S&DR was closed (as was the station) in 1966, just one month after Norton Hill colliery was decommissioned. The Somerset and Dorset Railway Heritage Trust took on the lease of the line in 1996, since which time its wonderfully committed volunteers have done a sterling job renovating the station and getting trains running once again. Although currently only half a mile long, it is, nevertheless, the only place where standard-gauge steam rides are available over any section of the S&DR. And this is just cause for celebration. Plans are afoot to double the length of the line, but as is the way with these things, this is dependent upon considerable funds being raised. An even more ambitious project is in the offing, namely to restore **Chilcompton's old railway station** (also closed in 1966), two miles distant from Midsomer Norton, and in time, connect the two stations. As Chilcompton is my home village, this certainly gets my vote.

"The other museum has exhibits pertaining to the war, with special emphasis on the Midsomer Norton Home Guard."

Even if you don't manage to get here on a day when trains are running – there are currently two full-size locos in operation – there's plenty more to see and do, including two museums: one, in the old Victorian stable block, displays an assortment of railway memorabilia, while the other, in a World War II **pillbox**, has exhibits pertaining to the war, with special emphasis on the Midsomer Norton Home Guard in the form of posters, phone sets, first aid kits etc – a case indeed for

Britain's smallest museum. You can also enter the signal box (rebuilt on the foundations of the original), have a nose around the goods shed and station outbuildings, and then grab some refreshments in a static buffet coach.

5 BOOKBARN INTERNATIONAL

Unit 1 Hallatrow Business Park, Hallatrow BS39 6EX ✆ 01761 451333
⌖ bookbarninternational.com

There are bookstores, and then there's Bookbarn International, which houses one of the largest selections of used, antiquarian, rare and new books in the world. This vast emporium, half a mile west of Hallatrow village, holds somewhere in the region of 1.5 million secondhand titles, on every conceivable topic, with each book priced at just £1. You could spend hours here scanning the distant rows of shelves, the likelihood being that you'll spend far more time here than you originally intended. Alongside the bricks and mortar shop, they also ship thousands of books to customers globally through the major internet sales sites; in fact, chances are that if you have purchased a used book online, it may well have come from here. Fenna, one of Bookbarn's directors, told me that they receive thousands of secondhand books each week, variously sourced from libraries, schools and charities, as well as people just having a clear out.

A fairly recent addition is the Darwin Rare Books room, named after the eponymous naturalist, who just happens to be the great-great-grandfather of William Pryor, Bookbarn's chairman. In here you'll find a sizeable acquisition of antiquarian, rare and collectible books – plus maps, comics and curios – some very reasonably priced, others requiring somewhat deeper pockets. Another good reason to visit is the Full Stop Café, where you can tuck into delicious veggie fare and scrummy homemade cakes and tarts. Events feature prominently here too, among them creative writing classes, music and poetry evenings, and a monthly Sunday Social complete with DJ.

¶¶ FOOD & DRINK

The Old Station Inn Wells Rd, BS39 6EN ✆ 01761 452228 ⌖ theoldstationandcarriage. co.uk. A short walk from Bookbarn, you get two for the price of one at this 1920s station hotel: a warming pub packed to the gunnels with all manner of tat (a trumpet, skis and, er, half a Citroen), and a restaurant within an old, bright red Great Western Pullman carriage –

not quite the *Orient Express*, but not a bad stab. There's a very creditable menu too, featuring the likes of Gressingham duck with forest berry sauce, and pork hock with cider gravy.

6 ST JAMES'S CHURCH
Cameley BS39 5AH ✆ 01761 452959

Somerset is blessed with some fine ancient churches, but for my money few are as enduring as St James's Church in the tiny hamlet of **Cameley**. Redundant since 1980, this time-warped gem dates from the 12th century, with various Jacobean and Georgian appendages thrown in for good measure, though thankfully it's one of the few churches hereabouts to have escaped a Victorian revamp. The exterior manifests contrasting architectural styles, the red Mendip sandstone tower set against the blue-grey lias stonework of the rest of the church. The most intriguing external feature, however, is the domestic-looking door, located up a shallow flight of steps to the left of the porch and giving access to the interior galleries.

The interior, too, is brimming with architectural oddities, from the gently sloping flagstones to the nave walls, which lean perceptibly outwards – stand at the back of the church and I defy you not to raise a wry smile. Elsewhere, the chunky medieval bench pews have been wonderfully warped and worn to a shine with age. More unusual aspects of the church interior include two raised galleries (accessed via the aforementioned exterior door), one for the general public, the other for the musicians, as well as a couple of private box pews, which were usually bought – and often custom-built – by the wealthiest members of the congregation. Although largely in poor condition, the medieval wall paintings betray sublime workmanship; in particular there's a fine representation of the Ten Commandments located above the chancel arch. In the chancel itself is a fantastically well-preserved 19th-century coffin bier, uncovered as recently as 2016 from the churchyard.

The graveyard is worth a gander too, the most notable collection of tombs and headstones those of the Rees-Mogg clan, including that of Lord William Rees-Mogg, former editor of *The Times* and father of local MP, Jacob. The church is usually open, but there is a number posted on the door that you can call if it's not. Approaching along the A37 from the south, take a left turn just before Temple Cloud and the church is located roughly a mile or so along a gently winding lane.

7 CHURCH OF ST MARY THE VIRGIN
Emborough BA3 4SG

Stranded in perfect isolation atop a shallow rise with far-reaching views of the Somerset countryside, the Church of St Mary the Virgin in **Emborough**, a small, scattered settlement on the edge of the Mendips, is one of a number of ancient churches in the area cared for by the Churches Conservation Trust. Every inch the country church, St Mary's manifests an unorthodox, reverse L-shaped ground plan, and is originally of 12th–13th-century origin, though subject to all sorts of historical tinkering thereafter. It finally became redundant in 1978 when it became clear that it could no longer muster a congregation. Unusually, the tower – distinguished by four slender corner pinnacles – occupies the central portion of the church, though you wouldn't know it once inside. In fact, the mostly Georgian interior is largely devoid of any ornamentation whatsoever – save for a few encaustic tiles on the chancel floor and some early 20th-century decorative plasterwork on the nave ceiling – but in no way does that lessen its impact. Much like the walls at St James's Church in Cameley (page 47), the walls here, separating the nave from the aisle, lean – somewhat alarmingly – inwards. As was typical of many churches built around this time, a raised gallery to the rear of the nave was built to accommodate the church musicians.

The Trust is responsible for maintaining, as well as finding new uses for, churches that are no longer used as places of worship. To this end, they've come up with a cracking concept, albeit with a terrible name: **champing**. If the idea of spending the night in a consecrated space is one that appeals, St Mary's is one of 20 or so churches around the country where you can do so, with the money raised from your stay going back into conserving these beautiful buildings. A room with a pew, anyone?

8 MELLS

The quietly refined village of Mells merits an extended visit by virtue of its historical associations and a splendid local walk through some abandoned ironworks. The history of the village is dominated by two families: the Horners, who purchased the estate following the dissolution of Glastonbury Abbey in 1539, and the Asquiths, one of whose number subsequently married into the Horner family. The walk described here follows a roughly circular fashion and should take no more than 90 minutes, notwithstanding the occasional diversion.

A village walk

The best place to start is the village shop (incorporating a community-run café), directly opposite which stands a striking triangular stone shelter by the celebrated architect **Edwin Lutyens** who, on account of his associations with both the Horners and the Asquiths, received multiple commissions. The shelter – which used to conceal one of the village's water taps – was designed by Lutyens in 1909 on behalf of Lady Horner as a memorial to her son Mark, who succumbed to scarlet fever. From here, head uphill; just around the corner stands Lutyens's **War Memorial** dating from 1921, its pedestal carved from Portland Stone and the slender Tuscan column, surmounted by St George slaying the dragon, hewn from Purbeck marble. From here head along Selwood Street, whereupon the fine 15th-century Tithe Barn hoves into view (though generally it's only open for functions), opposite which is **Mells Walled Garden** (✆ 01373 812597 🖱 thewalledgardenatmells.co.uk; 🕒 Mar–Oct, 10am–5pm daily; free admission). Officially still called the Rectory Garden, this was the site of the old monastic herb garden,

MELLS & THE END OF APARTHEID

Unbeknown to many, Mells played a significant role towards ending apartheid in South Africa. In the years running up to Nelson Mandela's release in 1990, Mells Park House (another Lutyens design for the Horner family, naturally, though it's not open to the public) was the setting for a series of meetings between the African National Congress (ANC) party and South African government officials in order to determine the fate of any post-apartheid agreement. Given the volatile political landscape in South Africa at the time – the ANC was banned and any prospective government officials would have been prevented from participating in talks with them – and the fact that Mells Park House was then owned by a South African mining company, it made this sleepy little corner of Somerset the ideal, if unlikely, hideaway.

The instigator of these meetings was Michael Young, former foreign affairs adviser to Edward Heath, and at the time an employee of the mining company. However, Young's involvement – among other things, he forged links with the ANC in exile – came at great personal risk and he was threatened on numerous occasions. In the event, Thabo Mbeki (leader of the ANC and future president of South Africa) was one of those whom Young persuaded to come to Mells. So clandestine were these meetings that very few people knew of them until some years later. These talks, and the negotiation process more broadly, were the subject of a film called *Endgame*, released in 2009.

the monastery itself having been pulled down following the Dissolution of the Monasteries. Despite having no background in horticulture, Sam Evans took over the business in 2017, the original owners having purchased it some nine years previous after a lengthy period of neglect. Laboured over with love, Sam has enthusiastically reinvigorated these thoroughly likeable gardens, centred on a lily-strewn pond and with a narrow raised terrace round the back offering glorious meadow views. Moreover, there's a rather ace café on site too (page 53).

Mells to Great Elm via Fussells Ironworks

✻ OS Explorer map 142; start at village shop in Mells ♀ ST730490; 2 miles; easy

This round trip is an enjoyable add-on to the village walk outlined on page 49, and also offers a fascinating glimpse into the area's surprisingly rich industrial and natural heritage, not least some significant remains of the old ironworks.

1 From the village shop, follow the road signposted to Great Elm for some 200yds before taking the footpath that bears right into the **Wadbury Valley** and tracks the course of the fast-flowing Mells River. After 100yds or so, just below a massive limestone rock face on your left, are the scant foundations of some old cottages. A little further on, perched above the water's edge, are the remains of the **Fussell's Upper Ironworks**, including the well-preserved engine house chimney; dating from 1744, these were the first of the Fussell family's ironworks to be established within the valley – there is some evidence to suggest that there were operations here, in some form or other, until as late as the 1960s.

2 In another 300yds or so, you come to the more substantial **Lower Ironworks**, which functioned roughly between 1780 and 1895. At the centre of the complex is **Valley House**, the former office building, closed in 1904 and now privately owned; at the time of my visit, it was being renovated – I was told by one of the workmen that the results will be spectacular. Head up the gently inclining path behind the house, with the high boundary wall on your right; at the end a clearing reveals the ruins of several structures, including workers' cottages and three tunnels, though these are inaccessible, partly because of safety reasons but also because they have become an important habitat for bats. After around 400yds, the path splits. Take the right-hand track along the stream, continuing through an increasingly wooded area (the path here can get quite boggy after rainfall), and after another 300yds you come to a bridge.

3 Cross the bridge to the south bank of the stream. Here it's possible to discern further evidence of the area's industrial past in the form of a **disused quarry** (opened by the Somerset

A little further along Selwood Street, dip down into New Street (ironically the oldest street in the village), the right-hand side of which is mostly consumed by a former boys' school. Beyond the gate at the end stands **St Andrew's Church**, whose battlemented tower is typical of so many churches in this part of Somerset. Described by the architectural writer Sir Nikolaus Pevsner as 'among the happiest churches in Somerset', its high and handsome interior holds several important memorials, the most conspicuous of which is a bronze equestrian statue

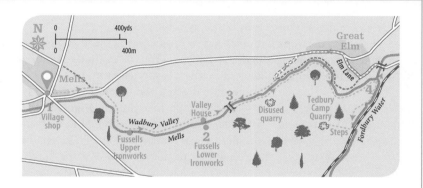

Quarry Company in 1910), just beyond which, and up to your right, is a small cave opening – scramble up and have a look. The path then continues until it reaches the confluence with **Fordbury Water**.

4 At this point, follow the path round to the right, so that the railway line (a mineral track serving nearby Whatley Quarry) and tunnel are on your left: some 200yds further on, you'll see some steep wooden steps, which ascend to the former **Tedbury Camp Quarry**; a vast, barren space, this was the sea floor in the Jurassic period, hence the many, easily identifiable fossilised oysters and tiny holes bored by marine worms. From Tedbury, retrace your steps (this time with the track and tunnel on your right) back to the confluence with Mells River, from where it's no more than a couple of hundred yards to the village of **Great Elm**. Once here, follow Elm Lane up and round to your left to the main road. After 300yds a path breaks off to the left and slopes back down into the valley. Continue back to Mells the way you came; you could continue walking along the main road back to Mells, but I don't recommend this.

by the renowned horse painter Alfred Munnings, dedicated to Edward Horner who fell during World War I; incidentally, Lutyens designed the plinth here, a miniature version of his Cenotaph in Whitehall. Don't miss, under the tower, Edward Burne Jones's lovely white peacock gesso plaque in memory of Laura Lyttleton, a Horner family friend, and, opposite, a wreath memorial to Raymond Asquith, again by Lutyens, with a red wall-carved inscription by the controversial sculptor Eric Gill. The graveyard, meanwhile, is a who's who of eminent personalities, among them war poet Siegfried Sassoon, author and theologian Ronald Knox, and Lady Violet Bonham Carter, daughter of prime minister Herbert Henry Asquith and grandmother of the actress Helena Bonham Carter; nose around a while and you'll find them. Lutyens's hand is felt here too, in the two rows of neatly clipped yew trees.

The door in the wall on the west side of the church is usually unlocked, in which case sneak through and into the grounds of **Mells Manor** – the house is off-limits to the public, save for special event days, but no-one should mind too much if you quickly scuttle through the garden. Originally the Horner family home, this grand Elizabethan mansion was largely rebuilt by Lutyens in 1925 following a fire and is now the family seat of the Asquiths – the present occupant is Raymond Asquith, great-grandson of former British Prime Minister Herbert Henry Asquith. Interestingly, the manor's tiny Catholic chapel attracts a far larger congregation than that of St Andrew's, thanks to influential figures such as the aforementioned Knox, whose presence here after World War I reinforced Mells as an important centre of Catholicism. Lutyens, inevitably, designed both the garden and the cast-iron gate piers at the bottom of the drive, which you exit before rejoining the main road. Immediately to your right is Lutyens's bus shelter, which is often overlooked owing to its rather inconspicuous location. Head across the grassy triangle and walk down Gay Street past a grouping of exceptionally pretty thatched cottages until you reach an early 18th-century **lock-up** on the right-hand side of the road; open the grille and take a peek into the black void. Take a look, too, at the weird-looking limestone grotto, possibly an old water trough, directly opposite. Back by the lock-up, turn right down Rashwood Lane (there is no street sign), at the end of which, just beyond the last house,

> *"The graveyard is a who's who of eminent personalities, among them war poet Siegfried Sassoon."*

A COUPLE OF JACKS & A JILL

Mells is said to have been the inspiration for the much-loved nursery rhyme, *Little Jack Horner*, the lyrics to which were first published in 1725. The story goes that, as steward to Richard Whiting, the Abbot of Glastonbury, Thomas Horner was tasked with delivering a Christmas pie to King Henry VIII; concealed for safekeeping within the pie were the deeds to 12 manors, one of which (that of Mells) was removed by Horner, who kept it to himself, hence the line 'he put in his thumb, pulled out a plum, and said what a good boy am I!' As improbable as this is, what is known is that Horner did indeed acquire the manor in 1543, and it's where the family remained until 1902.

The village of **Kilmersdon**, four miles north of Mells, boasts a similar (though no less dubious) claim to nursery rhyme fame, namely *Jack and Jill*. Local legend has it that in 1697, or thereabouts, Jack was heading uphill to fetch his pail of water when he was struck by a boulder from the local quarry and came crashing down, with Jill following in vain pursuit to try and save him. As you'd expect, the village makes great play of this, culminating in Jack and Jill races at the annual village fair in May. The hill itself (which starts near the church) is waymarked at various intervals with lines from the rhyme, while a plaque on the side of the primary school at the top of the hill recalls the supposed event.

a narrow mud track bears left and dips down through some woods, eventually emerging on to a gravel track running parallel to Mells stream; keep left as this track joins another road heading uphill and back on to Gay Street.

¶¶ FOOD & DRINK

Walled Garden Café Selwood St, BA11 3PN ✆ 01373 812597 ✎ thewalledgardenatmells. co.uk ◷ mid-Mar–Oct. Secreted away within the walls of its own, delightful garden, this seasonal café, with both indoor (the greenhouse) and outdoor (a sunny rose terrace) seating, serves up superb coffee and cake and Mediterranean-style lunches. Better still, at weekends and holidays during the warmer months the wood-fired oven gets an outing – try the veggie-packed garden pizza.

9 FROME

🏠 **Bistro Lotte** (page 56)

Derived from the Welsh word ffraw, meaning 'brisk' – as in the flow of its local river – **Frome** (pronounced 'Froom') sits upon high ground on the eastern fringes of the Mendips. Frome made its fortune from the proceeds of the cloth and woollen trades, but following the decline of these and other industries, it reinvented itself as a thriving market town, which it continues to be today. I must confess to having been rather ambivalent about Frome in the past, but it has grown on me, and locals I talk to tell me that it has changed beyond recognition in the last decade or so. They're a friendly bunch here, too.

Beyond the recent hype proclaiming Frome to be one of the coolest places to live in the UK – to be taken with a pinch of salt, of course – you'll find a spirited little town fermenting with bold new economic and political ideas. So much so that in 2015, every single member of the incumbent town council was booted out and replaced by the **Independents of Frome**, a coalition entirely made up of independent candidates. Even for a town where non-conformism has long prevailed, this was quite the small-scale political revolution. While the town's stock has certainly risen in recent times – increased pockets of gentrification and a growing band of celebrity residents partly testify to this – community is what matters here, with numerous social enterprises and community schemes to the fore. Wandering Frome's twisty cobbled lanes and countless galleries could comfortably detain you for a few hours – longer if your visit happens to coincide with one of the town's terrific markets, or if you try out one of the many fabulous places to eat and drink; the town possesses a particularly fine selection of restaurants.

A town walk

Rather than any specific sight, it's the overall feel of the place that is Frome's main appeal. As good a place as any to start is the **Black Swan Arts Centre**, one of several flourishing arts institutions sprinkled around town. An inn of sorts until the 1950s, the then crumbling building was repaired and transformed into an artistic hub in 1986; as enjoyable as the exhibitions are – which can be anything from paintings and prints to collages and drawings – more fun are the ground-floor studios where you can observe local artists at work, perhaps a jeweller or a sculptor.

A few paces away, the sweet little **Frome Heritage Museum** (✐ 01373 454611 ⬦ fromemuseum.wordpress.com ☉ Mar–Oct, 10.00–14.00 Tue–Sat) is a good place to swot up on the town's history. There may only be two rooms but they pack an awful lot in, from archaeology to the titans of local industry: J W Singer & Sons (art metalworkers), Fussell's (ironworks), Butler & Tanner (printers), Cockeys (lampmakers) are names that will resonate with those of a certain age but which sadly are no more. If you're lucky, you may get to see some of the so-called Frome Hoard; in 2010, a local metal detectorist unearthed a solitary clay pot in a nearby field that contained over 50,000 coins dating from AD3 – the largest coin hoard ever found in a single vessel in Britain and a find for which he was handsomely rewarded. This extraordinary cache is currently held by the British Museum (with some also in the Museum of Somerset in Taunton), but the museum's custodians are hopeful of acquiring at least a few of these coins in due course. Take time too to peruse the wall-bound timeline outlining the town's major happenings.

Heading down Market Place, cross the road and hook a left into **Cheap Street**, a narrow, pedestrianised street defined by its central leat (water channel) and an appealing array of independent shops. Emerging at the top by St John's Church, a quick zig-zag takes you to Saxonvale, a grubby brownfield site that's now the focus of a major regeneration programme. At its heart is the old textile and weaving mill dating from the late 18th century. This superb specimen is now home to the **Silk Mill Studios** (⊘ silkmillstudios.co.uk), with some 22 studios – printmakers, painters, framers, ceramicists and so on – as well as a gallery space hosting arts events, concerts and exhibitions. The studios are generally not open to the public, save for festival dates and open days, but there's no harm in popping along if you're particularly curious.

From here, it's a hop and a skip over to the **St Catherine's** quarter, known for its proliferation of independent shops selling vintage clothing,

MARKET MADNESS

If it's markets you're after, then Frome is your place. The big one is the not-for-profit **Frome Independent Market**, which takes place on the first Sunday of every month between March and December. The town centre is closed to traffic and taken over by some 200 stalls, showcasing everything from local food and drink to vintage fashion, furniture and collectibles. The Cheese & Grain (a popular live music and events venue) holds both the **Frome Farmers' Market** (which does what it says on the tin), on the second Saturday of the month, and the **Frome Country Market** (produce, plants, crafty things) every Thursday morning. Wednesdays and Saturdays are regular market days, which take place in the Cattle Market Car Park and at the bottom of Cheap Street. In addition to that little lot, there are a number of speciality markets, including a Vegan Market on the first Saturday of each month, also in the Cheese & Grain, plus the occasional Vintage Market or Steam Punk Fair– not forgetting, either, the Christmas Extravaganza market.

jewellery, flowers, vinyl records, and much, much more. Then take a slow (for it is very steep) walk up Catherine Hill, sneaking a right turn down Whittox Lane to the **RISE**, a brilliant church conversion that's now a gallery and café-cum-bakery; many of the original fixtures and fittings remain *in situ*, notably the magnificent organ.

⅋ FOOD & DRINK

Bistro Lotte 23 Catherine St, BA11 1DB ⌀ 01373 300646 ⊘ bistrolottefrome.co.uk ◠ 09.00–23.00 Mon–Sat, 09.00–15.00 Sun. Since opening in 2018, this cracking little restaurant has gone from strength to strength. Its keenly priced food (*moules frites, escargots, boeuf bourguignon*) and drink (wine and cider) are as authentically French as you'll find anywhere in Somerset – as is the ambience, with candle-topped wooden tables and low-key mood lighting. Service is spot on too.

The High Pavement 16 Palmer St, BA11 1DT ⌀ 07967 222862 ◠ 18.00–23.00 Fri & Sat. Occupying the ground floor of an old townhouse (which is indeed located on a high pavement), this posh, weekend-only restaurant has raised the bar, and then some, for all restaurants in Frome – and the emphasis is very much on Slow here, for that is how each dish is prepared. The cuisine is firmly of a Spanish/North African bent, with dishes such as cod *croquettas*, and harissa couscous with pine nuts and fried quail's egg. You'll find each weekend's menu posted on Facebook (f thehighpavement) on Mondays – and you must book ahead.

Palmer Street Bottle 11 Palmer St, BA11 1DS ⌀ 07971 012611 ⊘ palmerstbottle.co.uk ◠ Tue–Sat. Directly opposite The High Pavement, this superb little cheese and tap bar occupies a lovely, bright space with big bay windows and funky wooden tables and bench seating. Behind the reinforced concrete bar, a long row of taps dispense a fine selection of Bristol- and Bath-based brewery beers, as well as a selection of organic wines – and if you like them, you can buy a bottle and take your own away.

Thai Kitchen 8 King St, BA11 1BH ⌀ 01373 467370 ⊘ thaikitchenfrome.com ◠ lunch 09.00–15.00 Tue–Sat, plus 18.00–22.30 Fri & Sat. It's quite hard to find, but an awful lot of people seem to know about this ace little restaurant. With owner James greeting punters front of house and his Thai wife Puk working her magic in the kitchen, it ticks all the boxes: a short menu of appetising dishes (stir-fry beef in oyster sauce, fish cakes with curry paste) at ridiculously cheap prices, and you can bring your own bottle too.

10 NUNNEY

The village of Nunney is utterly dominated by its magnificent moated **castle** (English Heritage; free access), somewhat surprisingly one of just three in Somerset. The castle's history is slightly hazy, but what is known is that it was likely built in the late 14th century by wealthy local baron Sir John de la Mere, then remodelled in the 16th century by the Praters, a staunch Roman Catholic family from London. Its low-lying (almost street level) position ensured that it served no military purpose whatsoever; it was rather susceptible, as the one missing wall testifies. Bombarded by Cromwell's forces in 1645, then prey to gradual wear and tear, it finally collapsed on Christmas Day 1910 and the castle has pretty much remained this way ever since. Otherwise, many of the timbers, as well as stone and mullion windows and other bits and bobs, were pilfered by enterprising local residents back in the day – indeed you may notice some of these now adorning some of the cottages on Church Street. The castle's decline was halted in 1950 when it was purchased by Rob Walker, descendant of the whisky magnate Johnnie. As an interesting aside, Rob Walker was the owner of Formula One's first private racing team, which enjoyed considerable success in the 1950s and 60s through employing the likes of Stirling Moss and Graham Hill, who were among many from the racing fraternity to visit his then home at Nunney Court just down the road – this is now a private residence. Today the castle is still owned by the family but managed by English Heritage.

After nosing around the castle, make your way along Church Street to **All Saints' Church**. Situated on a small rise, it's worth a peek for its effigies, including one of de la Mere, and a fading mural of St George (minus the dragon). After visiting the sights, you could do worse than retire to the **George at Nunney** for a pint and perhaps a bite to eat. Nunney's big annual event is its **Street Market and Fair** on the first Saturday of August. Otherwise, there's loads more information on the village **website** (⊘ visitnunney.com); they also have a lively and informative Twitter account (@VisitNunney), run by Jeremy and Adrie, two well-informed locals who can give you the lowdown on just about any aspect of the village.

11 SHEPTON MALLET

🏠 **Maplestone Hall** (page 234) 🛖 **Greenacres** (page 234)

Shepton Mallet – a derivation of the Saxon name Scaep Ton, meaning Sheep Farm – doesn't rank very highly on most people's list of places to visit. This small market town has a reputation – a little unfairly in my opinion – for being a somewhat boring place where nothing very exciting ever really happens. Not that that has ever bothered the natives.

But the fact is that it is home to over 200 listed buildings (more than Wells as it happens) and boasts a clutch of attractions that would be the envy of more fashionable towns twice the size. Moreover, Shepton is the closest town to the Glastonbury Festival site, just three miles away at Pilton (as opposed to Glastonbury itself which is seven miles from Pilton), and is just a stone's throw from the Bath and West showground, the venue for the agricultural jamboree that is the Royal Bath and West Show.

"A model of the Babycham fawn that became the face of its mega-successful marketing campaign still stands on the site."

Check out the (stone) sheep on the roundabout on the A37 heading south of town. Like many settlements hereabouts, the town made its fortune in the Middle Ages from the wool trade, though several other industries have made their mark here over the course of time, including quarrying, cheese making and cider. The last of these remains an important fixture in town, though only just. The Shepton Mallet Cider Mill was only recently saved from closure thanks to the intervention of the Showering family, the same family who some 60 years earlier invented Babycham, an unfathomably popular sweet sparkling perry (a sort of proto-alcopop) in the 1960s and 70s. A model of the Babycham fawn that became the face of its mega-successful marketing campaign still stands on the site on Kilver Road, opposite Kilver Court.

Within the town itself there are one or two diversions worth investigating, starting with the **Market Cross**, a prominent, if not particularly graceful, monument originally erected in 1500 and recently scrubbed up. Close by, behind an ugly concrete civic building, the square, light-filled **Church of St Peter and St Paul** is worth a glance for its magnificent (if incomplete) late 14th-century tower, and even more impressive wood-barrel (or wagon) ceiling – indeed it was described by Pevsner as the country's finest – plus one or two other bits of detail, not least the lofty stone carved pulpit and a splendid effigy of a knight in the northeast window. Down at the opposite (southern) end of the High Street, the **tourist information office and heritage centre** (page 18) accommodates a sweet little one-room museum devoted to the town's traditional industries (cider, quarries). Its most curious exhibit, however, is a silver amulet (complete with the early Christian symbol chi-rho). Excavated from a 5th-century grave in 1990, it was a discovery that had historians rushing to proclaim that they had found the earliest

Christian burial site in Europe, though any excitement (it even made the national news) was short lived as it was later determined to be a fake.

Kilver Court Gardens
📞 01749 340422 🌐 kilvercourt.com

Once the site of the biggest woollen mill in the area, Kilver Court was purchased in 1996 by Somerset-born entrepreneur and fashion designer Roger Saul as the new headquarters for the high-end fashion label Mulberry, which he founded in 1971 just down the road in Chilcompton. Kilver's gardens were originally the 19th-century creation of industrialist Ernest Jardine, before being remodelled by the local Showering family (of Babycham fame, see opposite) in the 1960s. Their present incarnation is entirely down to Saul, who made restoring the gardens his next big project after parting company with Mulberry. I was lucky enough to spend an hour or so in his company, during which time he expounded upon his love of gardening and his vision for returning the gardens to their former glory. He started by creating the formal parterre before reworking some of the existing features, such as the rockery, waterfall, woodland stumpery, organic vegetable garden and lake – the flamingo house once kept a handful of these charismatic birds until some otters (or so it's thought) put paid to them. The garden's real wow factor though is the stupendous, 110yd-long herbaceous border, with over a thousand species planted in a sequence of beautifully choreographed colours, from dark and salad greens through to bronzes, browns and purples, then silvers and whites.

As if the gardens weren't spectacular enough in themselves, they are sliced through by the magnificent **Charlton Viaduct**, the longest of seven such structures built along a 26-mile stretch of the long-defunct Somerset and Dorset Railway (page 44). Originally raised in 1874, the viaduct was later widened to accommodate a doubling of the track size – standing underneath its massive arches, you can see quite clearly the contrast between the rough-hewn grey stone of the original structure and the red brickwork of the accompanying construction.

Alongside the gardens, the old textile mills have been regenerated to accommodate the Designer Village factory outlet (opened in 2011). Elsewhere, there's a garden nursery (take a look inside the ace Wiggly Shed), farm shop, café and restaurant – much of the menu leans heavily on spelt, which is cultivated on Roger's organic spelt farm at Sharpham

Park near Glastonbury (unfortunately not open to the public). Whatever your fancy, there's a little something here for everyone.

Shepton Mallet Prison
℘ 01743 343100 ⟁ sheptonmalletprison.com

'Some are seen pining under diseases, expiring on the floors, in loathsome cells of pestilential fevers and the confluent small pox', so wrote prison reformer John Howard in the late 18th century. Granted, Shepton Mallet Prison (aka Cornhill) is not an immediately obvious Slow destination, but it's one that I feel merits inclusion based largely on its history, which is as fascinating as it is long. Classified a Category C lifer prison – meaning prisoners who could not be trusted in open conditions but who were deemed unlikely to attempt escape – HMP Shepton Mallet was inaugurated in 1625, and, at the time of its closure in 2013, was Britain's oldest working correction facility. You can either wander at leisure on a self-guided tour or take one of the guided tours (costing a little extra; check website for times), which are led by former prison officers. By opting for the latter, you are rewarded with some colourful stories pertaining to prison life.

"Given the state of the cells, it's hard to believe that it's only been six years since it was decommissioned."

Notwithstanding the colossal, 75ft-high Grade II-listed walls, and the prison's supposed ghostly happenings (it styles itself as the country's most haunted prison), it's a stark, eerie place – by the same token, it's grimly compelling. The prison was extended and altered periodically from the late 18th century onwards, and included the installation of a tread-wheel (which those sentenced to hard labour would serve their punishment on) and the reconstruction/expansion of several wings, including B Wing (the Krays were incarcerated here for a short period as punishment for absconding from National Service), and C Wing, which was built for the purposes of housing female inmates. During World War II, it functioned as a military prison, both for the Americans and the British, before its resumption as a civilian prison in the 1960s. Given the state of the musty-smelling cells (with hard iron beds bolted to the floor, rusting basins and lavatory bowls, and peeling paintwork), it's hard to believe that it's only been six years since it was decommissioned.

After its designation as the County Gaol in 1884 – following the closures of Ilchester and Taunton prisons – a total of 25 executions were carried out at Shepton Mallet (including those of 16 American soldiers during World War II), some of which were conducted by Albert Pierrepoint, Britain's most prolific hangman. This has subsequently caused a problem for local property developers who have for some time been trying to get their hands on the place. Buried in unmarked graves deep within the prison walls are the remains of seven executed prisoners, but in order for anyone to be allowed to build upon the site, either these chaps need to be issued with a royal pardon (very unlikely), or permission must be sought from their relatives, an even more improbable scenario given how long ago these executions took place. Still, though its long-term future may be uncertain, the prison is due to remain open as a visitor attraction until 2020 at least.

12 WRAXALL VINEYARD

Wraxall BA4 6RQ ✆ 01749 860331 ⌖ wraxallvineyard.co.uk ◔ call ahead

There are a couple of excellent wineries in this part of the county, one of which is Wraxall, located a few miles south of Shepton Mallet just off the A37 – though don't come expecting the Loire Valley. Nevertheless, the vineyard's setting is sublime, positioned on a sunny, south-facing hillside with lovely views west to the Mendips. The name, Wraxall, is of medieval origin meaning 'a nook of land frequented by buzzards' (or something like that), hence the bird's logo on the label.

When Jacky and Brian moved down to Somerset from Edinburgh in 2007, ostensibly to retire, Wraxall was more or less derelict, and the vineyard, originally planted in 1974, was in a state of disrepair – in fact only one of the original grapes (Madeleine Angevine) was salvageable. Instead of retiring, the lure of returning the site to something like its former self proved to be an irresistible challenge, so they set about planting new varieties, namely Bacchus, Seyval Blanc and Pinot Noir. It took five years before the first harvest, and they now produce a quartet of still white and rosé wines – the pick of which is a luscious Pinot Noir rosé – alongside a couple of sparkling wines. The wine isn't produced on site – that's done just over the hill. Official vineyard tour dates (which includes tasting, of course) are listed on their website, but otherwise they're happy for anyone to pop along for a sample or two, though it is advisable to call ahead first. Whenever you choose to visit, there are few things more enjoyable, or Slower, than quaffing in a vineyard.

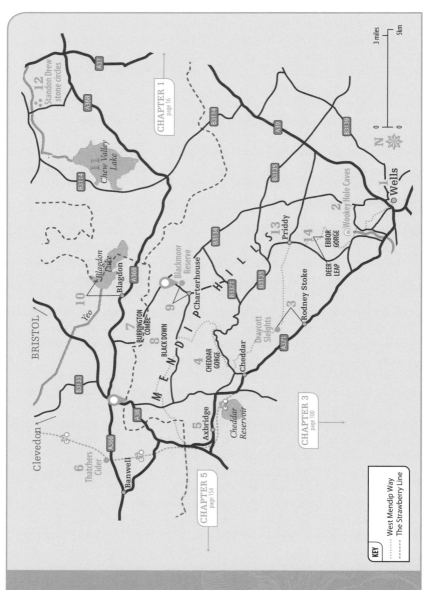

KEY
· · · · · West Mendip Way
— — — The Strawberry Line

CHAPTER 1
page 16

CHAPTER 3
page 100

CHAPTER 5
page 154

Standon Drew stone circles **12**

Chew Valley Lake **11**

A37

A368

B3114

BRISTOL

Clevedon

Thatchers Cider **6**

Banwell

A368

A38

B3133

Yeo

Blagdon Lake **10**
Blagdon

BURRINGTON COMBE **7**

BLACK DOWN **8**

Blackmoor Reserve **9**
Charterhouse

M E N D I P   H I L L S

CHEDDAR GORGE **4**

Cheddar

Axbridge **5**

Cheddar Reservoir

Draycott Sleights

Rodney Stoke **3**

A371

B3135

B3371

B3135

B3134

A368

DEER LEAP

EBBOR GORGE **14**

Priddy **13**

Wookey Hole Caves **2**

Wells **1**

A39

B3139

N

0   3 miles
0   5km

62

2
WELLS & THE MENDIPS

From Bath, this chapter takes us all directions south, roughly speaking. Southwest of Bath, **Chew Valley** and its two artificial lakes – Chew Valley and Blagdon – offer some of the best inland fishing and birding experiences anywhere in the country alongside some enticing waterside trails. Technically, Chew Valley is part of the **Mendips**, which feel, and look, like a tough little bit of Derbyshire dropped into the soft southern underbelly of Somerset. A distinctive limestone ridge pocked by innumerable cave systems and flanked by deep gorges, this is terrific walking country, though the wonderfully varied terrain permits all manner of adventurous pursuits, including mountain biking, caving and climbing.

Many visitors make an immediate beeline for the twin attractions of **Cheddar Gorge** (and its caves) and **Wookey Hole**, but there are greater rewards to be had by exploring the higher ground, such as **Charterhouse**, **Black Down** or **Priddy**, where you'll experience a quite different – and appreciably more peaceful – side to this charismatic landscape. It gets wet here mind, so come prepared.

The only urban centre of note in this area is **Wells**, which, on account of its magnificent cathedral ranks as England's smallest city, though it really couldn't feel any less like one. The cathedral, alongside the neighbouring Bishop's Palace and a smattering of other less obvious, though no less enjoyable, sites, make Wells an unmissable destination. Otherwise, the only other vaguely populous settlements covered within this chapter are Cheddar itself and **Axbridge**, the latter having retained its superb medieval core.

GETTING THERE & AROUND

Aside from the station at Yatton – 12 miles west of Bristol and on the Bristol to Exeter line operated by Great Western Railway ($\oslash$ gwr.com)

– there are no train lines running through the area covered in this chapter, so you'll be reliant on your own transport – be it two or four wheels – or buses. The few railway lines that once passed through this part of Somerset have sadly long since vanished, though one wonders how many more visitors Wells would receive were there still a line here – Wells station itself closed to passengers in 1951. Otherwise, you can walk or **cycle** one of the old trackbeds, such as the wonderful Strawberry Line (part of the old Cheddar Valley Line), which currently links Yatton with Cheddar. The Strawberry Line is actually part of the **National Cycle Network Route 26**, which continues north to Portishead on the Bristol Channel and south to Portland on the Dorset coast, a total distance of 81 miles. A section of the long-distance **Route 3**, meanwhile, cuts across the Mendips' central plateau, before continuing down through southwest Somerset and eventually to Land's End. The Mendips were tailor-made for **mountain biking**, with a number of rough and ready single-track trails, and while the terrain may look relatively obliging, don't be fooled – there are some challenging rides to be had here.

BUSES

There are no **buses** through the Mendips themselves, though an hourly service (126) runs along the A371 under the southern edge of the escarpment, linking Wells and Weston-super-Mare via several villages covered in this chapter, including Draycott, Cheddar and Axbridge. Otherwise, a number of services fan out from Wells to other parts of the county. This includes the Mendip Xplorer (service 376), a slightly misleading name given that it runs between Bristol and Glastonbury (via Wells) along the A37 and A39 (⊘ firstgroup.com).

WALKING

Above all, the Mendips offer glorious **walking**; though not especially pronounced, this terrain is not to be underestimated. Time permitting, you could tackle the 50-mile-long **Mendip Way**, which connects Weston-super-Mare and Frome; it's actually two constituent parts, but for the purposes of this chapter, it's the 30-mile-long West Mendip Way, connecting Uphill, near Weston, with Wells, that is of relevance. Otherwise, there are endless possibilities, a couple of which I have described in the chapter. You can also find a range of downloadable walking guides on the Mendips AONB website (⊘ mendiphillsaonb.org.uk).

WELLS & AROUND

1 WELLS

🏠 **Stoberry House** (page 235)

After the City of London (which let's face it doesn't really count), Wells is England's smallest city by virtue of its resplendent cathedral, which presides over a neat kernel of time-skewed medieval buildings. The Bishop's Palace and Vicar's Close complete an exceptional ecclesiastical enclave, though not to be outdone are a number of less conspicuous treasures, some of which I stumbled upon entirely by accident. All in all Wells and Slow make for happy bedfellows, and yet despite the crowds – and it can get very busy in summer – the place rarely feels overwhelmed. Small it may be, but this city packs quite a punch.

Wells first came to prominence under the Romans, who were drawn to the area by the natural springs, before the Anglo-Saxons held sway, initially under King Ine of Wessex who established a minster church here some time in the early 8th century. Indeed, the history and development of the city is irrevocably bound up with that of the cathedral and its bishops, none more so than Thomas Bekynton (c1390–1465) who was responsible for much of what you see today.

Exploring the city

Nowhere is Bekynton's influence more pronounced than the **Market Place**, which really comes into its own during the twice-weekly markets, held here on Wednesdays and Saturdays. Close together in the northeastern corner of the square are two contrasting gateways: one, the Penniless Porch, leads through to Cathedral Green – site of the magnificent Wells Cathedral (page 68) and the Wells and Mendip Museum (page 70) – while the turreted Bishop's Eye marks the entrance to the Bishop's Palace complex (page 71). On one side of the square, you'll notice a plaque in the pavement, which is actually a recreation of local girl Mary Rand's gold-winning jump at the 1964 Tokyo Olympic Games – a then world record of 6.76m. If you've never contemplated what jumping nearly 7m looks like (and really, why would you), you'll be impressed.

From the square, work your way down the **High Street**, either side of which are shallow water channels, another Bekynton contribution. At the far end of the High Street stands **St Cuthbert's Church**, which, believe it or not, some mistake for the cathedral – one can only imagine the disappointment. To be fair, it's an outstanding monument in its own right and worth more than a passing glance. Aside from the high, painted timber ceiling, with its carved and decorated angels, rosettes and shields, the most striking thing you'll notice is where the stone pillars darken, about a third of the way up. This the result of the church being raised some time in the 14th century – though how they achieved this is anyone's guess. Architecturally the standout feature (albeit one that has been largely destroyed) is the Jesse Tree reredos in the south transept, an exceptionally rare example of the legend in carved form; rediscovered in 1848, Jesse lies recumbent at the bottom with fragments of sculptures plastered elsewhere. For all that though, the church's main claim to fame is as the setting for the gruesomely funny demise of local journalist Tim Messenger at the village fete in the cult comedy *Hot Fuzz*, most of which was filmed in Wells – a fact that the city makes great play of.

Just behind St Cuthbert's are **Bubwith's Almshouses**, the oldest (1424) of the city's five almshouses, each of which is named after its founding bishop. Originally designed to provide accommodation, and sometimes other facilities, for those most in need – a precursor to the welfare state if you like – it's a function they still fulfil today. They're not public areas but it's unlikely anyone should mind if you take a wee peek through the gate. As it happens, I chanced upon an elderly gentleman who had been living here since his return from Greece some ten years previous. He proceeded to show me around the complex, with its fragrant, flower-filled garden and pocket-sized chapel, commenting that he wouldn't swap it for anywhere else. It wasn't difficult to see why. Across the road, on Priest Row, are the **Llewellyn's and Charles's almshouses**, two opposing rows of toy-like cottages not dissimilar to Vicar's Close (page 69), albeit on a much smaller scale.

Heading south from the High Street, on the far side of the recreation ground, is the superb 15th-century **Bishop's Barn** (thebishopsbarn. wordpress.com). A Grade I-listed building and Scheduled Ancient Monument with massive whitewashed stone walls and a magnificent cruck roof, the barn was, as the name suggests, originally part of the palace complex, and to that end was used as a grain store; thereafter it was utilised as a drill hall and arms dump, although those of a certain age may (or may not) recall seeing the likes of Status Quo and Supertramp perform here in the 1970s. Classified as vulnerable on the Buildings at Risk register, the Bishop's Barn is currently held in trust by Mendip District Council, whose quest it is to secure further funding for the ongoing programme of restoration. In the meantime, the barn continues to be used as a multi-purpose venue, primarily for the excellent Into the BARN programme, a series of community-led events staged at different times of the year. As an interesting aside, in 1867, W G Grace, England's greatest cricketer, played on the adjacent field, scoring a meagre three runs. Howzat(!) for a piece of trivia?

Located roughly half a mile east of the centre just south off Bath Road is the **Mendip Hospital Cemetery** (℘ 01749 674768 ⬧ mendiphospitalcemetery.org.uk), the burial ground for the Somerset and Bath Lunatic Asylum, which opened in 1848 and closed, as the Mendip Mental Hospital, in 1991. The site was almost lost to developers before the Friends of the Mendip Hospital Cemetery group stepped in in 2002 and became its sole custodians. Their stated aim was to preserve the cemetery as a nature reserve and to this end they've done a fantastic job, especially considering the state it was in. Following the autumn cut, there are wildflowers galore, and at any given time of the year you'll find the fields carpeted with snowdrops, primroses, foxglove and cowslip. Sparrowhawks are frequent visitors and you may also glimpse the occasional heron feeding down at the pond.

An estimated 3,000 burials took place here (the last was in 1963), and these would have been denoted by numbered iron gravemarkers – most have since been removed and boxed up, though clusters remain *in situ* here and there. Those that could afford it had a headstone, hence the presence of around 25 of these scattered randomly around the site. The cemetery chapel, which is in pretty good nick all things considered, holds the burial register alongside newspaper clippings, maps and plans, and photos of some of the deceased; many, remarkably, from the late 19th century. The cemetery is open most Sundays (and occasional Saturdays), details of which can be found on the website. To get here, take the turning next to the Britannia Inn on Bath Road, from where it's a five-minute walk along Hooper Avenue to a farm gate and then down the short track to the cemetery. The hospital itself is half a mile away in South Horrington and, although it has since been converted into flats, it's worth popping along to view the George Gilbert Scott-designed building, an austere, two-storey structure with a distinctive frontage.

Wells Cathedral & Vicar's Close
✆ 01749 674483 ⬙ wellscathedral.org.uk

Exerting a tremendous presence for miles around, **Wells Cathedral** is not only one of the finest ecclesiastical monuments in England but lays fair claim to being the first complete Gothic cathedral in the country. Begun in the late 12th century by Bishop Robert of Lewes, it was built on the site of an earlier church (of which there are a few extant remains) with subsequent additions further down the line. As a secular establishment, the cathedral survived more or less unscathed following the Reformation, though it did suffer fairly extensive damage during the later Civil War.

Seen for the first time, the massive west front is a startling proposition, its façade crawling with outstanding statuary including, centre top, Christ flanked by angels and, below, people ascending to heaven with their coffins, scenes from the Old and New testaments, as well as kings, queens, bishops and saints. The cool, cavernous interior is no less jaw dropping and if you're a fan of Gothic architecture (and even if you're not), you could spend hours absorbing the wealth of detail here – indeed, a repeat visit may be in order just to take it all in. Suffice to say that it's impossible to do this place justice in the short space I have here, so instead I've cherry-picked a few of its many arresting features.

The most striking aspect as you enter is the quartet of restraining – or scissor – arches, which were set in place (as were the partially obscured buttresses) once it became apparent that the hulking central tower was under threat of collapse. The nearby south transept is awash with flamboyant stone carvings, notably on the capitals, many of which have been adorned with some amusing vignette or other; wrapped around one particular capital frieze are four scenes, collectively known as *The Fruit Stealer*, with one scene depicting the farmer whacking the thief over the head with a stick as he tries to make off with a basket of apples. Look out too for the poor chap trying to extract a thorn from his foot and another grimacing with toothache. Observing the sand-coloured interior, it's hard to imagine that the cathedral was once painted throughout, tantalising glimpses of which remain here and there, notably on Thomas Bekynton's chantry chapel, which still bears its original mid 15th-century paintwork. Close by, high up in the quire, the **Jesse Window** (1340) – recently restored but which only survived being stoned during the Civil War thanks to its lofty position – ranks among the very finest medieval stained-glass windows anywhere in Europe.

The cathedral's single greatest triumph, however, is the octagonal **Chapterhouse**, a glorious, light-filled room centred on a single column of Purbeck marble supporting an elaborately ribbed ceiling; the room was formerly used for church legal proceedings (hence the stone seats), though today it's utilised for exhibitions and performances. The approach to the chapterhouse is via a sweeping stone staircase, which was made even more famous thanks to a photograph taken by Frederick Evans in 1903 entitled *A Sea of Steps* – have a look online. Lastly, if you get the chance, pop your head into the **Chained Library**, so named because books would, on occasion, go walkabout; it's worth a look for the Tudor ceiling alone.

Adjacent to the cathedral is the 14th-century **Vicar's Close**, one of Britain's best-preserved examples of a medieval street, which probably explains its ongoing popularity as a film and television set – *Poldark* and *Wolf Hall* were both fairly recent visitors. The Close comprises two symmetrical rows of cottages, harbouring 27 lodgings housing members of the Vicars' Choral (the men's choir), as well as vergers, organists and other administrative staff from the cathedral. Plans are afoot to restore one of the cottages to its original state for visitors to view, but for now you'll have to content yourself with a stroll along this

GOING FOR A SONG

Formed in AD909, the **Wells Cathedral Choir** is one of the finest in the world. Currently led by organist and master of the choristers, Matthew Owens, the choir comprises the 12 Vicars' Choral (the men), and 18 boys and 18 girls, though the boys and girls (who were only introduced in 1994) are separate choirs and only sing together on special occasions; all choristers are educated at the Wells Cathedral School, one of just five specialist music schools in England. There are plenty of opportunities to hear the choir in action: Evensong (17.15 Mon–Fri & 15.00 Sun), Eucharist (09.45 Sun) and Choral Matins (11.30 Sun). In October, the **new music wells festival** is a week of retrospective organ and choral music, attracting some of the world's most renowned composers, as well as premiere performances by the cathedral choir. If you're not fortunate enough to catch them in the flesh, there are dozens of recordings available. Schedules are posted on ⌀ wellscathedral.org.uk.

medieval masterpiece. The Close is actually linked to the cathedral via the Chain Gate, which you may have passed under, but unless you've special dispensation this is not accessible to the public.

Wells & Mendip Museum
☎ 01749 673477 ⊘ wellsmuseum.org.uk ☺ Mon–Sat

A few paces along from Vicar's Close, the small but eminently enjoyable Wells and Mendip Museum is jam-packed with fascinating stuff, and you're quite likely to spend more time here than you initially planned.

"You'll find a stone memorial honouring local hero Harry Patch, the last surviving combat soldier from World War I."

I know I did. This being the Mendips, it's no surprise that much is made of the area's geology, with cave exploration to the fore; to this end a great debt is owed to the pioneering speleologist and founder of the museum, Herbert Balch (1869–1958). A mock-up cavern displays all manner of cumbersome-looking equipment, for instance rope ladders, hammers and harnesses, and gas and carbide lamps. Here, too, are some intriguing fossil remains – many unearthed by Balch himself – from the various cave-dwelling animals (bears, hyenas, elephants) that once lurked within, mainly mandibles, skulls and other bone fragments; somewhat more grisly are the skeletal remains of a newborn baby embedded within a clump of rock.

Hidden away in a darkened room, beyond cabinets packed with fossils and minerals, is a beautifully worked collection of early 19th-century Victorian samplers, delicately embroidered pieces that schoolgirls, some as young as seven, were obliged to complete as part of their education; many are impressed with a moral or religious text, some movingly so. One in particular caught my eye; it read 'Eleanor Morris is my name, Wales is my nation, Carmarthenshire is my dwelling, place and Christ is my salvation, when I am dead and in my grave and all my bones are rotten, in this sampler you will find my name when I am quite forgotten'. Hanging on the walls above the staircase is a group of statues that once graced the cathedral's West Front; it's a rare opportunity to see close up the exquisite craftsmanship involved. On the front lawn you'll find a stone memorial honouring local hero Harry Patch, the last surviving combat soldier from World War I prior to his death, aged 111, in 2009 – a fact that earned him nationwide fame.

The Bishop's Palace

✆ 01749 988111 ⊘ bishopspalace.org.uk; see ad, 4th colour section

'An extensive palace, adorned with wonderful splendour, surrounded with flowing waters, and crowned with a fine row of turreted walls,' so recalled the playwright Thomas Chaundler in the 15th century. Fast forward some 600 years and the venerable Bishop's Palace – deep in the shadow of the cathedral – appears to have changed little since then. Encircled by a wide moat, itself fed by the wellsprings from whence the city takes its name, the palace has been home to the Bishop of Bath and Wells for some 800 years, among them Cardinal Thomas Wolsey and George Carey. Beyond the Gatehouse entrance, a baize-like croquet lawn fronts the **Great Hall**, the third-largest secular medieval hall in England after Westminster and Canterbury. Largely despoiled during the Reformation, its current shell – roofless and minus two walls – provides a picturesque backdrop to lush gardens, which extend across the South Lawn to a grassy bank just below the crenellated ramparts, themselves bookended by chunky bastions. A walk along the ramparts affords lovely views of the palace's medieval deer park (sadly deer-less these days) and away to Glastonbury Tor and the Mendips.

The palace itself retains some fine architectural detail – not least the magnificent cross-ribbed vaulting in the Undercroft – alongside one or two noteworthy exhibits, including the dazzling gold leaf coronation cope worn by the Bishop of Bath and Wells for coronations; the only other bishop to receive the honour of escorting the monarch on such occasions is the Bishop of Durham. The Long Gallery, meanwhile, is hung with portraits of former bishops – keep an eye out for Bishop Mews who has a clearly identifiable black patch on his cheek, strategically placed to cover a musket wound sustained during one of the many campaigns he fought in. More worthwhile is Bishop Burnell's beautifully proportioned **Chapel of the Holy Trinity**, distinguished by a series of richly coloured windows comprising fragments salvaged from French churches destroyed during the 1789 Revolution.

The real joy of this place though is the **outer gardens**, whose 14 acres make for a splendid retreat on a warm summer's day and where I spent a couple of hours lazily mooching around. Above all there's the lovely arboretum with hornbeam, foxglove and birch trees, alongside a profusion of wildflowers, which, depending upon the season could be snowdrops, bluebells or orchids. Here too you'll find a bountiful kitchen garden (the results of which sustain the excellent Bishop's Table café; see below) and a little orchard with a fabulous play area for kids – for my money this is the best picnic spot in the city. Elsewhere, the five wells, including the holy well of St Andrew, have been neatly landscaped into a series of manmade pools, one featuring a mini waterfall.

FOOD & DRINK

The Bishop's Table Bishop's Palace Gardens, BA5 2PD ✆ 01749 988111
⬧ thebishopspalace.org.uk ◔ Apr–Oct 09.30–18.00, Nov–Mar 09.30–16.00 daily.
Overlooking the croquet lawn, this smart, glass-fronted café offers cracking breakfasts (including vegetarian and vegan options) and lunches (lamb and chilli burger, Somerset Ploughman's), plus coffee and cake, of course.

The Good Earth 4–6 Priory Rd, BA5 1SY ✆ 01749 678600 ⬧ www.thegoodearthwells.
co.uk ◔ 09.30–16.00 Mon–Fri, 09.00–17.00 Sat. What started out as a wholefood store in the 1970s (which is still here) has become something of a local institution, at least judging by the number of punters that make a beeline for this cracking veggie café. And you should stop by, too, be it for a cup of freshly roasted coffee (made using organic origin espresso beans) and a wedge of lemon polenta and poppy seed cake, or a slice of pizza or quiche with salad (£6.95) at lunchtime (from noon). On the way out, take a peek inside the adjoining shop, stocked with beautifully crafted household items.

Goodfellows 5 Sadler St, BA5 2RR ✆ 01749 673866 ⬧ goodfellowswells.co.uk ◔ daily, but check the website for specific hours. An inland seafood restaurant in Somerset doesn't initially seem to quite fit with the Slow ethos, but rest assured, Goodfellows is the real deal when it comes to its fishy intentions; Brixham crab, and tuna carpaccio, and king scallops with wild mushrooms are just some of the mouthwatering possibilities; if you can't decide, have a bash at the tasting menu (£48). The restaurant's open-plan kitchen allows diners to watch owner/chef, Adam Fellows, hard at it. Meanwhile, his wife Martine runs the adjoining deli/patisserie, whose delectable selection of cakes and pastries should assuage any sweet-toothed cravings.

2 WOOKEY HOLE CAVES

⅄ Wookey Farm Campsite (page 235)
✆ 01749 672243 ⬧ wookey.co.uk ◔ mid-Feb–Dec, daily; Dec–mid-Feb, Sat & Sun

An intricate system of deep pools and intricate subterranean rock formations, Wookey Hole may have acquired its name from the old English word *wocig*, meaning 'animal trap'; what is known is that humans inhabited these depths at least 50,000 years ago. Although there was some initial exploration of the caves here in the late 19th century, it wasn't until the celebrated caver and geologist **Herbert Balch** pitched up in the early 1900s that the extent of what once lurked within came to light – quite literally. Balch spent much of his career systematically exploring and mapping these caves, unearthing all manner of artefacts in the process, many of which are on display at Wells Museum (page 70). Following his work, the caves opened to the public in 1927. Wookey has also been a world-renowned cave-diving site ever since F G Balcombe completed the first successful dive here in 1935 – indeed these were the first cave dives to take place anywhere in Britain. Since that time, the caves' complex of flooded passages have proved irresistible to a succession of expert divers – the record for Wookey (and until 2008 the record for the British Isles) is 90m, set by John Volanthen and Rick Stanton in 2005; both Stanton and Volanthen were among the first divers to reach a group of children stranded in caves in Thailand in 2018, an incident that made international news.

The principal attraction among many others here at Wookey Hole are the visits to the caves, by guided tour only, and lasting about 45 minutes. Many of the standard cave formations, such as stalagmites and stalactites, are present to some degree or other. Wookey's signature cave is Chamber 20, which opened to the public as recently as 2015; the largest of the 25 chambers so far discovered within the system, it features a subterranean lake but is more notable for its rarely seen fluted rock formations, which manifest themselves as corrugated surfaces or ridges – compositions that are more commonly found in Chinese cave systems.

Exiting the caves, you enter Dinosaur Valley (yes, really), setting for a herd of life-size prehistoric beasts in full-on animatronic mode. The pick of the many other attractions scattered around the site is an interactive 4D cinema experience, which is sure to raise a giggle or two if nothing else. Elsewhere, there are enough dollops of tack to keep younger ones entertained, but in truth it's all looking just a little tired these days.

THE MENDIPS & SURROUNDING AREA

Wedged between tracts of gently rolling farmland south of Bristol and the northern fringes of the iron-flat Levels, the Mendips – an area covering just 22 miles (east to west) and peaking at 325m – don't get the acclaim that they should. Richly textured by history and nature, this sparsely populated limestone escarpment is permeated with fissures, tunnels and chambers that have given rise to all manner of dramatic formations: deep canyons, dry valleys and rocky outcrops. Another distinctive feature of the Mendips are its dry-stone walls – many of which have existed since medieval times – that criss-cross the largely treeless plateau. The odd, isolated farmstead aside, there's very little human activity here – indeed, there are but a couple of villages located on the ridge itself.

The toponymy of Mendip is unclear, though the most likely explanation is that the name derives from the medieval word 'Mynes-Deepes' (as in 'Deep Mines'), which would seem reasonable given that the area has been worked commercially for lead and zinc since Roman times. Indeed, history has firmly left its mark on the Mendips: Iron Age hillforts, abandoned mine workings, burial mounds and World War II remains are just some of the features that litter the landscape. This wonderfully diverse topography guarantees limitless opportunities for leisure pursuits: caving, climbing, mountain biking, horseriding, fishing, birdwatching and, of course, walking, the possibilities for which are limitless; it's one of my favourite walking destinations anywhere, and not just in Somerset. For the purposes of this chapter, it's the Mendips' western and central plateau (designated an AONB in 1972) that is covered. Of interest to anyone wishing to learn more about the landscape, **Mendip Rocks** is a programme of events taking place between July and October, ranging from cave and quarry tours to all manner of guided walks (industrial, archaeological and geological among others); information on the various events can be obtained from ⊘ mendiphillsaonb.org.uk.

3 RODNEY STOKE & DRAYCOTT SLEIGHTS

Wedged between the Levels and the Mendips, 4 miles northwest of Wookey Hole, **Rodney Stoke** is one of Somerset's nine so-called Thankful Villages (villages that suffered no casualties during World

War I), and is named after the Rodney family, two of whose number – Sir Thomas and his son, Sir John – were lords of the manor, as well as prominent 14th-century politicians. As good a reason as any to stop by is the 12th-century, Grade I-listed **St Leonard's Church**, tucked away at the bottom of the village.

Inside beyond the rood screen – a superb example of Jacobean woodcarving – in the Rodney Chapel, is an assemblage of exceptional monuments dedicated to the eponymous family. By far the most ostentatious is the floor-to-ceiling tomb of George Rodney, which still betrays hints of colour here and there, though a more impressive architectural proposition is the stone tomb and effigy of Thomas, helmet to one side and his feet resting on a dog's back. The sword above his tomb was stolen in the 1960s, and the helmet likewise some years later; while the sword was never found, the helmet was recovered when the dealer who acquired it took it to the Victoria and Albert Museum in London, whereupon it was promptly identified and returned. Reposed within an arched canopy under the window is a similarly resplendent effigy of Anna Lakes, wife of George, this one hewn from Somerset alabaster. Back in the nave, take note of the pews with their beautifully carved ends, a common feature of many a Somerset church. Outside, to the rear of the church, is an upright Grade II-listed grave slab, remarkable for both its age (12th century) and its two extremely rare incised crosses, which commemorate a double burial.

While here, it'd be remiss not to hop across the main (A371) road for a stroll around **Rodney Stoke National Nature Reserve**, an alluring mix of woodland and grassland rolling down the south-facing slopes of the Mendips. Adjacent is **Draycott Sleights Nature Reserve**, a steeply sloping scarp comprising limestone grassland (in Somerset speak, 'sleight' means sheep pasture) and rocky outcrops; a well-signposted mile-long circular trail starts by the entrance on New Road, which bisects the reserve. As in so many places on the Mendips, the commanding views make the short trek up here worth the effort; it's a great spot for a picnic no less. Both reserves are species-rich, harbouring numerous communities of butterfly and dragonfly, as well as resident brown hares, roe deer and muntjac, while various raptors patrol the skies.

"Rodney Stoke is one of Somerset's Thankful Villages (villages that suffered no casualties during World War I)."

CYCLING THE STRAWBERRY LINE

Running between Yatton and Cheddar – a distance of ten miles – the Strawberry Line (⌀ thestrawberryline.org.uk) takes its name from the railway (which was officially called the Cheddar Valley Line, and was part of the Great Western Railway) that transported local strawberries, produce and passengers until its closure in 1965. Following the old trackbed (part of the **National Cycle Network Route 26**), it's off-road nearly all the way and mostly flat too, making it a wonderful Slow proposition for families with little 'uns; that said, if you do have young children, it might be best tackled in bite-size stages, which is what we did with our daughter.

A lovely bit of sculpture heralds the start of the route at **Yatton**, whereupon the wide and flat track passes through open countryside and, on your right, the Biddle Street SSSI, whose distinctive rhynes and ditches (for this is on the margins of the Levels) are home to an array of flora (meadowsweet, flag iris) and fauna (dragonflies and damselflies, reed and sedge warblers and myriad butterfly species); look out, too, for nesting boxes which have been specially constructed for kestrels and barn owls. Crossing the River Yeo (and a main road), you bypass Congresbury village and continue down a longish stretch (keeping an eye out for apple orchards – page 83) to **Sandford**, which is roughly the halfway stage. Here, the old station (☺ Apr–Oct, Sat & Sun) has been restored as a wonderful heritage centre packed with memorabilia and, outside, a vintage carriage and sentinel shunting engine – a good spot to pause for some light refreshment. From Sandford, it's a few short rotations to **Winscombe** where the old station area has been recast as an attractive green space with a picnic area, bits

¶¶ FOOD & DRINK

The Cider Barn Latches Ln Crossroads, Draycott BS27 3RU ⌀ 01934 741837. If nothing else, curiosity is likely to lead you to investigate this conspicuous roadside barn positioned right on the B371. Run by the affable Jason, the Barn has become one of the most popular watering holes in the area, which may have something to do with its fine selection of local ciders and real ales, delicious homemade food (shepherd's pie, chilli) and constant hubbub of lively chatter. There's often live music too, including an open-mic night on the first and third Wednesdays of the month. Given all that, there's a good chance you'll end up staying here longer than you anticipated – and that wouldn't be a bad thing at all.

4 CHEDDAR GORGE

⋏ Petruth Paddocks (page 235)

Cheddar Gorge is often rated one of Britain's finest natural phenomena, a claim that's not without substance. If nothing else, it's certainly England's largest canyon – an impressive fact for starters. A true river gorge, of sculpture and a historical timeline. Beyond here lies Shute Shelve Tunnel (the only tunnel en route) before the line loops into Axbridge. The last section, from Axbridge to Cheddar, skirts the eastern rim of the Cheddar Reservoir, before ending, rather unceremoniously, at a light industrial complex on the edge of Cheddar itself, though this was the location for the old station yard, some remains of which are still visible.

There are several very welcome, and welcoming, pit stops en route, as well as further possibilities in Winscombe and Axbridge (page 82). The best of these is the **Strawberry Line Café** located at Yatton Railway Station (01934 835758 strawberrylinecafe.co.uk 07.30–15.30 Mon–Fri, 09.30–16.00 Sat & Sun). Occupying the formerly disused waiting room on platform 1, this bustling little café

– part of the Strawberry Line Community Interest Company, a very laudable project to help people with learning disabilities assimilate into mainstream society – serves up scrumptious homemade grub (soups, quiches and fishcakes, breakfasts, coffee and big wedges of cake). Happy, courteous staff, a wood-burning fire, games and books for kids, and old black-and-white photos of the railway round things off perfectly. This place fully deserves your support. And rather handily, between April and October, the café also has **bike hire** available (£8 for 3 hours, £12 for 6 hours, plus helmet & lock), including one disability-adapted tricycle.

Plans are afoot to extend the route east between Cheddar and Wells (and then on to Shepton Mallet), and north between Yatton and Clevedon, though this is unlikely to happen any time soon.

Cheddar was formed millions of years ago by glacial meltwater, the resultant river creating the massive fissure you see today. The most exciting approach to the gorge is along the B3135 from the east. Until 1800, there was no carriage road through here; instead access would have been by horse or pack mule, or on foot – these days a narrow, tightly twisting road shadowed by towering cliff sides wends its way through the two-mile chasm. Whatever your mode of transport, this demands concentration, not least because there are so many distractions; in addition to the gorge's awesome natural beauty, feral Soay sheep – with their distinctive, shaggy chocolate coats – and wild goats cling improbably to the sides, while buzzards, falcons and kestrels circle high above. Unsurprisingly, it's a landscape beloved of climbers, the gorge presenting some of the country's most challenging terrain. These days, the gorge is owned by the National Trust, though the caves and other attractions, as well as the parking facilities, are not.

Cheddar and tourism have long gone hand in hand. The village had in fact established itself as a popular tourist attraction long before the opening of the caves, thanks in large part to the opening of the Great Western Railway branch line through Cheddar in 1869. The railway line has long gone, and these days it's the caves and its attendant attractions that sustain the local economy. The crowds (in summer at least) can

WHEY THERE!

Cheese has been the currency of Cheddar since the late 12th century, when the first authentic Cheddar was made here – the cool, stable temperatures and lush pastures were deemed perfect for its production. At one time Cheddar was solely the preserve of the King's Court: both Henry II and Charles I were said to be partial to the stuff – as, evidently, was Captain Scott, who took 3,500lb of the stuff with him for his 1901 Antarctic expedition aboard *Discovery*.

Although Cheddar is now produced the world over, only a dozen or so farms in the West Country (Somerset, Devon, Dorset and Cornwall) are licensed to use the EU PDO (Product of Designated Origin) as West Country Farmhouse Cheddar, meaning that those producers must use traditional Cheddar-making techniques, otherwise known as 'Cheddaring': this involves cutting the cheese into blocks before stacking and turning them at regular intervals to drain the whey – it must also be aged for a minimum of nine months. Barely half a century ago, there were some 400 producers in Somerset making authentic Cheddar, a number that dwindled rapidly owing to, among other things, the decline in the number of farms and the absence of protected status for the

name. Officially, the only Cheddar made in Cheddar itself these days is by the Cheddar Gorge Cheese Company (cheddaronline. co.uk), where you can actually watch the cheese being made and pick up some to take home. You can also buy the stuff at the Original Cheddar Cheese Company (originalcheddargorgecheese.co.uk), who opened Cheddar's first cheese shop in 1870. The taste of Cheddar depends upon a number of factors, including location, time of year and what the cows have been eating. Generally speaking, the taste will vary from the gentle, creamy flavour of a mild (sold at around three months) to the distinctly nuttier, sweeter taste of a mature (or extra mature), which is traditionally cloth-bound and sold nine to 15 months after production. Some locally produced cheese is still stored within Gough's Cave (see opposite), its constant low temperature and humidity perfect for maturation.

You can find decent Cheddar in many farm shops, though the three regarded the best are Keen's in Wincanton (keenscheddar. co.uk), Montgomery's in North Cadbury (montgomerycheese.co.uk), as well as the Westcombe Dairy near Evercreech (westcombedairy.com).

be off-putting, as can the litany of souvenir shops and cafés lining the main road. Car parking, too, is a pain, though there are designated pay-and-displays dotted about, which cost around £5 a day. The village of Cheddar itself is nothing to get too worked up about, though there are one or two agreeable pubs should you wish to stick around.

Cheddar Caves

⟋ 01934 742343 ⟋ cheddargorge.co.uk

Cheddar's star turn is **Gough's Cave**, named after the eponymous explorer who discovered, and then opened, these caves in the late 19th century – though anecdotal evidence suggests that the cave was probably shown to visitors some decades earlier. By this time though, the far smaller **Cox's Cave** just down the road was already well established as one of the country's leading show caves, having been discovered in 1837 – indeed, Gough and the eponymous Cox brothers would go on to become keen rivals. Around 800m of Gough's Cave are open for self-guided visits, with several caverns on show, including St Paul's Cathedral, whose walls and ceilings have been stained a rich ochre by iron oxides, and the calcium-rich Diamond Chamber, home to some of the caves' most impressive stalagmite deposits. One of Europe's most important late Upper Palaeolithic sites, Gough's Cave has yielded remarkable evidence of early modern human culture, for example a human skull sculpted into a bowl – in fact there's no shortage of evidence to suggest that cannibalism was a common practice back in the day. The caves' most famous excavation was the near-complete skeleton of a man discovered in 1903, thought to be 9,000 to 10,000 years old; known as '**Cheddar Man**', the old boy's remains (Britain's oldest complete skeleton) currently reside in the Natural History Museum in London.

To be honest, a visit to Gough's Cave alone suffices, but given that the ticket includes a further four attractions, which run the length of the main (B3135) road, you may as well take in as much as you can, time permitting. These include Beyond the View, a 270° cinematic presentation; Dreamhunters, a cleverly conceived multimedia walk-through experience located inside Cox's Cave; and the intermittently illuminating Museum of Prehistory. Finally, there's Jacob's Ladder, with its 274 knee-trembling steps to the top of the gorge, and superlative views once up there. It's worth noting that there is also a separate entry fee for Jacob's Ladder if that's all you want to do, though you can avoid

GORGE WALK

For a very different, and very dramatic, perspective of the gorge, allow yourself a couple of hours for the Gorge Walk. It's a popular, well-worn trail, but no less enjoyable for being so – though if you want it (almost) all to yourself, make as early a start as possible. Begin on Cufic Lane, diagonally opposite the National Trust office; from here, the well-signposted walk continues in an easterly direction along the northern rim, with the main gorge road some 500ft below on your right. Descending and then crossing the road at Black Rock (which, at about 1.7 miles, is roughly the halfway point), the path climbs steeply to the top of the gorge (so the road is once again on your right) – however, you'd do well to rein in any curiosity and stay well away from the edge as there's no protection on this south side from the almost sheer drop. The views from here, not only of the gorge, but westwards across the fenlands of the Somerset Levels, and Cheddar Reservoir to the Quantock Hills, are fantastic. During early summer you'll likely come across the endemic **Cheddar Pink** wildflower emerging from cracks in the limestone; the county flower no less, it's not found anywhere else in Britain. Continuing in a westerly fashion, the walk concludes with a descent of Jacob's Ladder (page 79).

paying this altogether if you complete the Gorge Walk (see box, above). Incidentally, there are good savings to be made by purchasing tickets (which are otherwise quite expensive) online.

If you're around in late June, consider having a look at what's going on as part of the **Top of the Gorge Festival**, which, strangely enough, occupies a site at the top of the gorge, and features all manner of adventurous activities (caving, climbing, archery, foraging and bushcraft among others), alongside music, film, food and drink.

5 AXBRIDGE

🏠 **Oak House Hotel** (page 235)

A sedate little market town lying at the foot of the Mendips and pushed up hard against the A371, Axbridge is a real charmer. That said, it probably doesn't get the visitors it should – in part, I would assume, because of its proximity to Cheddar just down the road – not that the locals particularly mind. Granted its Royal Charter in 1202, when King John sold most of the royal manor of Cheddar to the Bishop of Bath and Wells, the town established itself as a major centre of the wool and cloth trades, industries that prospered here well into the 17th century. The town's handsome medieval square – for centuries the site of markets and fairs – preserves a neat kernel of pastel-coloured tenements and wood-framed buildings, though many of these are now concealed behind modern façades; it's just a shame that car parking is allowed here. Take a little walk up the High Street too; there aren't many streetscapes of this ilk left anywhere in the country these days.

The square's focal point is **King John's Hunting Lodge**, a misnomer if ever there was one: the eponymous king wouldn't have known anything about it, given that he perished some 250 years before it was built in the mid 15th century; moreover it was never used for hunting, nor was it ever a lodge – still, why should that matter? Regardless, it's a superb, three-floored timber-framed jettied building that, over the course of time, has variously functioned as a post office, pub, barbers, and numerous different shops, including a saddlers, bakers and confectioners.

These days the building is home to a fine local **history museum** (𝒸 kingjohnshuntinglodge.co.uk; ☉ Apr–Oct), its weirdly configured rooms crammed with many a splendid artefact – indeed it's as much fun negotiating the rickety stairs and slanting floors as it is perusing the exhibits. A number of the items on display manifest macabre provenance, including mantraps, the old town stocks and prison door, a coffin and bier from the former workhouse, and a skeleton (not inside the coffin I hasten to add) of a Roman foot soldier, found during a dig at a local garage. For me, though, two

"The town's handsome medieval square preserves a neat kernel of pastel-coloured tenements and wood-framed buildings."

things really stood out: a mid 15th-century wall painting (albeit largely effaced) of St Christopher that was discovered in a house in nearby West Street, and the Axbridge Nail, a substantial specimen dating from 1627 that once stood outside the Lamb pub opposite; used for the collection of tolls from the market (hence the term 'pay on the nail'), bronze pillars of this type (of which very few still exist) were more typically found in ports such as Bristol, but such was Axbridge's importance as a trading town that it was deemed necessary to have one here.

There are many good reasons to visit Axbridge, another being the wonderful **Roxy Cinema** (𝒸 axbridgeroxy.org.uk), a short walk up the High Street from the main square, at number 36. Formerly *The Lion* coaching inn, the building was purchased derelict by Juliet and David McClay in 1997. Describing themselves as economic migrants from London and New York, Juliet explained to me that initially they were

AXBRIDGE EVENTS

They like their events here in Axbridge. The three-day **Blackberry Fair and Carnival** at the end of September sees the main square transformed into one big fairground while a procession of floats wend their way through the town's narrow streets. The big one though is the **Axbridge Pageant**, the caveat being that it's held once every ten years, such is the organisation – the cast extends to some 400 people (and animals) – and finance required; excitingly, the next one is scheduled for August 2020. First performed in 1967, this hefty historical re-enactment recalls key moments throughout the town's history, for example King John hunting, the visit of Henrietta Maria (wife of Charles I), the coming of the railway in the 1860s, and the 1973 Basle air disaster that killed a generation of local mothers. I've never actually attended but, by all accounts, it's quite a spectacle. A somewhat more regular affair is the **farmers' market** – one of the county's best – on the first Saturday (09.00–13.00) of each month in the square.

unsure as to what to do with the place, but eventually decided that it would make the perfect movie theatre, and it opened as such in 2012. Its one screen and 34 seats (recycled from the Colston Hall in Bristol) make it one of the country's smallest cinemas, if not *the* smallest, while the programme is invariably a mix of vintage and contemporary films. You can book your tickets online or purchase them from the sweet little Art Deco-style box office just inside the entrance; there's also a 1950s-style cocktail bar to the rear. Make a date at the Roxy and you're unlikely to want to watch a film anywhere else again.

⫴ FOOD & DRINK

The Almshouse Tea Shop The Place, BS26 2AR ☏ 01934 733720 ♨ thealmshouseteashop. co.uk ⏱ 10.00–16.00 Wed–Sun. Occupying a superbly restored 15th-century almshouse (as the name suggests), this is a super place to replenish after an outing on the Strawberry Line (walkers, cyclists and dogs all welcome), whether it's for coffee and cake, late breakfast or something more substantial for lunch; they also do the occasional three-course evening supper (Almshouse by Candlelight), for which bookings are required – just mind your head on the beams.

The Lamb The Square, BS26 2AP ☏ 01934 732253 ♨ butcombe.com. Directly opposite King John's Hunting Lodge, the town's perennially popular boozer – a late 15th-century coaching inn – has everything one could ask for of a local: pub games, warming wood-burning fires, a cheery atmosphere and, as one of several local Butcombe pubs, reliably good beer – the food's not half bad either. You'll like it very much.

6 THATCHERS CIDER

Myrtle Farm, Sandford BS25 5RA ✆ 01934 822862 ⌁ thatcherscider.co.uk

Apples were first pressed at Myrtle Farm in 1904 by William Thatcher; since then, Thatchers has gone on to become one of the country's largest cider producers. However, it remains a family-run business to its core, currently on its fourth generation of owners (Martin is the current incumbent), and well on its way to training up the fifth generation – the company, it seems, is in safe hands.

Unlike so many brewery and distillery tours, Thatchers is worth every penny. Over the course of two hours, you get to see the canning centre, fermentation plant and packing area, as well as other parts of the site depending upon what operations are going on. Inside the slick, now almost entirely automated, canning centre, our chirpy guide Phil reeled off a list of impressive numbers: nine cans a second come off the production line, which equates to 30,000 per hour, 1.5 million per week, and more than 70 million per year – and that's not counting kegs and bottles. Everything bar the harvesting of the apples is done on-site (30,000 tonnes of which are pulped each year), though they do have their own, extensive orchards nearby. Otherwise, they take their apples from a small group of local farms, most of whom have been supplying Thatchers for years.

"They take their apples from a small group of local farms, most of whom have been supplying Thatchers for years."

You'll also get to see the 11 enormous oak vats – these timeless specimens date from the 1870s and are still used for maturing a select range of ciders. Happily, the tour concludes with a tasting session, which typically includes a number of vintage and artisan ciders that you won't find anywhere else. Once finished, I suggest retiring to the pub for yet more imbibing, and then going to the shop to take a few samples home... Well, that's what we did anyway.

⫙ FOOD & DRINK

The Railway Inn Sandford BS25 5RA ✆ 01934 611518 ⌁ therailwayinn.com. Thatchers fabulous on-site pub-cum-restaurant sports a gorgeous handcrafted wooden bar and a comfy lounge-like area with plunging, brown leather armchairs and sofas, and timber ceilings bearing old picking ladders and tankards. The food is top drawer, with a menu featuring lots of Thatchers-infused dishes (no surprise there) such as mussels in a cider and leek sauce, and cider and honey glazed gammon with fried duck egg and spiced pineapple chutney.

Burrington Combe & Dolebury Warren

❋ OS Explorer Map 141; start: car park at the end of Doleberrow (a narrow lane just off the A38), at the foot of Dolebury Warren ♀ ST446590; 5 miles; easy to moderate: this is a mostly level walk through mixed woodland, fields & heathland with some occasional light scrambling

This richly diverse route begins along a wooded valley and crosses into open moorland before encountering the dramatic limestone gorge of Burrington Combe. More woods follow before Dolebury Warren comes into view, complete with the substantial earthen ramparts of an Iron Age hillfort and one of the best viewpoints in the Mendips.

1 At the car park, go through the gate and follow the level track along the bottom of the wooded combe. After half a mile, 100yds after passing a sign for Dolebury Warren on your left, fork left. To your right is **Rowberrow Warren**, a mixed woodland site though predominantly spruce, pine and larch. When you come to a crossing of tracks (with fields in front of you), about a quarter of a mile later, keep more or less straight on. Go through another gate, with woodland to your left and open moorland on your right, and continue along the track for a short distance.

2 At a gate with a private footpath sign (behind which is a large wooden cabin hidden among the trees), turn right towards the open moorland. The scenery here is wonderful, and hints at what lies beyond the ridge, up on **Black Down**. After some 200yds, at a crossing of tracks, turn left and walk towards Burrington Combe, the deep rocky valley clearly visible straight ahead. After about 500yds the track narrows and descends – keep going (ignoring some subsidiary paths) and then, after a sharp bend in the dip, take the left fork as the path rises; at this point the path runs along the face of the hill and then descends quite steeply. Heading down (steady as you go), you pass the entrance to **Goatchurch Cavern** on your right, with another entrance to the same cave a little further down (you can do no more than stick your head in). Cross the stream (though this was actually dry when I was last there), on the other side of which is **Sidcot Swallet**, another small cave, though you cannot enter this one either; at this point you'll likely hear traffic from the road, which is some 200yds straight ahead.

3 At the road, you've reached **Burrington Combe** (page 86). Handily there's a path running parallel to the road; walk along here, passing **Aveline's Hole** (page 86) on the other side of the road and, on your left as you round the corner, the **Rock of Ages** (page 86) – pause a moment to read the fading plaque. A little further, on the opposite side of the road, you'll see the Burrington Inn; 150yds after this, take a left turn up Link Lane. The lane ascends, bearing

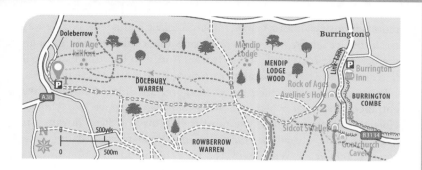

left; continue for 400yds before following the signposted track between hedges on the right (just before the house). Continue through the woods, ignoring any turnings to the left and carry on for a quarter of a mile. Pass the scant ruins of the late 18th-century **Mendip Lodge** – erstwhile home of poet and playwright Reverend Thomas Sedgewick Whalley – on your left and continue straight on; after 75yds, when the main track swings right, carry straight on, to the right of a ruined building. Beyond the wooden barrier, turn left up the sunken track, with old walls on either side. After a quarter of a mile (ignoring the first three gates on your right), go through a gate on your right and into a field by the National Trust sign for Dolebury Warren.

4 Proceed alongside the fence to its corner, then keep going along the line of hedgerow trees to reach another fence. Here, take the gate on your right to enter scrubby woodland; bear half left, gaining height as you reach **Dolebury Warren**, an exposed grassy ridge partially covered with commercial forest. Carry on past a small wooded area on your left towards the well-preserved earthen ramparts of the **Dolebury Warren Iron Age hillfort**. The outstanding feature of the walk, Dolebury Warren is thought to have acquired its name during the medieval period when it was used for breeding rabbits, a rich source of both meat and fur at that time. The **views** from the summit are fantastic, extending south over the Mendips, southwest to the Quantock Hills, east across Chew Valley Lake, and northwest over the Severn Estuary, beyond Steep Holm and Flat Holm, towards south Wales. It can get mighty blustery up here, mind.

5 Head straight through the fort and continue along the shallow cut grass track until you reach a gate and a stony downhill path. Walk down here to another gate, then bear sharp left by the pink house and continue down to the lane; walk 200yds along the lane back to the car park.

7 BURRINGTON COMBE

A deep limestone gorge honeycombed with caves and underground streams, Burrington Combe is a welcome, low-key alternative to its more famous neighbour, Cheddar Gorge. Like Cheddar, the combe was cut in the ice age by the action of streams that could not sink through the permeable rock while it was frozen. And, also like Cheddar, you'll find feral goats and sheep scampering among the precipitous ledges here.

Entering the combe, the sides of the gorge are dotted with tiny cave entrances (none of which are accessible), with names like Lionel's Hole and Elephant's Hole. The most well known of these, however, is **Aveline's Hole**, a cave in which human skeletal remains dating back some 10,000 years were discovered in 1797, supposedly by two boys out chasing a rabbit. Further excavations in the early 1900s by the University of Bristol Speleological Society (under whose auspices the cave still belongs) uncovered the remains of a further 21 bodies dating from a similar period, thus confirming this as Britain's oldest cemetery; the cave actually takes its name from one William Aveline, tutor of William Dawkins, the man who made the first major excavations here in 1860. More recently, in 2010, members of the cave team uncovered some rare wall engravings that are believed to date from around the same time as the aforementioned remains; unfortunately, there is no access to the cave.

About 200m from Aveline's Hole, diagonally opposite the car park as you round the corner, there's a large outcrop on your left, immortalised in or around 1762 by the Reverend Augustus Toplady of Blagdon, who, it is said, wrote the hymn '**Rock of Ages**' while sheltering from a storm in a crevice in the rock, as the wall-bound plaque indicates. However, many scholars have cast doubt on the authenticity of this supposed event.

¶¶ FOOD & DRINK

The Crown Inn The Batch, Churchill BS25 5PP ✆ 01934 852995 ☞ the-crown-inn.co.uk. A proper pub, of which there seem to be fewer and fewer of these days, the convivial Crown is, along with the Queen Victoria in Priddy, one of our two favourite hostelries in the Mendips. Its pleasingly scruffy interior – chipped wood-panelled walls and comfortably battered tables and chairs – is frequently full of locals enjoying the excellent selection of ciders and bitters while tucking into filling dishes like cauliflower cheese and cottage pie in front of wood-burning fires. A most rewarding way to round things off after the walk to Burrington Combe and Dolbury Warren (see box, page 84). Cash only.

MOUNTAIN BIKING THE MENDIPS

The Mendips are made for **off-road biking** – as an increasing number of enthusiasts are discovering. Most bikers start at Burrington Combe. From the first car park upon entering the Combe (from the east), there are two main possibilities: either take the bridleway north on to Burrington Ham or the one south on to the open moorland of Black Down, where you've a choice of several paths fanning out beyond Beacon Batch. The most obvious destination from here is Rowberrow Warren – where there are lots of fabulous downhill woodland tracks – and then onwards to the village of Shipham for some well-earned refreshments; you can also take a loop around Dolebury Warren or head south towards Charterhouse and Cheddar Gorge.

Alternatively, and slightly easier, start at the car park further along the gorge by the Burrington Inn and cycle 150yds to Link Lane on the opposite side of the road. Heading up the lane, you can either take a right in between the hedges, which takes you through Mendip Lodge Wood and on to Dolebury Warren (as in the walk on page 84), or carry straight on towards Black Down or Rowberrow Warren (as above). Whichever route, or routes, you take, the OS141 Cheddar Gorge and Mendip Hills West map is a useful aid. Although biking here is doable at any time of the year, this predominantly limestone range can get pretty darn muddy in all but the driest months. Then there is of course **Cheddar Gorge**, which, although on road, is a stunning (and if going up it, calf-cramping) ride at any time of the year; it's often a destination for major races such as the Tour of Britain.

GUIDED BIKE TOURS & BIKE HIRE/REPAIR SHOPS

Bad Ass Bikes Old Garden Centre, Burrington Combe BS40 7AT ✆ 01761 462011 ⊘ badassbikes.co.uk. A few paces down from the Burrington Inn, this outfit does servicing and repairs only.

Bike the Mendips ✆ 01761 463356 ⊘ bikethemendips.com. Owner Adrian offers a range of guided bike rides for all abilities as well as other excursions such as foraging and bushcraft survival.

Mendip Snowsport Lyncombe Drive, Churchill BS25 5PQ ✆ 01934 834877 ⊘ mendipsnowsport.co.uk. It's somewhat bizarre to find a ski centre in Somerset, but these folk also offer guided mountain-biking trips in the Mendips.

8 BLACK DOWN

A windswept, gorse-covered plateau criss-crossed by a well-worn network of paths and strewn with mounds from the time when these upland slopes functioned as a decoy town during World War II (see box, page 88), Black Down is the largest area of common land within the Mendips AONB. It's also my favourite destination anywhere in these hills, a wonderful spot for aimless rambling, though you can also take it in as part of the walk outlined on page 84. Moreover, on a clear day, the views across to the Bristol Channel, including the islands of Steep Holm and Flat Holm, are unbeatable. There's also a good chance of encountering wild Exmoor ponies – as I have done on numerous walks hereabouts – whose persistent grazing allows the rough grasses and

DECOY & DESTROY: OPERATION STARFISH

One of the more unusual mechanisms of air defence employed by the British military during World War II was the creation of **decoy towns** in order to divert enemy bombs away from their intended targets – often major cities like Bristol. Black Down, at the very heart of the Mendips range, was the site of one of the first decoy towns which was constructed following the bombing of Coventry in 1940, though there were eventually a dozen in the Bristol environs and more than 800 nationwide.

This complex – and, on the face of it, ingenious – defence and deception strategy involved lighting decoys designed to simulate night-time Bristol, which included devices to mimic the comings and goings of Temple Meads railway station. Another method employed was the use of urban decoy (or diversionary) fires, which were designed to replicate the fire effects the enemy would expect to see when their target had been successfully set alight, thus duping the second wave of attackers into bombing the same target. These were also known as 'Special Fires' (SF in military jargon), a term from which the codename **Starfish** derived; in turn, Starfish became the designated name for the nationwide programme of decoy sites.

These diversionary tactics were also intended to draw in the Luftwaffe to within range of anti-aircraft fire – it occasionally worked too, as the events of August 1940 demonstrated, when three Heinkel He 111s came down in the vicinity.

Most decoy towns were systematically cleared following the end of the war, which makes the existence of numerous well-preserved remnants on Black Down all the more important. These include three **control bunkers** that housed the generators, one of which is clearly visible near the Tynings Farm entrance on the southern boundary. Unsurprisingly, it's in a poor state of repair and sealed off – note the ungainly looking brick wall outside, built to protect the bunker's occupants from bomb blasts. Otherwise, the most obvious surviving features are the hundreds of strategically sited earth mounds (or tumps) and stone cairns, designed to prevent enemy gliders from landing on the flat terrain.

For all its ingenuity, it's difficult to gauge just how effective Operation Starfish actually was. Given that Bristol was subjected to some of the heaviest bombing of the war, it's probably fair to suggest that it was only moderately successful at best.

BANGERS & CRASH!

Once or twice a month, between March and October, this otherwise peaceful part of the Mendips is awoken from its slumber by a bit of crash, bang and wallop! Mendips Raceway (mendipsraceway.com), on the edge of Batts Combe Quarry between Charterhouse and Shipham, has been hosting stock car and banger racing since 1969; though this may not be many people's idea of Slow, in terms of pure entertainment it's hard to beat. A full schedule of races is posted on the website.

scrub to flourish; expect little more than a curious glance from these beautiful animals. The summit point for Black Down is **Beacon Batch**, which, at 1,066ft, is the highest point in the Mendips; it's denoted by a trig point atop a Bronze Age burial mound.

9 CHARTERHOUSE & BLACKMOOR RESERVE

A wonderfully isolated spot roughly midway between Cheddar and Burrington Combe, **Charterhouse** is little more than a crossroads with a handful of buildings. These include the Charterhouse Centre – an old school that is now an outdoor activity centre and administrative headquarters for the AONB – and **St Hugh's Church**, originally an old welfare hall for lead miners before its current incarnation – it also functioned as a first-aid and anti-gas centre during World War II. The church's dour exterior hints little at its lovely interior, with carved white-oak furnishings, though note that it is only open on Sunday afternoons in the summer.

Behind the Charterhouse Centre, a road leads down to a small car park and **Blackmoor Reserve**, a compelling landscape that was once at the heart of the Mendips' extensive lead and silver mining industry, hence its designation as a Scheduled Ancient Monument. While surface remains are an important visible manifestation of this once vast industrial wasteland, the landscape has otherwise been spectacularly reclaimed by nature. Surprisingly, given the historically high levels of toxic materials in the surrounding landscape, the hummocky ground supports a high number of flourishing, metal-tolerant plant communities such as Alpine pennycress and sea campion.

This is also **adder** country so, between March and late summer, keep a keen eye out for the UK's only venomous snake (it's greyish with a distinct zigzag along its back); generally though, adders keep a low profile and will only bite if trodden on (you'll soon know) or if they

Charterhouse, Black Down & Velvet Bottom

❋ OS Explorer Map 141; start: Blackmoor Reserve car park, just behind Charterhouse Outdoor Activity Centre ♀ ST505556; 5 miles; moderate difficulty: occasional inclines taking in road, moorland, fields & flat-bottomed valleys

A walk steeped in archaeological interest, this fabulously varied route begins at the old lead-mining territory around Blackmoor before continuing to Black Down, a wide expanse of open moorland that was the site of one of the country's first decoy towns during World War II (see box, page 88). From here, the walk proceeds across open fields before a gentle descent through ancient woodland towards the deliciously named Velvet Bottom, one of Somerset's loveliest reserves. The walk finishes at Ubley Warren, with further lead mine workings.

1 At the car park, facing the small hill and with the road behind you, take the path to your left, which rises gently (there are intermittently spaced stones on your right), and after about 100yds follow the left fork. Continue along this path for 200yds and, just before a small tree, you'll see a few steps to your left; go down these and follow the mostly slag-covered path down and around to the left of the reeds. Walk across the hummocky ground (so-called 'gruffy' ground), cross the stile into a field, and continue alongside the wall to reach the road.

2 At the road, turn right, and after 200yds turn left on to **Rains Batch**, a long, narrow lane that ascends gently for half a mile to the twin transmission masts – you can't miss them. Here, join the bridleway just to the left; this path narrows and becomes increasingly rocky as you gain elevation (hence can be quite tricky underfoot when wet). You eventually reach a gate, which you go through to emerge on to **Black Down**, a sweeping, wind-bitten expanse that could have been plucked straight out of Exmoor.

3 From the gate, take the slightly rutted path straight ahead. Continue walking for about 400yds, whereupon you reach **Beacon Batch**, the Mendips' highest point. At the trig point of Beacon Batch, take the left track (a distinctive reddish-brown colour) and continue walking flat and straight for about half a mile, ignoring the first three paths that you meet (each of which crosses the path you are on more or less diagonally). At a T-junction, turn left and walk along a wide grassy path until you reach the southern edge of Black Down. Before leaving Black Down through the gate, you can't fail to see a **bunker** just to your right, constructed during World War II when this whole area was turned into a decoy town (see box, page 88), though it's now sealed up. You'll also very likely encounter **wild ponies** up here; on my outing, I saw half a dozen or so of these beautiful animals braving what was a bitterly cold day.

4 Go through the gate and head down the stony bridleway towards **Tynings Farm**, on your right. At the road, turn left and walk along here (you are now on the West Mendip Way) for about

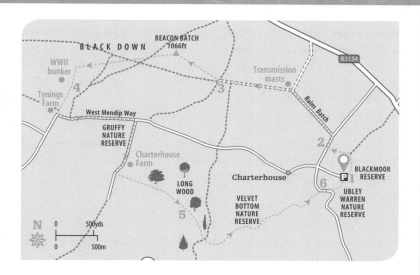

800yds, past the entrance to the **Gruffy Nature Reserve** on your right. Some 400yds further on, turn right on to the tarmac farm road towards **Charterhouse Farm**; the distinctive lumpy ground of the Gruffy reserve to your right is another reminder of this area's importance as a mining centre (see box, page 94). Approaching Charterhouse Farm, take the right-hand fork, following the road past the farm as it turns into a stone track. At the end of the field beyond the farm, go through the gate on your left and walk along the edge of the field following the wall to your right – follow the boundary all the way to the end of this very long field.

5 At the far corner of the field, go through the gate and take the wide rocky path veering slightly to the left and down into the lower section of **Long Wood**, which in late spring is awash with bluebells and wild garlic. At the bottom, go through another gate and keep walking straight ahead until you reach a couple more gates and a sign to **Black Rock**. Heading right here takes you to Cheddar Gorge (a wonderful walk in itself), but for this walk you need to go left through the gate by the information board. You are now entering **Velvet Bottom Nature Reserve**, a long, snaking valley of mostly rough grassland. Like Blackmoor, Velvet Bottom was at the centre of mining operations here in the Mendips, manifest today in heaps of glistening black slag, the remains of old settling dams and shallow circular depressions known as buddle pits where the ore was washed out. It's a fabulous landscape; you may spot badgers and rabbits here too.

▶

> ## Charterhouse, Black Down & Velvet Bottom (continued)
>
> 6 Just beyond the reserve, you'll see the road; cross this at a slight diagonal and enter **Ubley Warren Nature Reserve**, characterised by the same uneven 'gruffy' ground that has shaped nearby Blackmoor; more distinctive here though are the vertical wall cuttings in the bedrock, otherwise known as rakes (which are the result of lead veins running close to the surface that have been excavated). Follow the path round to the left and you'll reach a gate by the road – turn right here and you're back at the car park.

feel particularly threatened, though there's a small crumb of comfort in knowing that, except in extremely rare cases, bites are not fatal. In any case, watch your step. You may also want to think twice about bringing your dog up here, too.

10 BLAGDON LAKE & VILLAGE

Immediately west of Chew Valley Lake, the smaller **Blagdon Lake** predates the former by nearly 50 years, having been completed in 1905. It's also far more low-key than Chew, despite its reputation as one of the country's great fly-fishing venues, its bountiful stocks of brown and rainbow trout drawing anglers from all over the world. Like Chew Lake, there are few permissible footpaths, so it's disappointing to learn that it's not possible to circumnavigate its seven-mile-long perimeter. There is, though, a truncated footpath starting up in the northwestern corner (just beyond where the dam wall ends), which then edges Butcombe Shore and Butcombe Bay.

Blagdon village

A busy, scattered village, Blagdon is perched high above the lake, affording terrific views as you head down towards the water. Given how steep the gradients are hereabouts, I was amazed to learn that a railway line once served the village; between 1901 and 1963, the Wrington Vale Light Railway – constructed and owned by the Great Western Railway – operated both passenger and freight services (the latter for the purposes of transporting materials for the dam) between Wrington and Blagdon. As you near the bottom of Station Road, just before reaching the lake, on your left is what's left of **Blagdon Halt station**: a section of platform, alongside which you can clearly identify the contour of the old trackbed, station lamp posts, and the old waiting room and ticket office, which is now part of a larger private residence. As incongruous as that is, it can't detract from a strong sense of nostalgia one feels here. Here, too, is the body of a 'TOAD' brake van built in 1922.

Blagdon is also home to **Yeo Valley Organics** (yeovalley.co.uk), the largest organic dairy producer in the UK and best known for its natural yoghurt pots, as well as producing butter and ice cream, not to mention more than 2,000 tonnes of milk each week. Yeo Valley was set up in 1974 by Mary and Roger Mead and is now run by their son Tim and his wife Sarah, though Mary still happily tends to the 400-strong herd of Friesian cows. I met with Sarah at Yeo Valley HQ, which, refreshingly, is not your average company headquarters, and had a natter over coffee in the superb Yeo Valley Canteen (see below) overlooking Blagdon Lake. We were joined by executive chef Paul Collins, who has worked at several top-rank establishments including The Dorchester and The Grove hotels. Paul, who also gives food demos here, expounded upon Yeo Valley's strong sustainable credentials, explaining that their three-star rating from the Sustainable Restaurant Association is as a result of nothing going to landfill, everything in the kitchen being recycled (food waste is recycled through an anaerobic digester), and the entire premises being run on their own, self-generated solar power.

Sarah then showed me around the **Organic Garden** (01761 461425 theorganicgardens.co.uk Apr–Sep, 11.00–17.00 Thu & Fri), less than half a mile away at Holt Farm, which is also the location of both the dairy and the family home. Here, Sarah has designed a series of artfully themed gardens (Bronze, Glasshouse, Gravel), alongside wildflower meadows carpeted with Camassias, a woodland copse and birch grove. Best of all though is the posh veg patch, which sustains both The Canteen and the equally brilliant Garden Café, housed in the former milking parlour here at the farm. As if she's not busy enough, Sarah also co-ordinates **Valleyfest** (valleyfest.co.uk), a small-scale, family-friendly gathering held across the first weekend of August; there's oodles of stuff going on, from music, theatre and circus to foraging and wildlife walks.

¶¶ FOOD & DRINK

The Canteen Blagdon Ln, BS40 7YE 01761 461425 yeovalley.co.uk/the-canteen. 08.30–17.00 Tue–Fri. The country's best office canteen? Probably. Different? Absolutely.

The space looks fantastic, bearing, as it does, Sarah's idiosyncratic stamp: light fixtures culled from saucepans and colanders, brightly coloured murals, and floor-to-ceiling windows – you'll not find another restaurant in Somerset with better views. The food is a different class too, maybe toasted sourdough with mushrooms, spinach and poached egg, or beet burger with Yeo Valley crème fraiche – and at around £10 a main, it's a steal. Most of the ingredients are sourced, as you'd expect, from the farm and garden. The one caveat is that, being a staff canteen, it's only open for breakfast and lunch Tuesdays to Fridays, though there is the occasional evening event; bookings are required for all meals but you can pop in for coffee at any time.

MINE'S SOME LEAD

Although evidence points to some form of mining hereabouts during the Iron Age, it wasn't until the Romans arrived that lead production became a serious concern. The main direct evidence for Roman mining in the Mendips – one of the country's pre-eminent lead sites – was the discovery of inscribed lead ingots (typically bearing the names of emperors such as Vespasian), known as pigs. Lead was also mined for its silver, a small but important component of the ore.

Oddly, almost next to nothing is known about the industry during Saxon times, though what we do know is that lead output increased substantially during the medieval period as smelting technologies advanced. The owner of the land, and thereby the mines, at this time was the Bishop of Bath and Wells. Indeed, a charter granted by Richard I to one Bishop Reginald proclaimed that the bishop was allowed 'the right of mining lead wherever they could find it on their own land in Somerset, freely, quietly, and honourably, and without any contradiction or impediment'. This then provided the bishop with both a handsome income and a readily available material to roof their churches. Following another fallow period, the Mendip Hills Mining Company resumed lead production in 1844, sinking ever deeper shafts. However, during the latter half of the 19th century the gradual depletion of ore extracts, alongside the exploitation of rich ore reserves elsewhere in the world (which simultaneously flooded the market and lowered the price), led to the eventual collapse of the industry hereabouts.

The most tangible relics of the region's lead-mining past are the distinctive bumps and grooves (known locally as 'gruffy' ground) that are the result of intensive ore extraction, buddling pits (circular depressions for washing and separating the ore), and rakes (mineral veins appearing as rock-cut clefts). More impressive are what are considered to be the most intact lead smelting tunnels anywhere in the country, which date back to the 1860s. Elsewhere, big dumps of glassy, black smelter slag still cover large areas of Blackmoor reserve, which, in fact, appear intermittently all the way down to **Velvet Bottom**.

11 CHEW VALLEY LAKE

Nearer to Bristol than Bath – it's just ten miles or so south of the former – Chew Valley Lake opened in 1956 for the purposes of supplying drinking water to the city and its surrounding area, though construction came at a cost, as it necessitated flooding the village of Moreton (listed in the Domesday Book) as well as extensive tracts of farmland; it's said that during dry periods the old village bridge can be seen poking above the surface of the water. It has since become one of England's premier **fishing** and **birdwatching** centres, with more than 250 species of birdlife catalogued in the lake environs; wintering wildfowl is especially prominent. Among internationally important species to be found on the open water are shovelers, black-headed gulls and the lesser black-backed gulls, while birds of national importance include gadwalls and great crested grebes. The lake's extensive reedbeds, meanwhile, support significant numbers of reed warblers and bitterns. It's little wonder that twitchers are in their element here. Bar one hide on one of the nature trails, permits must be obtained in order to use the other five hides, which

"It's said that during dry periods the old village bridge can be seen poking above the surface of the water."

are clustered around the southern end of the lake; Herriot's Pool and Heron's Green Bay are considered the best spots. These can be purchased at **Woodford Lodge**, located just outside Chew Stoke on the lake's western shore, which is also where fishing permits are sold; there's a very creditable restaurant here too, or you could just swing by for a beverage, a most agreeable option on a warm summer's evening.

As it's designated both a Site of Special Scientific Interest (SSSI) and a Special Protection Area (SPA), and privately owned by Bristol Water, public access to the lake is limited, unless that is, you fish, watch birds or sail. There are currently very few areas where it's possible to walk, although a recreational trail around Chew Lake, in conjunction with Sustrans, has been proposed, so may well be up and running by the time you read this. For now, you can content yourself with a couple of short nature trails on the northeastern shore, though they're not particularly well signposted; look for the sign that says Picnic Spot Two. Starting from the car park (£2 all day), the **Grebe Trail** is a ¾-mile hard-surfaced loop skirting the lakeshore, while the slightly longer, and only partially surfaced, **Bittern Trail** (no dogs or bikes) is largely shaded by sycamore wood, but features reeds, willow and grassland too; from the open-access hide about halfway along, there's every chance of seeing Canada geese, coots and herons, and possibly cormorants.

12 STANTON DREW STONE CIRCLES

Stanton Drew BS39 4EW 🖉 0370 333 1181; English Heritage

Unlike its far more famous counterparts at Avebury and Stonehenge, you won't find hordes of day trippers piling into the village of Stanton Drew to view its remarkable stone circles. Nor will you find the phalanx of facilities that typically accompany those more hallowed sites; payment (£1), for example, is via an honesty box – it's all refreshingly low-key, and much Slower. That, and the fact that Stanton Drew, which lies just outside the Mendips range, is so far off the beaten track means that you'll probably have the place all to yourself, save for a few cows. While these stones may lack the drama of the aforementioned sites, their historical resonance is not in question. In fact, Stanton Drew constitutes the third largest set of prehistoric standing stones in the country, dating broadly from around 3000–2000BC, possibly earlier.

"It is so far off the beaten track that you'll probably have the place all to yourself, save for a few cows."

Sited on a working farm – hence the rather frisky cows presented more of a distraction than the stones themselves – the complex comprises three interrelated stone circles, the largest of which is, surprise, surprise, called the **Great Circle**; with a diameter of 113m and counting 26, mostly recumbent, stones, it's second only in size to Avebury. Among the many inevitable legends that abound here, the most often told supposes that guests at a wedding were turned into stone as punishment for partying on the Sabbath, lured into doing so by the devil himself – enjoyable as that tale is, more prosaically the stones are likely to have formed part of an important ceremonial site. The two much smaller stone circles lie in close proximity.

The circles here may well have provided the inspiration for John Wood the Elder's Circus project in Bath (page 31) following his survey of the site in 1749, though the stones were first studied by the celebrated antiquarian John Aubrey in 1664. Much more recent research (1997) identified remnants of a vast henge (ditch) alongside a series of pits, the likelihood being that these would have once held large timber

A TASTE OF SOMERSET

The taste of Somerset is, of course, cider, though you'll find plenty of cheese devotees around the county. But there's stacks more scrumptious stuff besides, including local wineries, oysters from Porlock and eels from the Levels.

1 The vines at Smith & Evans. **2** Cheddar cheese storage at Wookey Hole. **3** Porlock Bay Oysters. **4** Thatchers have been producing cider since 1904. **5** Guildhall market, Bath.

HELEN HOTSON/S

IAN WOOLCOCK/S

CHRISTIAN MUELLER/S

COASTAL SOMERSET

Timeless seaside resorts, the country's only Grade I-listed pier, dune-backed beaches and exhilarating cliff walks ensure that Somerset's coastline has something for everyone.

1 The harbour at Porlock Weir has been operational for at least 1,000 years. 2 Clevedon is home to England's only intact Grade I-listed pier. 3 The Low Lighthouse at Burnham. 4 Weston-super-Mare's Grand Pier. 5 Fossil-rich Kilve Beach is Somerset's equivalent of Dorset's Jurassic Coast.

ALAN DAVIES

HISTORICAL SOMERSET

Castles at Dunster and Nunney, standing stones at Stanton Drew, and an Iron Age hillfort at South Cadbury are just a few of Somerset's many historical highlights.

TRAVELLIGHT/S

1 Westonzoyland Pumping Station Museum. 2 The grand interior of the Bishop's Palace, Wells. 3 Crunchie-coloured Montacute House. 4 Radstock Museum celebrates local mining history. 5 Stanton Drew Stone Circles date broadly from around 3000–2000BC. 6 The Watchet Boat Museum displays a fantastic collection of local boats.

EXPLORING SOMERSET'S WILD PLACES

Wildlife watchers will be in their element thanks to world class birdlife on the Levels and fantastic fishing at Blagdon, but if you fancy expending slightly more energy, how about trekking the valleys of Exmoor or mountain biking in the Mendips.

1 Mountain biking over the Mendips. 2 Tarr Steps, Exmoor National Park. 3 The iconic Exmoor pony. 4 Exmoor's Snowdrop Valley. 5 Murmuration at Shapwick Heath National Nature Reserve. 6 Fishing on Blagdon Lake. 7 Common cranes, the Levels. 8 Red deer are a common sight on Exmoor. 9 Westhay Moor National Nature Reserve.

ACCELERATORHAMS/ISTOCK

MIKE WOODHEAD/AMLI, SWT

ENPA

MIKE CHARLES/S

10 View across the Quantock Hills. 11 Horseriding is a great way to take in the scenery from North Hill. 12 A population of wild goats inhabit Cheddar Gorge. 13 Rock climbing at Cheddar Gorge.

TOM MEAKER/S

MRTOM-UK/ISTOCK

EXMOOR RIDING

poles, thereby indicating the presence of a large temple, which in turn suggests that the site is probably much older and more elaborate than initially thought.

You can get information about the site from the village's Druid's Arms pub, whose garden is, somewhat incongruously, the location for three more colossal stones collectively known as **The Cove**, which are thought to predate the main stone circles by around 1,000 years and were, in all probability, the remains of a long barrow, or chambered tomb; the pub itself suffices for a quick beverage before pushing on. Note that dogs are not allowed on-site.

13 PRIDDY & AROUND

In many ways Priddy is the quintessential Somerset village, with its thriving community school, farm shop, church and, most importantly of all, a rather fine hostelry (page 98). The focal point of the village is its handsome green, the site of Priddy's most idiosyncratic feature, the thatched Hurdle Stack, which harks back to the wool trade that once flourished hereabouts. The green had the focal point of the annual sheep fair since 1348, but following the sad demise of that event (last held in 2013), it's now the wonderful **Priddy Folk Festival** (priddyfolk.org) that takes centre stage here each July. The village is also useful as a starting base for any number of walks, including a couple of my favourites.

Within easy walking distance of Priddy, and punctuating the skyline of nearby North Hill in a broadly linear arrangement, are a series of prominently sited mounds, Bronze Age tumuli collectively known as **Priddy Nine Barrows**; it's believed that they were excavated in the early 19th century though unlike Stoney Littleton Long Barrow near Bath (page 41), it's not possible to enter any of them. Beyond here, though on private land and less discernible, are the **Priddy Circles**, four earthwork enclosures that may or may not be linked to the barrows themselves. The

"Priddy's most idiosyncratic feature, the thatched Hurdle Stack, harks back to the wool trade that once flourished hereabouts."

land around Priddy was once extensively worked for its lead ore, most intensively at the former St Cuthbert's lead works south of the barrows. The abandoned hollows and spoil heaps of the old workings (which functioned until 1908) are now part of the **Priddy Mineries** nature reserve, which supports a diverse range of flora and fauna, including several species of dragonfly.

You can take in all these sites on a broadly **circular walk** starting up by the village church. From here, head southeast across a series of fields to Eastwater Farm, before reaching Wells Road; after passing a couple of roadside cottages, bear left on to a path towards Priddy Pools (signposted). From the pools, head due north to North Hill and the barrows, beyond which (across another road) are the Circles; you can then return to Priddy along Nine Barrows Lane and back down past the church.

¶¶ FOOD & DRINK

Hunter's Lodge Inn Old Bristol Rd, BA5 3AR ✆ 01749 672275 ⊙ 11.30–14.30 & 18.30–23.00 daily. Standing on its lonesome at the intersection of two unnamed roads (hence easily missed), the Hunter's has been run by the inimitable Roger Dors for more than 50 years – yes, really! It looks, and feels, like a place where time has stood still, and that's just the way the locals like it, not least the many cavers who hang out here. Fairly priced beer straight from the barrel (including Potholer, of course), unfussy but pleasing food, and good cheer – what's not to enjoy? No credit cards and no mobiles.

The Queen Victoria Pelting Drove BA5 3BA ✆ 01749 676385 ⬦ thequeenvicpriddy.co.uk ⊙ noon–23.00 daily. There's nowhere in the Mendips quite like the Vic, especially if it's good food, good beer and good chat you're after – oh, and toasty fires. Walkers, cyclists, children, dogs and muddy boots all welcome. It's renowned locally for its winter makeover when the exterior becomes one giant gingerbread house. I love it.

14 DEER LEAP & EBBOR GORGE

A walk along the delightfully named **Deer Leap** (a short drive from Priddy along Pelting Drove) is my family's default Sunday afternoon outing; not because we can't be bothered to do anything else but because, on a clear day, this elevated, southwest-facing ridge affords views that are bettered in few places anywhere else in Somerset: the Levels and Glastonbury Tor, the Quantocks, and the Bristol Channel – even Steep Holm on a clear day. A patchwork of sloping fields, divided by dry-stone walls and old ladder stiles, it's mostly rough pastureland (grazed in summer by cows and sheep) with large patches of scrub and gorse woven into the landscape. You're quite likely to see buzzards and other birds of prey, but the wind can really blow here so be prepared – if you've got a kite, there are few better places to get airborne.

We'll often combine a walk along Deer Leap with a quick romp around **Ebbor Gorge**, half a mile or so further down the road towards Wookey. It is almost deserted compared with Cheddar Gorge – we rarely encounter more than a dozen or so people here at any one time. The gorge was created some 270 million years ago following the collapse of a huge cavern. Defined by craggy limestone outcrops and towering cliffs cloaked in ancient ash woodland, the caves that pockmark the gorge once sheltered both humans and animals, among them cave bears, wolves and arctic lemming, as recent finds testify.

The main, moderately strenuous trek through the gorge doesn't take much more than an hour. From the car park (thefts do occur here so lock up), descend to the valley floor, sheltered by thick, damp woods – ideal conditions for the ferns, mosses and fungi that grow here – before a fun little scramble up through a narrow ravine, at the top of which the path loops round to a clifftop plateau (another deserving picnic spot) where you can pick out the distinctive shape of Glastonbury Tor and the brooding outline of Exmoor. From here, a stepped path brings you back down to the bottom of the gorge, before further steps rise again back to the start point. There are also a couple of shorter, easier paths, one of which is suitable for wheelchairs and pushchairs.

SEND US YOUR SNAPS!

We'd love to follow your adventures using our *Slow Travel Somerset* guide – why not tag us in your photos and stories via Twitter (@BradtGuides) and Instagram (@bradtguides)? Alternatively, you can upload your photos directly to the gallery on the Somerset destination page via our website (bradtguides.com/somerset).

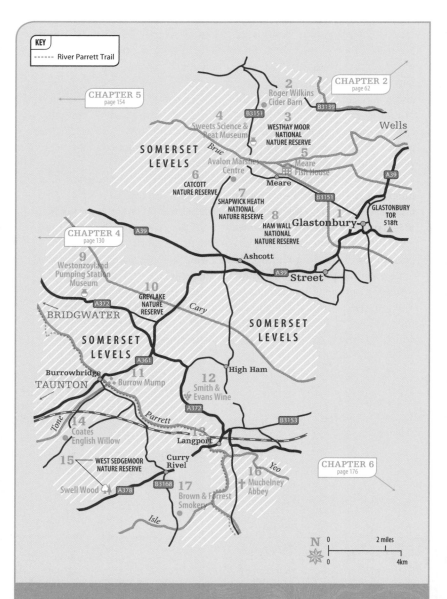

------ River Parrett Trail

CHAPTER 5
page 154

CHAPTER 2
page 62

2
Roger Wilkins
Cider Barn

B3139

B3151

Wells

4
Sweets Science &
Peat Museum

3
WESTHAY MOOR
NATIONAL
NATURE RESERVE

SOMERSET
LEVELS

Brue

Avalon Marshes
Centre

5
Meare
Fish House

Meare

A39

6
CATCOTT
NATURE RESERVE

7
SHAPWICK HEATH
NATIONAL
NATURE RESERVE

B3151

1

GLASTONBURY
TOR
518ft

8
HAM WALL
NATIONAL
NATURE RESERVE

Glastonbury

CHAPTER 4
page 130

A39

Ashcott

A39

Street

9
Westonzoyland
Pumping Station
Museum

10
GREYLAKE
NATURE
RESERVE

Cary

SOMERSET
LEVELS

A372

BRIDGWATER

SOMERSET
LEVELS

A361

Burrowbridge

TAUNTON

11
Burrow Mump

High Ham

12
Smith &
Evans Wine

A372

Tone

Parrett

B3153

14
Coates
English Willow

13
Langport

15
WEST SEDGEMOOR
NATURE RESERVE

Curry
Rivel

Yeo

CHAPTER 6
page 176

Swell Wood

A378

B3168

17
Brown & Forrest
Smokery

16
Muchelney
Abbey

Isle

N
0
0

2 miles
4km

GLASTONBURY & THE SOMERSET LEVELS

3
GLASTONBURY & THE SOMERSET LEVELS

Glastonbury is a town quite unlike any other, a place where folklore and legends thrive, among them that a young Jesus visited here with Joseph Arimathea, while another supposes that this was the final resting place of King Arthur, though that seems fanciful at best. Whatever its legends and myths, the town's Christian sites are many, from the magnificent ruins of the once all-powerful abbey and the Chalice Well to Glastonbury Tor, one of the West Country's most enduring landmarks.

If there was one part of Somerset that I enjoyed researching above all others, then it was probably the **Somerset Levels and Moors**, to give them their full and proper name. Fringing Glastonbury and extending across parts of the north and centre of the county, the wholesale transformation of this deeply rural, pastoral landscape over the last 30 or so years has been nothing short of remarkable. Where once it was intensively worked for peat, today it's an area of pristine chequerboard fields, extensive wetlands and languid rivers. Water is, in many ways, the defining feature of the Levels, with flood risk a fact of life – as the locals have found out to their cost too many times to mention, not least in 2014 when catastrophic flooding made the national headlines.

Above all though, the Levels are home to some of the finest **birdlife** anywhere in the country and, whatever the time of year, there's more than enough here to satisfy even the most ardent twitcher. Not that you have to be a serious fan of winged fauna to appreciate the scale and diversity of birdlife present: I'm certainly not (or at least I wasn't), but I frequently found myself caught up in the thrill of trying to spot the likes of avocet, bitterns and great white egrets. Not forgetting the murmurations of course. In fact such is the importance of the Levels' biodiversity that 13% of the Levels are designated either as Sites of Special Scientific Interest, Special Protection Areas or Ramsar sites. Historically and archaeologically, too, the Levels are of national significance, manifest in some of the country's most ancient discoveries, including Iron Age and Roman settlements and timber trackways, though these have long since been buried deep within the old peat bogs. There are, however, more obvious reminders of the county's illustrious past, such as the Fish House in Meare and Muchelney Abbey.

Wildlife-watching aside, the Levels afford ample but undemanding **walking** opportunities, with the flat, wide open spaces providing ideal terrain for cyclists with an aversion to hills. Another way to appreciate the fragile beauty of the Levels is to get out on to the water itself, with several local outfits offering water-bound activities. The wide panoramic views, both from inside looking out and from outside the area looking in are consistently breathtaking; take yourself off up to higher ground – for example the Mendips or the Blackdown Hills – and you'll be rewarded with a unique perspective of a unique landscape.

GETTING THERE & AROUND

Thanks in part to its relatively central location within the county, Glastonbury is well served by public transport – well, **buses** at least. The principal route is the Mendip Xplorer (service 376), which runs between Bristol and Glastonbury via Wells along the A37 and A39 (⌂ firstgroup.com). Other useful services include bus 77, which starts in Wells before passing through Glastonbury and then continuing south down to Somerton and Yeovil (page 189), bus 29 southwest to Taunton (page 146), and bus 75 east to Bridgwater (page 141), which also passes through Ashcott, Shapwick and Catcott on the Levels. The southern part of the Levels is covered by the number 54 Yeovil to Taunton bus, which calls at Pitney, Langport and Curry Rivel en route. In terms of **trains**, there's nowhere that comes remotely close to Glastonbury or the Levels, the principal lines lying some distance west and south of here.

If **driving** around the Levels, note that may of the lanes are quite narrow and bumpy in places. Nearly all the reserves have decent parking facilities, some of which are pay and display.

WALKING & CYCLING

The Somerset Levels are, of course, prime **walking** and **cycling** territory, particularly if you enjoy these pursuits in their more gentle forms. There are endless possibilities for aimless rambling around the reserves,

ℹ TOURIST INFORMATION

Avalon Marshes Centre Shapwick Rd, Westhay BA6 9TT ✆ 01458 860556
⊘ avalonmarshes.org
Glastonbury St Dustan's House, 1 Magdalene St, BA6 9EL ✆ 01458 832954
⊘ glastonbury.co.uk
Langport Bow St, TA10 9PR ✆ 01458 253527 ⊘ langport.life

most of which are also well suited to two wheels, although some of the old drove tracks can be quite rough in places. The trackbed of the old Somerset and Dorset Railway running through Ham Wall and Shapwick Heath is superb – and of course there's the added bonus of potentially seeing some fantastic wildlife en route. The Avalon Marshes website (⊘ avalonmarshes.org) details a series of excellent rides around the Levels. The long-distance **National Cycle Network Route 3** (which has already crossed the Mendips by this point) traverses the Levels en route to Devon and Cornwall. If you fancy cycling around the Levels, one excellent local bike hire company is **Parrett Trail Bikes**, based in Langport (✆ 01458 253626 ⊘ parretttrailbikes.co.uk).

One long-distance walk that you might consider tackling (or part of it at least) is the 48-mile long **River Parrett Trail**, which begins at the river's source in Cheddington, Dorset, and ends its journey at Bridgwater Bay, taking in historic sites such as Muchelney Abbey and Burrow Mump along the way. The Avalon Marshes website also has a dozen or so downloadable heritage walks of varying lengths.

1 GLASTONBURY

🏠 Magdalene House (page 235) **🏡 Middlewick Holiday Cottages** (page 235)

Whatever your preconceptions of Glastonbury, they're probably true. Ordinarily this'd be a fairly mundane little market town, were it not for a high street teeming with psychedelically painted shops, cafés and healing centres bearing names like Man, Myth and Magik, The Speaking Tree, and the Chocolate Love Temple, and an assortment of oddball characters – hippies, druids, knights, pixies (not real ones) – nonchalantly going about their business. But that's really only the half of it. With over 70 different faith groups present, it's little wonder that Glastonbury retains its own unique personality; there's nowhere else quite like it in Somerset, or, for that matter, the country. Central to it all is the abbey, though there's plenty more to keep you occupied if you've got the appetite and the stamina, including the Chalice Well and, nearby, the engaging Rural Life Museum. Not forgetting Glastonbury Tor, which is within easy walking distance of the town centre.

About halfway up the High Street, wedged between a pair of shops, is the **Tribunal**. Dating from the early 15th century, this handsomely weathered, two-storey medieval townhouse takes its name (erroneously as it turns out) from the time when it was purported to have been a bishop's court, though there's never been any evidence to support this and it was, quite likely, just a merchant's house. Today, this venerable old building holds the **Glastonbury Lake Village Museum** (English Heritage), which recalls the history of the long-since vanished Glastonbury Lake Village, a local Iron Age island settlement discovered by amateur archaeologist Arthur Bulleid in the late 19th century. Among the many items retrieved by Bulleid (most of which were in an excellent condition owing to the preservational qualities of the peat-rich soil), the most impressive was a stash of some Bronze Age bone jewellery.

GLASTONBURY ABBEY

Magdalene St, BA6 9EL ✆ 01458 832267 ⌨ glastonburyabbey.com

Founded in the 7th century, possibly even earlier, Glastonbury Abbey can lay fair claim to being the country's oldest Christian site. Enlarged by St Dustan in the 10th century, it suffered a catastrophic fire in 1184, which pretty much gutted the entire complex and necessitated a complete rebuilding job. Following that, the abbey never looked back, casting its territorial claims as far north as Wales and the Midlands, and all the way down to the south coast, becoming an ecclesiastical powerhouse that was second only to Westminster Abbey in London. The burial place of kings Edmund I, Edgar I and Edmund II, its influence spread far and wide; it's also claimed that Glastonbury had the largest collection of books outside the library of Alexandria in Egypt. Upon the Dissolution of the Monasteries in 1539, many of the buildings were plundered and stripped, leaving the complex to crumble. Above all though, the abbey remains central to the Arthurian story (see box, opposite), which, despite the dubious associations, has fired the imagination of pilgrims and visitors for centuries.

TALL TALES OR TRUTHS?
GLASTONBURY'S LEGENDS

The **Arthurian** legend is ubiquitous, in history, folklore and place names all over Britain. In truth, there are few parts of the British Isles that don't have some sort of claim on the chap, however tenuous it may be, and Glastonbury is no different. For it was here, in the abbey, that Arthur was allegedly laid to rest following his death in battle; it is then supposed that his queen Guinevere was buried here some time later. The reality though is that no such thing happened – a fact more or less confirmed following further, more extensive archaeological research in 2014. Instead, this was most likely the result of some carefully crafted PR spin on the part of the monks in residence at that time. Glastonbury also has claims to **Camelot**, Arthur's court, but then so do many other places, including Cadbury Castle in south Somerset (page 185), Winchester, parts of Cornwall, and Brittany, in France, though by far the strongest contender for this particular accolade is Caerleon in south Wales.

The earliest Glastonbury legends, however, concern one **Joseph Arimathea**, who, depending upon the source, was either one of Christ's disciples or his great uncle. Either way, it is said that Arimathea first paid a visit to Glastonbury with the infant Jesus, returning some years later to preach the gospel. Then there is the tale of the **Holy Thorn**, which supposes that some time soon after Christ's death Arimathea made the journey to nearby Wearyall Hill, whereupon he planted his thorn staff into the ground; the staff took root and overnight a tree sprouted forth. It's said that the tree flowers but twice a year, once to recall the birth and another to recall the death of Christ – and indeed it's true that it does flower roughly around these times, weather permitting. There are numerous descendants of the tree around town, including one at the abbey and another in the grounds of St John the Baptist's Church. One thing that is most certainly true is that each Christmas the eldest child from a local school cuts a sprig from the tree at St John the Baptist's, which is then sent to the Queen, whose breakfast table it adorns. It was Arimathea, too, who supposedly brought the **Holy Grail** with him to the Chalice Well (page 107), but again, there's nothing to support such an event ever happening.

Abbey museum & grounds

Before exploring the grounds, it's worth learning a bit more about the abbey's history in its absorbing **museum**. Many of the objects on display – stone-carved heads, grave markers and effigies of monks – were either salvaged following the fire in 1184 or retrieved following the dissolution of the abbey. Keep an eye out, too, for some of the smaller exhibits, notably a sublime collection of oyster shell palettes (still retaining some pigment) and fragments of blue stained glass from windows commissioned by Henry Blois, erstwhile abbot of Glastonbury and grandson of William the Conqueror. Not to be outdone (though it has no connection to the abbey) is the joyful *Madonna and Child* sculpture by the celebrated, and controversial, artist Eric Gill; originally commissioned for St Mary's Church, located near the abbey, in 1928, it went walkabout for about 40 years before being rediscovered in a local cemetery and then put on permanent display here in 2011.

The centrepiece of the abbey complex is the magnificent, roofless shell of the **Lady Chapel**. One of England's finest late 12th-century monuments, this largely Romanesque structure retains an extraordinary sense of grandeur that not even a few relatively modern accretions can quash. Its stonework, in particular, betrays some wonderful detail, including carved figures of the Annunciation, Herod and the Magi, alongside other richly sculpted ornamentation, bits of which, remarkably, still bear traces of the original paintwork.

In an unassuming spot adjacent to the Lady Chapel, a small sign deems this the burial site of **Arthur and Guinevere**, though in truth it's probably nothing of the sort. Indeed, the claim that it was such, which first surfaced in 1191, was most likely a crude attempt by monks to raise much-needed funds by increasing pilgrim numbers following the catastrophic fire seven years previous. Beyond the large void where the nave of the Great Church once stood are the not insubstantial remains of the **choir**, looking as if it's been spliced in half. Its two hulking transept piers overlook the site of where Arthur and Guinevere's tombs supposedly once were (marked by another low-key plaque), their remains having been transferred here from the aforementioned grave (in 1278). Whatever the truth of Arthur's alleged burial here, what is known is that any remains were lost for eternity following the abbey's dissolution. Looking straight ahead from the choir's far end, it's easy to see why this was once the longest abbey in all of Europe – it's the best spot from which to appreciate the scale and splendour of these ruins.

"Looking straight ahead from the choir's far end, it's easy to see why this was once the longest abbey in all of Europe."

The most complete of the abbey's remaining buildings is the **Abbot's Kitchen**, whose stone roof was a riposte to thieves intent on pilfering lead from the roof of the Great Church. Ignore the fact that (yawn) it's been mocked up as a medieval kitchen, and instead admire the wealth of architectural detail: eight thick stone ribs that arch upwards to a lantern ceiling and four splendid corner fireplaces. You can wander at leisure around the monastic ruins, herb gardens, ponds and orchards – all of which make for tranquil picnicking spots. The free guided tours of the abbey grounds, which take place daily on the hour, are well worth joining.

RURAL LIFE MUSEUM
Chilkwell St, BA6 8DB ✆ 01458 831197 ⬦ swheritage.org.uk ⊘ Tue–Sun

Completely overhauled in 2017, the splendid Rural Life Museum occupies the renovated farmhouse and cowsheds of Abbey Farm, a working unit owned by the Mapstones until 1972. And they've done a great job. A thoroughgoing, and thoroughly entertaining, trawl through Somerset life in its many wonderful guises, themes covered include community trades (carpentry, coopering and gloving among them), social and domestic life, and a variety of different themes such as celebrations, religion, folklore and the arts (keep an eye out for the Glastonbury bin). But as you'd expect, it's farming and food production that features most prominently, from traditional industries like dairy farming and cider-making (check out the magnificent press from 1792) to similarly well-established but less familiar local practices like willow growing and eel farming. Two of the more curious exhibits I stumbled across were a mummified cat – these were traditionally hidden in walls and chimneys to ward off evil spirits – and Evelyn Waugh's ear trumpet telescope.

Once you've surveyed all that, make your way over to the timeless **Abbey Barn**, dating from 1340 and one of just four such structures in the county left that were owned by Glastonbury Abbey. Now used for temporary exhibitions, you can take a peek inside at its majestic wooden ceiling. Out in the small orchard you'll find an old corrugated **shepherd's hut**, a pleasingly primitive dwelling that provided its owner with all the basic necessities (bed, stove, seating and storage areas) required to see him through a long, tough season.

THE CHALICE WELL
85–89 Chilkwell St, BA6 8DD ✆ 01458 831154 ⬦ chalicewell.org.uk

'A place of great spiritual significance for many faiths' is how Natasha Wardle, project manager at the Chalice Well, describes these tranquil gardens. Natasha, who has been working here for 19 years, explained to me that people from all over the world have been coming to the Well for at least 2,000 years, to take the waters and to be healed, and for many it remains *the* most spiritual of all Glastonbury's many sacred sites. The gardens were owned by the poet and playwright Alice Buckton from 1913 to 1944, though it was the visionary spiritualist Wellesley Tudor Pole – probably best remembered for the One Minute Silence, which played out at 21.00 each evening on the BBC from 1940 until the mid 1950s – who founded the Chalice Well Trust in 1959. Fascinating characters both, the lives of Buckton and Tudor Pole are worth exploring further if you have the time. Buckton even made a silent film about the town in 1922, entitled *Glastonbury, Past and Present*. Good luck getting your hands on that.

The Red Spring is known as such on account of the blood that flowed from the Holy Grail when it was supposedly brought here by Joseph Arimathea shortly after Christ's death, though more prosaically it's because of its dense iron oxide properties. As it is, the chalybeate water issues forth from the Lion's Head fountain, and flows down to the abbey fish pond; indeed it may be these iron deposits that have spawned such ginormous fish. The mildly ferrous taste is, as you might imagine, an acquired one, though you're advised not to drink too much – a sip'll do. While the water's source remains unknown, what is known is that there was a covered bathhouse here some time in the 18th century, as evidenced by some shallow remains, into which water tumbles from a mini waterfall. The well itself, which sits at the top of these ample, beautifully landscaped gardens, invites further opportunities for quiet contemplation.

GLASTONBURY TOR

Rearing up sharply from the iron-flat Levels and visible for miles around, Somerset's giant mystic hill (518ft) is yet another local landmark bound by legend – among them that the hill was home to one Gwyn ab Nudd, Lord of the Celtic Underworld. The best way up the tor is via a circular walk starting in the town centre: at the top of the High Street, turn right on to Chilkwell Street then left up Dod Street; cross the field and walk along Stone Down Lane before turning right along a path through a field, where you begin the ascent (in any case it's all well signposted). Return down on the exact opposite side, which brings you out near the Chalice Well – you can of course do this in reverse. Although it's not an exacting climb, a reasonable level of fitness (and some half-decent boots) helps. Crowning the hill is **St Michael's Tower**, which is all that

GLASTONBURY FESTIVAL

Conceived in 1970 by local farmer Michael Eavis, the Pilton Festival was just a small hippy affair, the headline act a then relatively little-known band called T-Rex; there were 1,500 people in attendance and it cost £1, which included a bottle of milk from Eavis's farm. Held intermittently thereafter until 1981, the **Glastonbury Festival of Contemporary and Performing Arts** (glastonburyfestivals.co.uk), as it was by then known, went supernova in the late eighties and is now the largest, and greatest, greenfield festival in the country, with an attendance that these days tops the 170,000 mark. It hasn't all been plain sailing mind: in 1990 violence broke out between security guards and New Age travellers (aka 'The Battle of Yeoman's Bridge'); in 1994 the iconic Pyramid stage went up in flames just a week or so before the event; and, in 2005, the mother of all thunderstorms resulted in large parts of the site drowning under 4ft of water. The weather is, of course, an occupational hazard at Glastonbury, and heaven knows (excuse the pun) the festival has had its fair share of mud-filled mayhem over the years.

The vast site – which is actually on Eavis's own Worthy Farm – accommodates everything from comedy and cabaret to art and meditation, but ultimately it's all about the music. You'll have to be quick (or lucky) mind, as tickets, which cost around £250, are usually snapped up within minutes of going on sale. Following a fallow year in 2018, the festival returned all guns blazing in 2019, with headline sets from Stormzy, The Killers and The Cure.

survives of the original 14th-century church. But of course you come here for the views, which are stupendous: on a clear day it almost feels as if there's not a single part of Somerset that you can't see. Expect to take quite a buffeting from the wind, however; it blows hard up here.

FOOD & DRINK

The George & Pilgrim 1 High St, BA6 9DP 01458 831146 georgeandpilgrim. relaxinnz.co.uk. Imposing 15th-century public house and hotel whose graceful stone frontage, bearing fine mullion windows, conceals a delightful warren of Gothic-like alcoves. The snug bar serves up a tip-top selection of draught beers, and the food ain't half bad either. Some say the place is haunted…

Rainbow's End Café 17A High St, BA6 9DP 01458 833896 rainbowsendcafe.com 10.00–16.00 daily. Family-run for more than 30 years, this friendly old place tucked away down a tight alley is the original Glasto veggie café; a colourful salad bar is complemented by regular favourites such as spicy carrot and dahl soup and daily specials like cannellini bean casserole. In warmer weather there's a lovely little suntrap courtyard out back.

THE SOMERSET LEVELS

There are few more enchanting landscapes anywhere in Britain, let alone Somerset, than the Levels, the largest lowland wetland remaining in the UK. A vast area covering some 160,000 acres between the Blackdown Hills and the Mendips, it's a relentlessly flat landscape of smooth green

"With numerous rivers meandering across the pancake-flat landscape, the threat of flooding is ever present."

fields, wetlands and rivers, artificially drained and irrigated to allow productive farming. In every aspect, the Levels are a place apart from the rest of the county. However, with numerous rivers – including the Axe, Sheppey and Brue in the north, and the Cary, Yeo, Tone and Parrett to the south

– meandering across the pancake-flat landscape (which averages just 26ft above sea level), the threat of flooding is ever present, as the locals found out to their cost in 2013/14 when two months of rainfall left some 10% of the area underwater for several weeks – and longer in some places.

The ideal springboard for exploring the Levels is the **Avalon Marshes Centre**, just beyond the village of Meare on the fringes of Shapwick Heath National Nature Reserve; from here, you can strike out towards either Westhay Moor or Ham Wall reserves – these three almost contiguous reserves form the greater part of the **Avalon Marshes** project, a landscape that has been transformed in just a few decades from working peatland to the flourishing wetlands present today.

The beauty of the Levels is that there is no best time to be here. Every season is different and special – and this is especially true when it comes to its **birdlife**; whether it's wintering wildfowl, long-legged waders, birds of prey or the starling murmurations, the Levels provide a world-class habitat for some 150 species, not to mention all the different types of butterflies and dragonflies here. Meanwhile, the reintroduction of cranes on **West Sedgemoor**, the Levels' southernmost reserve, has been one of the most exciting wildlife projects to take place anywhere in the UK in recent times.

2 ROGER WILKINS CIDER BARN

Lands End Farm, Mudgley, nr Wedmore BS28 4TU ℘ 01934 712385 ⌔ wilkinscider.com
⊙ 10.00–20.00 Mon–Sat, 10.00–13.00 Sun

There's nowhere else in Somerset quite like Roger's gaff – in fact, come to think of it, there's no-one in Somerset quite like Roger. This much is evident the moment you step inside the agreeably tatty, corrugated iron and brick barn tucked away at the end of a muddy lane in the village of Mudgley overlooking Westhay – and that's exactly the way anyone who has ever beaten a path to Roger's barn door likes it. The man himself has been doing his thing for about 1,000 years (well, that's what his website says) and in all that time, little, if anything, has changed: none of your imported concentrates or fancy bottles here, just dry and sweet farmhouse cider dispensed from ginormous wooden barrels. You'll not be charged for it either (and you can drink as much as you want) – you can, though, order flagons to take away, and there's also cheese, pickle, chutney and oodles of other stuff to buy. So come on in, take a seat in the lounge bar (it's not what you think), and enjoy the company – a word of warning though: you might find yourself here for a while.

3 WESTHAY MOOR NATIONAL NATURE RESERVE

⌂ Double Gate Farm (page 235)

Owned and managed by the Somerset Wildlife Trust, Westhay Moor – the Avalon Marshes' northernmost reserve – is not dissimilar to Shapwick Heath (page 115) in that it was once a significant peat harvesting area. Unlike Shapwick though, it's much less travelled, hence you can enjoy this peaceful landscape, consisting mostly of open reedbeds, in relative solitude.

"You can enjoy this peaceful landscape, consisting mostly of open reedbeds, in relative solitude."

I had Richard Atkins, treasurer of the SWT (and a good friend to boot), show me around the reserve on a cool and breezy February afternoon. We started at the car park at the bottom of **Dagg's Lane Drove**, before breaking off into the heart of the reserve along a wide grass track (or cross drove) edged by alder, birch and willow. Either side of the track are large areas of raised mire (or bog), which, as Richard explained, is one of the country's rarest and most threatened habitats, having been seriously depleted following centuries of peat cutting. Since being re-established here, however, plants such as sundew, and rare mosses like sphagnum, have continued to flourish – as far as wetland restoration projects go, the one here at Westhay has unquestionably been one of the most successful.

Continuing along the track, it eventually joins up with **London Drove**, from where we walked along to the **North Hide**, one of six hides on the reserve. This hide is a splendid new two-storey affair; as elsewhere on the Levels, winter is really the best time to observe birds here (including grey herons, bitterns and marsh harriers), and although it was fairly quiet at the time of my visit, we did see a couple of great white egrets as well as a bunch of cormorants hanging out in a tree some distance away. As if to emphasise the ever-increasing numbers of species visiting the Marshes, in 2017 two night herons were spotted on Westhay, an event that caused much hysteria among the birding fraternity. It was the first time that this bird had been recorded breeding anywhere in the UK, though don't expect to see them – as their name suggests, they are nocturnal feeders.

FOOD & DRINK

The Duck at Burtle Station Rd, Burtle TA7 8NU ✆ 01278 238282 ⬦ theduckatburtle. co.uk. You can barely move for (pretty average) gastro pubs these days – albeit you won't find many in this part of the world – but the Duck is one that consistently manages to keep its standards high. It's centred on a long, curving bar (always a welcome sight) with squishy sofas and wood-burning stove. The restaurant offers a fine menu that very much trades on the local ingredients (breaded Somerset brie, slow-cooked pork belly with apple mashed potato and a cider sauce), though while here you should really try the duck burger or pan-fried duck breast (unless you're a vegetarian, that is).

The Sheppey Lower Godney BA5 1RZ ✆ 01458 831594 ⬦ thesheppey.co.uk. The Levels is starved of decent places to eat and drink, but this vibrant pub, in the hamlet of Godney just a couple of miles from Westhay, is the one exception. It's nothing to look at from the outside – in fact, if you didn't know better, you'd probably give it a wide berth – but inside, it's fun and it's funky. One smartly designed space leads to another, and then another, before you reach a decked terrace overlooking the River Sheppey, a wonderful spot when the sun shines. You'll not eat better for miles around, with a menu particularly strong on fish and veggie dishes (Sheppey fish stew, wild mushroom croquettes with baba ganoush), best enjoyed with a beer from the well-stocked bar. Popular at weekends with lunching families. Look out, too, for evenings of live music; they get some good bands down here.

4 SWEETS SCIENCE & PEAT MUSEUM

Blakeway, nr Wedmore BS28 4UE ✆ 07830 211544 ⬦ sweetstearooms.co.uk ◷ Wed–Sun

A scruffy-looking roadside shack culled entirely from recycled materials, Sweets is, first and foremost, a café/tearoom, and a jolly good one it is too, renowned for its big breakfasts and especially popular among cyclists. But there's a museum here too, and what a bonkers trove it is!

Established by peat farmer Merv Sweet, distant cousin of Ray of Sweet Track fame (see box, page 116), it is, ostensibly, a museum dedicated to science, technology and the peat-digging industry, though there are things here that defy categorisation: a tomahawk, a muzzleloading pistol found on Westhay Moor, an eel-catching machine and, er, a model of Paddington Bear. Pride of place, however, is a cabinet stuffed with mangled bits of a Junkers 88 bomber shot down in 1944 and recovered by Merv and his brother Clive when they were out digging one day in 1986; it wasn't a bad effort either, given that the wreckage lay buried some 35ft beneath the surface.

5 MEARE FISH HOUSE
St Mary's Rd, Meare

Standing in splendid isolation at the entrance to the village of **Meare** (meaning 'lake'), the **Fish House** is the country's sole surviving monastic fishery. Built for nearby Glastonbury Abbey around 1330, the Fish House was the occasional residence of the official responsible for the fishery, before it was abandoned following the Dissolution of the Monasteries. The estate was quite the complex in its day, comprising a series of ponds, orchards, vineyards and gardens, alongside St Mary's Church and the adjacent Manor House (now a farm), which is where visiting abbots would stay. The monks certainly weren't slow to exploit Meare Pool, the neighbouring lake, in those days richly sourced with pike, roach and eels – expensive and prestigious commodities back then. Once caught, the fish were held within one of the aforementioned ponds before being boated down to the abbey once a week.

Long since stripped bare – largely owing to a fire that gutted the building in the late 19th century – the interior originally consisted of two floors (as evidenced by the gnarled old beam running its length), downstairs comprising a main hall flanked by a parlour and service room, and upstairs there were two bedchambers. In truth there isn't much to see, but it's an impressive structure

"The Fish House was the occasional residence of the official responsible for the fishery."

and offers a cooling retreat on a hot day. The key for the House can be obtained from the aforementioned Manor House Farm, located around 350yds to the west (next to the church); it can be reached by road or via a pleasant little walk through the meadow; there's usually somebody there.

6 CATCOTT NATURE RESERVE

West Drove, nr Burtle TA7 8NQ; Somerset Wildlife Trust

If you've an aversion to crowds, such as those that regularly descend upon Ham Wall (page 117), then Catcott, a short distance from Shapwick Heath on the western margins of the Avalon Marshes, and one of the lowest parts of the Levels and Moors, is the place for you. Formerly arable land (carrots were once the big thing here), it was taken over by the Somerset Wildlife Trust in the 1970s, who subsequently converted it to the fabulous wetland you see today.

I was lucky enough to join Kevin Anderson, a SWT visitor guide, for a little jaunt around the reserve and, as the old adage goes, what Kevin doesn't know about birds isn't worth knowing about. We started at the Low Hide (next to the car park), which looks out over grazing meadow

MOOR MURMURATIONS

Between November and February, Shapwick Heath's main draw is the **murmurations**, the name given to large groups of starling flocks. Although not uncommon elsewhere in the UK, it's widely acknowledged that few parts of the country can rival the Somerset Levels when it comes to this marvellous spectacle. These great swarms – which can be anything from a few hundred to hundreds of thousands – generally peak in December and January when the resident community is joined by a large migrant population from northern Europe. Given these huge numbers, it's hard to believe that the starling is on the critical list of birds most at risk, but sadly it is.

Flying swiftly in co-ordinated formations, it's believed that starlings gather in such large numbers for two reasons: firstly, to keep themselves warm (the sheer volume of birds is enough to raise the air temperature by a few degrees) and secondly, to deter possible predators such as peregrines and sparrowhawks – safety in numbers and all that. The birds generally target the reedbeds, as these provide them with a safe and warm environment in which to kip down for the night, before their departure early the next day in search of food, a journey that can take them as far as the coastal mudflats at Bridgwater Bay some 20 miles away.

Although most people head down here at dusk, just before the starlings roost, it's much more fun to observe this spectacle at sunrise; not only will the crowds be thinner, but the dawn explosion is even more dramatic. Having done both, I can vouch for that. Although Shapwick Heath is their preferred destination, starlings do also roost at Ham Wall. Either way, there is a Starling Hotline (✆ 07866 554142), which reports where the birds roosted the night before, though this by no means guarantees that they'll be in the same place the next day.

that's naturally flooded in winter before slowly drying out in spring for the cattle to move in. For this reason, winter is the best time to enjoy **Catcott Lows**, and on this particular day it was abundant with wildfowl: teal, wigeon, pintail and shoveler, with the odd heron gliding in too. This is also a popular sport for hen and marsh harriers, though we saw neither on this occasion. From here we walked up **Higher Ropes Drove**, which, Kevin explained, was also known in the 19th century as the Leather Track on account of the waste that would often be dumped here by local leatherwork and sheepskin industries (the renowned Clarks's shoe factory is just up the road in Street) – and, as if to prove it, he picked up a large, remarkably well-preserved hide, declaring that it was most likely around a hundred years old.

We went into the woods (glimpsing a roe deer), beyond a series of ponds harbouring three species of newt, including a large population of great crested. From here a boardwalk took us to the **Great Fen**, which has been converted from peatland to reedbed and open water in just the last ten years, and it's stunning. We took to the elevated Tower Hide, and although there was little going on in terms of bird action (it's better here in spring and summer), we did witness a solo flying display from a great white egret. The whole site is well signposted, and although it's not suitable for bikes, it makes for a wonderful couple of hours of rambling.

7 SHAPWICK HEATH NATIONAL NATURE RESERVE

Shapwick Rd, Westhay BA6 9TT avalonmarshes.org/explore/nature-reserves/ shapwick-heath

Covering an area of some 500 acres in the very heart of the Somerset Levels, Shapwick Heath is the flagship reserve of the Avalon Marshes complex, a vast patchwork of reedbeds, lakes, ditches, wildflower meadows and wet woodlands teeming with brilliant wildlife, including over 60 species of birds (bitterns, great egrets and marsh harriers among them), dragonflies and butterflies, water voles and otters. For many though, Shapwick is synonymous with the murmurations (see box, opposite).

Designated a National Nature Reserve in 1961, most of the area now covering Shapwick Heath was once peatland, which originally formed here thousands of years ago. Peat was extracted by the Romans who used it to burn fuel, and it continued to be harvested commercially until

THE SWEET TRACK

The Sweet Track was one of a series of ancient timber causeways that cut across the Levels thousands of years ago. A simple yet ingenious concept, the Sweet Track was a raised walkway that ran for roughly a mile across a reedy swamp linking Westhay Island in the north with the Polden Hills to the south, comprising long wooden planks made of oak, ash and lime that were kept in place by sharpened pegs driven slantwise into the ground on either side. A superb example of early Neolithic engineering, its function was almost certainly dual purpose, namely to facilitate easier movement across this extensive, boggy terrain and also to provide access to hunting, grazing and fowling areas.

The catch is that these days you can't actually see it, owing to its aerobically preserved state deep within the soil. There is, however, a replica section of the Sweet Track located just off the main cycle path that runs through Shapwick Heath Nature Reserve (it's well signposted), reached via a spongy, peat-laden footpath through the thick fern woods. If you want to see part of the original Sweet Track, now a Scheduled Ancient Monument, then you'll have to venture to the British Museum in London.

There's plentiful evidence to suggest that similar trackways existed elsewhere in western Europe, particularly throughout the peatlands of central Ireland. Dendrochronology (tree-ring dating) established that this track was built in or around 3806BC, which, at the time of its discovery in 1970 by local peat farmer Ray Sweet (hence the name), made it the oldest known wooden trackway in Britain. However, it later lost its crown to the Post Track, which was discovered running parallel to the old Sweet Track, predating it by around 30 years. In 2009, a peat bog next to the notorious Belmarsh Prison in southeast London was the unlikely, and somewhat less exotic, location for the discovery of an even older timber platform.

as recently as the 1990s; a small working peat industry does still exist, but for how much longer is anyone's guess.

A most enjoyable walk, or bike ride, through Shapwick Heath – and one we've done as a family on a few occasions – starts by the bridge about 400yds south of the **Avalon Marshes Centre** on the Shapwick Road (page 103). From here, the wide path runs arrow straight down through the reserve along the trackbed of the old Somerset and Dorset Railway to Ham Wall Nature Reserve (see opposite), some two miles distant. Running parallel is the **South Drain**, an early 19th-century manmade waterway constructed for the purposes of transporting peat and other agricultural produce. There are several well-placed hides en route, including a couple just off the path, overlooking Noah's Lake –

where there's a good possibility of spotting otters and water voles – and on the main path itself, where the superb **Tower Hide** (the lower part is wheelchair accessible) affords terrific head-on views of the reedbeds, where you're quite likely to see herons and egrets mooching about. Locals say that the peat banks on Shapwick are the best place on the Levels to spot kingfishers, though that doesn't necessarily mean it makes them any easier to see. Heading in the other direction (west) from the bridge for about half a mile brings you to Canada Lake, and beyond here Catcott (page 114).

8 HAM WALL NATIONAL NATURE RESERVE

Main entrance on the Meare–Ashcott Rd, BA6 9SX ⊘ rspb.org.uk/hamwall

Directly opposite Shapwick Heath lies Ham Wall National Nature Reserve which, although far more compact, is equally as lovely. In fact, Ham Wall attracts greater numbers than all the other reserves, partly due to its excellent facilities, which include a large car park (£3/day), toilets and visitor centre (☺ w/ends 10.00–16.00). Previously worked by the peat industry, the reserve came under the auspices of the RSPB in 1994 and is now a thriving wetland comprising reedbeds, open water, grasslands and woodland. And, as elsewhere on the Levels, it's all about the birds. Ham Wall's most celebrated residents are **bitterns**, which were first bred here in 2008, and the reserve is now home to one of the largest populations in the country – to hear their distinctive, fog-horn 'boom' is quite something. Otherwise, expect to see marsh harriers and hobbies, while the nearby reedbeds of Walton Heath attract great-crested grebes and kingfishers, among others species. There are plenty of viewing platforms and hides dotted along the reserve's four trails, one of which – the Reedbed Trail – is wheelchair and buggy accessible.

9 WESTONZOYLAND PUMPING STATION MUSEUM

Hoopers Ln, Westonzoyland TA7 0LS ⊘ 01278 691595 ⊘ wzlet.org ☺ 13.00–17.00 Sun, plus special event days

Located in lovely rural isolation a mile or so from the village of the same name, the Westonzoyland Pumping Station Museum is not only the sole surviving pumping station still working in steam (with all the buildings still standing), but it also offers a fascinating glimpse into a small part of Somerset's little-known industrial heritage. So successful was the pumping station here at Westonzoyland following its inauguration in 1831, that a further five stations were eventually constructed along the River Parrett, though by the 1950s these original stations had been superseded by diesel counterparts; their function, however, essentially remained the same, namely to drain low-lying land – a much-needed requirement in these parts.

The museum's star attraction – and the only engine original to the site – is the Easton and Amos Steam Land Drainage System, a formidable unit installed in 1861 that was capable of pumping out 100 tonnes of water a minute (or, if it's easier to imagine, seven full baths a second). The largest centrifugal pump in the UK still in working order in its original location, it last saw action in the early 1950s. Elsewhere, the exhibition hall holds a substantial assemblage of beautifully restored pumps, boilers, engines and turbines, many of which were made within the county by locally renowned foundries such as Easton & Johnson in Taunton and Culverwell in Bridgwater. You can't miss the magnificent Marshall Portable Boiler out in the courtyard – an impressive unit, it powers every single steam engine on site.

As wonderful as these timeless pieces are, the best time to visit is on one of the **Steam Days** (check website for details), when all the machines are at full throttle; these usually take place once a month as well as on bank holidays and on other special occasions, for example the Steam on the Levels weekend in mid-May, when the museum really goes to town. On Steam Days, you can also ride the **Westonzoyland Light Railway**, a dinky narrow gauge that transports visitors around the site courtesy of its three locomotives.

10 GREYLAKE NATURE RESERVE

A361, TA7 9BP; RSPB

By the standards of the Levels, Greylake Nature Reserve is a relatively young landscape, having been converted from arable farmland around 15 years ago. Seasonally flooded, it's a mixed habitat, though predominantly reedbed and rough grassland, with occasional large areas of open water; along with West Sedgemoor (page 124) it's one of the most important sites in the country for wintering wildfowl and waders. In fact, given its small size (certainly compared with other reserves on the Levels), the range of birdlife present is mightily impressive.

One of two trails (both of which should take no more than 30 minutes to complete), the well-defined **Reedbed Loop** skirts a vast swathe of

6ft-high reeds before breaking off into the heart of the reedbed itself to a hide where (in spring) you can view booming bitterns; you may even see otters mucking about here. The main hide lies at the end of the wheelchair-accessible **Easy Access Trail** (also accessed via the Reedbed Loop), its proximity to the water affording fabulous opportunities to see ducks (wigeons, teals, shovelers) and waders (lapwing, snipe) up close and, in summer, little egrets and herons. It's also a fantastic spot for observing year-round raptors – marsh harriers, merlins and peregrines in particular.

11 BURROW MUMP

Burrow Bridge TA7 0RB; National Trust

Four miles south of Greylake on the A361, it comes as something of a surprise to suddenly see a rather large knoll emerge from the otherwise pancake-flat terrain. It's an even more startling sight when surrounded by water, not an infrequent occurrence in these parts. Standing at the foot of two rivers, the Parrett and the Tone, Burrow Mump – which rather oddly translates as 'Hill Hill' – was presented to the National Trust in 1946 as a memorial to honour all the Somerset men and women who fell

FLOODS ON THE LEVELS

Floods, unfortunately, have long been a fact of life on the Levels. Way back in 1607 more than 2,000 people drowned as a result of coastal defences in the Bristol Channel being breached, an event that was repeated in 1872, when this part of Somerset remained underwater for nigh on six months. More recently, there was widespread flooding in 2007 and 2012, though it's the memories of the events of 2013/14 that remain pretty raw around these parts.

During December 2013 and January 2014, unprecedented amounts of rainfall fell upon the Levels, resulting in some 17,000 acres being submerged for weeks on end – some villages, like Muchelney and Thornley, were heavily flooded for more than two months. The Environment Agency subsequently came in for some sharp criticism from locals, not only for being far too slow to react to the situation, but also for failing to implement appropriate preventative measures in the first place – first and foremost, questions were raised over the lack of proper dredging of the rivers and rhynes. Since those grim days, rivers have been dredged and giant pumps have been installed in several locations, while longer-term proposals include the construction of a tidal barrage and the requirement that a number of roads be raised, all of which means that, in theory at least, the events of 2013/14 should never again be repeated.

during World War II. The hill, just 70ft high, has certainly seen its fair share of action over the years, having been used as a refuge for Royalist soldiers during the Civil War and then again occupied by the king's army during the Monmouth Rebellion. And like Glastonbury Tor, visible in the distance, there are legends associated with this place too. It's said that **Alfred the Great** used the hill as a lookout while fighting the Danes around the end of the 9th century; though this may remain unsubstantiated, records indicate that he did establish Athelney Abbey nearby, of which nothing now remains.

"It's said that Alfred the Great used the hill as a lookout while fighting the Danes around the end of the 9th century."

Surmounting Burrow Mump today, and most likely built atop an older, medieval chapel, is the roofless but otherwise almost totally intact ruin of the 18th-century Church of St Michael, a designated Grade II-listed building and Scheduled Ancient Monument, though it is not possible to enter. You can, though, content yourself with some wonderful, far-reaching views (across the Levels) once you've completed the short but exhilarating little scramble up from the car park.

12 SMITH & EVANS WINE

Higher Plot Farm, Aller Rd, Langport TA10 0QL ✐ 01458 259075 ⬧ smithandevans.co.uk

Somerset may be a relatively minor player when it comes to England's wine counties, but this part of the country does boast a coterie of excellent wineries, of which Smith & Evans is one. A long-established wine trader, Guy Smith and his wife Laura Evans (a film editor) spent five years looking for a suitable wine-growing site, which culminated in them finding this sunny, steeply sloping terrace overlooking the southernmost reaches of the Levels, and with it, providing stunning views across to the Blackdown Hills, the Mendips and Exmoor. Both the white lias limestone (a soil common to both the Burgundy and Champagne regions of France) and the unique macroclimate (it's very dry here) combine to make this the ideal spot for harvesting their two excellent wines: a dry white (Pinot/Chardonnay) and a sparkling wine. Planted in 2008, their first yield was in 2010, and since then volume has grown year on year, to the point where, in 2018, they produced in excess of six tonnes of grapes, which translates to some 5,000 bottles. Visits are generally by appointment only but the shop is usually open if you fancy a little tipple and/or wish to purchase a bottle or two. They also produce cider with apples harvested in the neighbouring ancient orchard. You'll likely be accompanied around the vineyard by Bert, the adorable family lab.

13 LANGPORT

It's probably fair to say that Langport has never been the most fashionable of places, but much has changed for the better here in recent times. Admittedly, the main drag, Bow Street, still looks decidedly grubby in places (thanks mainly to the traffic thundering through) – and no, your eyes aren't deceiving you, many of the buildings along here do tilt backwards.

Depending upon your source, Langport variously translates as 'Long Town', 'Long Port' or 'Long Market' (the Domesday Book refers to it as 'Lanporth', which seems vaguely Welsh to me) – but whatever its meaning, its history is as fascinating as it is, erm, long. In many ways, this spirited little market town, which claims to be the country's smallest, is defined by its river, the wide and muddy **Parrett**, which cuts across the A378 at the west end of town. Indeed, Langport grew rich on its waterway, with people and goods (chiefly corn and salt) traded here from Roman times right up until the 20th century.

Hard as it is to believe now, Langport was, for a period in the mid 19th century, one of the most powerful financial centres in the country. For this it had to thank Vincent Stuckey, founder of Stuckey's Banking Co (a past constituent of NatWest) in 1826, whose note circulation was second only to the Bank of England at that time. Upon Stuckey's death in 1854, his nephew **Walter Bagehot** (1826–77) took over as secretary. Not only Langport's most famous citizen, but one of Britain's most influential personalities, Bagehot (pronounced 'badge-it') was the pre-eminent political economist of his time, editing both *The Financial Times* and *The Economist*, the latter for 17 years (even today, the magazine retains a weekly column, 'Bagehot's Notebook', in his name). Such was the depth of his work (notably *The English Constitution*, published in 1867) that his writings still remain relevant today. While Bagehot may not necessarily be a household name, he is quite the celebrity here in Langport, so much

"Langport was, for a period in the mid 19th century, one of the most powerful financial centres in the country."

so that he has a garden named in his honour, located behind the town hall on North Street. An information board here relays the story of Bagehot's life.

In terms of sights, most things of interest are located at the western end of Bow Street. First off there's **Great Bow Wharf**, which has been subject to an extensive programme of regeneration. Part of this involved the complete rehabilitation of the early 19th-century warehouse, which has been converted into an excellent community hub, complete with the excellent Kitchen café (see below). Across the way, a dozen smart new eco-homes have been erected.

Beyond the wharf, and across the three-arched Great Bow Bridge, is **Shakspeare Glass and Arts** (✆ 01458 252477 ⏣ shakspeareglass.co.uk), the workshop of nationally renowned glass-blower Will Shakspeare, who has been at this game for more than 30 years. You'll catch Will hard at it in his workshop most days, crafting sublime pieces (baubles and bowls, tumblers, vases and the like) that are heavily influenced by the local colours and landscapes – cast your eyes over his gorgeous Hedgerow and Somerset collections, for example. If you fancy having a blow yourself, and this definitely looks like one of the trickier crafts to master, then Will offers glass-blowing classes. There's also a gallery and a coffee shop here.

¶¶ FOOD & DRINK

The Halfway House Pitney Hill, Pitney TA10 9AB ✆ 01458 252513 ⏣ thehalfwayhouse. co.uk. This is everything a village pub should be: rough-hewn beams and chunky slate flooring, woody aromas from a crackling fireplace, and a gentle undertow of good conversation. Factor in a fantastic selection of real ales and farmhouse ciders, plus wholesome lunches for under a tenner, and this really does tick all the boxes. Moreover, there's invariably something going on here, be it a quiz or steak night, a barbecue or a beer festival.

Kitchen at the Wharf Bow St, TA10 9PN ✆ 01458 254354 ⏣ kitchenlangport.co.uk ⏲ 09.30–15.00, plus Fri 17.00–20.00 daily. Occupying the old (but newly renovated) warehouse down on Great Bow Wharf, Kitchen certainly looks impressive with its stripped, white-wood flooring and thick timber beams, not to mention a sunny riverside terrace – and the food is very good, too: sourdough sandwiches, crisp salads and brunches are big pluses on the menu.

Pitney Farm Café Glebe Farm, Woodbirds Hill Ln, Pitney TA10 9AP ✆ 07769 173682 ⏣ pitneyfarmshop.co.uk/pitney-farm-café ⏲ 10.00–17.00 Tue–Sat. In the pretty little village of Pitney, 2½ miles northeast of Langport, the lovely Lily oversees this sweet, larch-clad hut, which she had built from scratch. Sit yourself down at one of the scaffold-board tables, take in the view of the long fields through the big windows (it's not often you get a view like this), and kick back with a delicious cup of coffee and a slice of homemade cake. Lily also rustles up scrumptious lunches (such as porky potato cakes with poached eggs and wilted kale), which are prepared with organically grown ingredients from the farm. It's really rather delightful.

14 COATES ENGLISH WILLOW

Meare Green Court, Stoke St Gregory TA3 6HY ✐ 01823 490249 ✐ coatesenglishwillow. co.uk ◷ 09.30–17.00 Mon–Sat, tours 11.00 & 14.30 Mon–Fri; see ad, 4th colour section

Coates English Willow, which celebrated its 200th anniversary in 2019, is currently run by the fifth-generation of the eponymous family, namely Jonathan and Nicola – the chap who got the whole thing going back in 1819 was one Robert Coate. Willow weaving is as deep-rooted a Somerset tradition as cheese and cider, albeit one that's far less prevalent, and this is the only place in the country where willow is grown on a large-scale commercial basis – the deep peat and damp soil that's so prevalent here on the Levels is ideal for harvesting this fantastically pliable crop. Aside from the production of baskets, furniture and the like, willow is also used to make artist's charcoal, which is done by burning willow sticks at very high temperatures in non-oxygenated air; this now not only accounts for roughly half of their business here, but also to about 80% of the world's total production of artist's charcoal.

As fascinating as many aspects of the **tour** are – which takes in the drying and sorting barns, soaking pits, charcoal kilns and machine room (up to 180 bundles can be stripped in one day by machine, as opposed to eight by hand), you'll be far more distracted by the basket makers, two of whom were hard at it crafting willow coffins when I visited – indeed, as Nicola told me, the manufacture of willow coffins now accounts for a large part of their business. The level of skill required to become a weaver is quite something; indeed, a typical apprenticeship takes around three years, although, as Nicola pointed out, attracting potential willow weavers is (unsurprisingly, perhaps) not easy these days. The tour aside, there's oodles to see and do here, and kids are especially well catered for: the fun **sculpture trail** goes through nearby woodland, where they can identify a dozen or so different willow creatures. There's also longer trails that continue down to and along the River Tone.

The **museum**, meanwhile, amply demonstrates just how versatile willow is, with cradles, beehives, sparrow traps and fish traps (as once used on the nearby Parrett), and postal baskets among the many wonderful items on display. While baskets (in their many guises) are the mainstay of the current business – Fortnum & Mason is one of their most prestigious clients (hampers of course) – they've also been commissioned to provide props for a number of films, such as shell baskets for *War Horse*, eel traps for *Robin Hood*, and chairs for *Sweeney Todd*. Once you've exhausted this little lot, retire to the very lovely Lemon Tree Coffee House and for a cup of coffee and a home-baked scone or slice of cake.

15 WEST SEDGEMOOR NATURE RESERVE & SWELL WOOD

Access to **West Sedgemoor Nature Reserve** (Curry Rivel TA10 0PH ✆ 01458 252805 ⌖ rspb.org.uk ⊙ by pre-booked guided walk only), which is under the auspices of the RSPB, is slightly different from others

THE RETURN OF THE CRANE

One of the most exciting events to happen on the Levels in recent times was the introduction of 93 **common cranes** on West Sedgemoor Nature Reserve (⌖ thegreatcraneproject.org.uk), the first 21 of which were released in 2010. Until then, this majestic bird had been absent from the South West for over 400 years, and had only made a comeback in the UK in the 1980s when a small population started breeding on the Norfolk Broads. They had become extinct in the UK during the medieval period, killed off thanks to a combination of hunting and the draining of their traditional wetland sites.

West Sedgemoor was chosen as the site for the project owing to its relative seclusion and size, as well as the feeding opportunities it could afford the birds. The eggs (which were collected from Germany) were hatched and hand-reared at The Wildfowl and Wetlands Trust in Slimbridge in Gloucestershire before being released here, and it was another five years before the first second-generation chicks (ie: the offspring of the original founding flock) were born, in 2015. While the reintroduction programme, now complete, has been an unqualified success, post-release monitoring continues, and the success or otherwise of the project will ultimately depend upon breeding productivity, something that won't be fully known for a few years yet. However, at last count, in 2018, there were at least 56 of the original 93 cranes alive, and an additional 17 second-generation birds in the group. This survival rate is actually pretty good given that, typically, only 50% make it through to adulthood. The first of the second-generation birds are now also at breeding age (at least three years old).

on the Levels, in that it can only be visited on a pre-booked guided walk; that said, there are some lovely views from the elevated public footpaths to the south of the reserve at Swell Wood (see below), where hedgerows also teem with birdlife. This extensive tract of wet grassland, which is subject to a carefully controlled water management system, provides ample refuge for southern England's largest community of wildfowl (mallards, shovelers, teal) and breeding waders (lapwings, snipe and redshank), though it's the curlew that causes the biggest stir here as it's one of the country's most endangered bird species – although at Sedgemoor numbers are actually on the up, which is cheering news indeed. It's well worth signing up to a walk, though these do get booked up quickly.

Between March and June, **Swell Wood** (A378, TA3 6PX) – an ancient deciduous forest just off the A378 on the southern fringe of West Sedgemoor Nature Reserve – is the location for the largest **heronry** in

I was fortunate to have Damon Bridge, RSPB Conservation Officer for the Somerset Levels and Moors, take me out to a section of the Parrett Trail near **Aller Moor**, just west of Langport (which is where the cranes seemed to have settled upon as their favourite gathering spot) in the hope of a sighting – though this was by no means a given, seeing as they have a habit of slinking away among the tall vegetation. But we did get lucky and it was a genuine thrill to catch a glimpse of these charismatic creatures skulking around the fields foraging for grub. If you do go seeking cranes, don't forget your binoculars (better still, a telescope if you've got one handy), as you're unlikely to get within a few hundred metres of them. They roost at night, standing in shallow water as a group before heading out to the fields the next day to feed, mostly on arable stubbles

and in pasture where they probe for worms, insects, tasty roots and seeds. The best time to catch sight of them is early morning before they get disturbed by farming operations or people out walking. The cranes are present on the Levels and Moors all year round, but are hard to spot in summer months when the hay meadow grasses are tall, so the best time is autumn, winter or early spring.

The release population at West Sedgemoor represents around half of the UK population, though they haven't all remained in Somerset, with some now breeding in Wales, Gloucestershire and other counties in the South West. Elsewhere, the native Norfolk population has increased over the past few years, with birds now also successfully breeding in the Fens in Cambridgeshire and Suffolk, on the Humberhead Peatlands of Yorkshire, and in the wilds of northeast Scotland.

the South West, if not the country; in a good year, there can be up to 100 pairs of grey herons here. Nesting cheek-by-jowl in improbably bulky constructions perched high among the treetops, the sight of so many of these birds crammed together is quite something. As colonial nesters they much prefer their own company (though little egrets have recently muscled their way in here), and typically return to the same site each year, though nests do require rebuilding.

"Nesting cheek-by-jowl high among the treetops, the sight of so many of these birds crammed together is quite something."

There are two well-signposted nature trails through Swell Wood, both starting at the car park (there are no other facilities here), one of which has a dedicated heron hide, though it's sometimes the case that you may only be able to hear them (an unmistakeable guttural bark) as opposed to see them. Your best bet is to get here as early as you can. Notwithstanding the star attraction, the woods are a lovely spot for a gentle ramble, especially in spring when the floor is carpeted with bluebells. Note, again, that dogs are not allowed anywhere on either West Sedgemoor or at Swell Wood.

16 MUCHELNEY ABBEY

⌂ **The Parsonage** (page 235) ⛺ **Thorney Lakes Caravan and Camping** (page 235)
Muchelney TA10 0DQ 🖉 01458 250664 ☺ Apr–Oct; English Heritage

While not quite in Glastonbury's class, Muchelney Abbey, in the tiny village of the same name, was, nevertheless, a heavyweight ecclesiastical institution back in the day. Most likely founded by Athelstone in or around AD692, the abbey experienced its most sustained period of growth in the 12th century, with further piecemeal development in the 13th century. Little, though, was spared of Muchelney following its dissolution in 1538, and most of the complex was levelled within just a few years; thereafter it was used as farmland and, until relatively recently, orchards.

The abbey's sizeable footprint is clearly mapped out by the ruins of low walls, which are great scrambling territory for kids. Excavations have revealed four stages of growth here at Muchelney, the earliest dating from the Saxon period. That church was later swallowed up by a far bigger one built by the Normans, who pitched up in their boats (which tells you much about the landscape at that time) some time in the 12th century; the last of these phases revealed substantial Gothic elements.

One of just two buildings to survive unscathed following the dissolution was the Abbot's Lodge. A first-rate architectural specimen, both inside and out, what is most striking about it is the combination of blue lias stone and gorgeous, honey-coloured hamstone, the latter quarried at Ham Hill near Yeovil – you'll see it everywhere on your travels in this part of the county, though it becomes even more prominent the further south you go. Inside the antechamber (which now functions as the ticket office), a flight of wonderfully well-worn stone steps not dissimilar to those at Wells Cathedral (page 68) ascend to the Abbot's Chamber, whose fine timbered ceiling is trumped only by a magnificent 15th-century hamstone fireplace surmounted by two recumbent lions. From here another, narrower, set of steps leads to a sequence of three small rooms, each of which sports its own unique wooden ceiling, the most impressive of which is a barrel roof in the painted chamber, so-called on account of its 500-year-old patterned, if patchy, fresco.

On the same floor, the Cheese Room is arguably the most interesting of them all, by virtue of its superb coffered ceiling, stone fireplace and cambered floor; moreover, there's a display of decorated tiles (originally part of the parish church), each of which depicts a local scene – the one that caught my eye had herons fishing for eels, two of the county's most iconic species. Back downstairs, a massive wall now separates what were originally two kitchens, though they do still retain their fine timber roofs. Grafted on to the side of the lodge is the one remaining (south) cloister, albeit now completely enclosed. It holds some fantastic sculptural work, not least a beautifully carved figure of a headless St John the Baptist with a lamb resting on a book (possibly the Bible). One can only imagine what this part of the abbey complex must have looked like before the three remaining ranges were torn down. Completing this fine ensemble is the thatched monastic latrine, of which this is one of very few surviving examples; it may even be the only one.

"The thatched monastic latrine is one of very few surviving examples; it may even be the only one."

17 BROWN & FORREST SMOKERY

Bowdens Farm Smokery, Hambridge TA10 0BP ✐ 01458 250875 ☝ brownandforrest.co.uk

If it needs a good smoking, then the good folk at Brown and Forrest Smokery, located four miles south of Langport on an upmarket

EEL BE 'AVIN' YOU

They may not be everyone's cup of tea, but eels are quite the delicacy down 'ere in this part of Somerset. An order of predatory elongated fish, the European eel is as mysterious as it is delicious. Each spring, the larvae of these eels depart from their breeding grounds in the **Sargasso Sea** in the North Atlantic Ocean and embark upon an epic journey to Europe's western seaboard, a journey that, incredibly, takes up to three years; by the time they've reached these shores, they've become **elvers**, or glass (baby) eels. Entering the Severn Estuary, they migrate upstream before finding their way into the rhynes and ditches of the Somerset Levels, whose dark, silty and slow-moving waters provide them with the ideal habitat in which to feed

and grow – they've also got the remarkable ability to slither across wet grass, which is of course plentiful hereabouts. Several years later, having matured from 'yellow' to 'silver' eels (by this stage they can be anywhere between eight and 20 years old and up to a yard long), they head back to the Sargasso Sea to spawn and then die. It really is the most extraordinary of animal migrations.

None of this, though, really answers the question of why they come here in the first place, and it's this, alongside the question of their entire life cycle, that has long vexed scientists. Although the eel is currently on the list of critically endangered species, it's not entirely clear how at risk it actually is, though the population does appear to have stabilised in recent years.

industrial estate in Hambridge, are the people to do it – and while eel is their flagship product, they pretty much smoke anything and everything here. Originally founded by Michael Brown in 1981, the business was taken over in 2004 by Jesse Pattison, who had been living and working in Suffolk as an agricultural sales rep, though he had known, and trained under, Brown beforehand. Among Brown and Forrest's many prestigious clients are Fortnum & Mason, the Grosvenor House Park Lane, and a number of Michelin-starred restaurants, though Jesse has always been adamant that they won't be going down the route of supplying supermarkets.

The smoking process is as ingenious as it is simple, and involves the use of just two modest, upright wood-fired ovens, one for hot smoking, and another for cold smoking. The former is used to smoke most meats, such as duck, lamb and chicken, as well as eel of course, while the latter – little more than a brick cupboard (known as a London Kiln in the capital) – is mostly used for salmon, haddock, trout and cheeses. Once the oven is fired up and good to go, the meat is initially roasted at high temperature over an open fire before sawdust is added to give it that smoky taste. On my visit there, Jesse explained to me that, because of its delicate flavour, eel (which looks a bit like trout but has nowhere near as powerful a taste) has to be smoked with beech sawdust, as opposed to oak, which is traditionally used for smoking salmon and trout. It's possible to see the smoking process on one of the Smokery's three open days, which take place at various times during the year. Otherwise, the unpretentious daytime-only **restaurant** (⊘ 09.00–16.00 Mon–Sat) serves up terrific food for breakfast and lunch – you'll just have a hell of a job deciding which dish to try (preface all the following with 'smoked'): mackerel, sausages, lamb fillet, salmon scotch egg… In warmer weather they place tables outside, from where there are lovely vistas of the surrounding countryside. It's also worth stopping here to visit the **shop** (⊘ 09.00–16.00 Mon–Sat), which is groaning with goodies – so you're unlikely to leave empty-handed.

SOMERSET ONLINE

For additional online content, articles, photos and more on Somerset, why not visit ⊘ bradtguides.com/somerset.

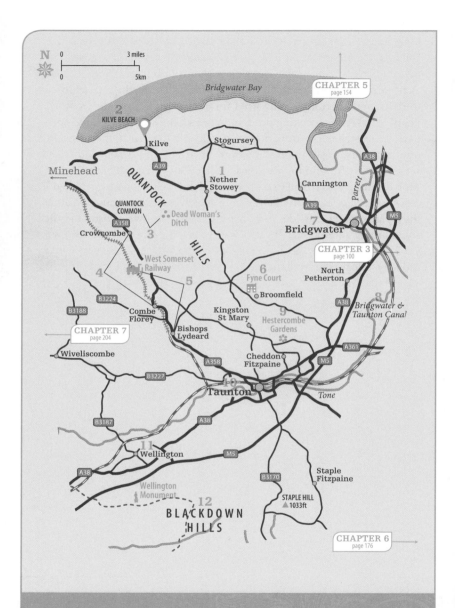

FROM THE QUANTOCKS TO THE BLACKDOWN HILLS

4

FROM THE QUANTOCKS TO THE BLACKDOWN HILLS

While neither **Taunton** nor **Bridgwater**, two of Somerset's largest towns, merit extended visits, both are worth a diversion on account of a clutch of eminently enjoyable museums. Taunton is also home to the county cricket team, so if you can spare the time (and like cricket), this makes for a wonderfully relaxing day out. Like so much of Somerset though, it's the countryside around here that offers the greatest rewards. First up are the **Quantocks**, which, although of modest height and lacking the drama of nearby Exmoor, present superb walking possibilities. There's plenty of cultural sustenance here too, thanks to the pre-eminent Romantic poet Samuel Coleridge, one-time resident of **Nether Stowey**, and a flourish of red sandstone churches in the villages of Bishops Lydeard, Crowcombe and Combe Florey, all worthwhile destinations in themselves.

One, very leisurely, way of exploring the Quantocks is aboard the delightful **West Somerset Railway**, which chugs serenely through rolling countryside and along a short stretch of coastline before reaching Minehead (covered in *Chapter 5*). Even if you're not a fan of steam, this is an unmissable experience. Ranged along the Somerset/Devon border, and even less visited than the Quantocks, are the **Blackdown Hills**, which present further, gentler rambling opportunities. The Blackdown Hills overlook the charming little market town of **Wellington**, which is well worth a Slow morning's exploration.

GETTING THERE & AROUND

The **M5** bisects this central part of Somerset, skirting Bridgwater, Taunton and Wellington along the way – three towns that are well served by public transport. Both Taunton and Bridgwater lie on the main **train** line between Bristol and Exeter (with frequent services to both), and in addition, there are roughly hourly services from London Paddington to Taunton (✐ gwr.com). Fans of steam won't want to miss out on the wonderful **West Somerset Railway** (page 139), which links the village of Bishops Lydeard, near Taunton, with Minehead on the coast.

BUSES

Dozens of **buses** fan out from Taunton, including the 21 to Bridgwater, the 22 to Wellington, the 29 to Glastonbury (*Chapter 3*) and Wells (*Chapter 2*), and the 54 to Langport (*Chapter 3*) and Somerton (*Chapter 6*). Buses to the Quantocks are more sporadic, though villages along its flanks are reasonably well served; buses 16 and 24 travel the A39 between Bridgwater and Minehead, stopping at Nether Stowey, while bus 28, which runs roughly parallel to the West Somerset Railway on the A358 between Taunton and Minehead, serves Combe Florey and Crowcombe among other villages. For more information, check ✐ firstgroup.com/somerset.

WALKING & CYCLING

Walkers have plenty of choice in this particular area, with both the Quantock and Blackdown hills providing ample opportunities to stretch one's legs. While neither of these ranges are particularly demanding, they shouldn't be underestimated – and if you want to go all out, there's the long-distance Coleridge Way. Moreover, these hills aren't especially well travelled, so the chances are that you'll have them (almost) all to yourself. Although there are more exciting parts of Somerset for **cycling**, there are one or two spots where you can get pedalling, such as the Bridgwater and Taunton Canal towpath, which is part of National Route 3.

THE QUANTOCK HILLS

🏠 **The Old Cider House** (page 235), **Parsonage Farm** (page 235) 🏠 **The Old House** (page 235)

Designated England's first Area of Outstanding Natural Beauty in 1956, the Quantock Hills tend to fly under most people's radar, possibly because of their proximity to Exmoor or possibly just because they're just not that well known. Either way, this 12-mile ridge, wedged in between Bridgwater, Taunton and Minehead, is an alluring mixed landscape of ancient oak woodland, secluded combes and open heathland stalked by red deer and wild ponies. It's fabulous, and still mostly untouched, walking and riding country with numerous scenic trails, among them the long-distance **Coleridge Way**, named after the great Romantic poet **Samuel Taylor Coleridge** (see box, page 134), the one name you'll come across time and again here in the Quantocks. Coleridge lived in **Nether Stowey**, one of the Quantocks' few sparsely populated villages and hamlets. It was here too that I went to school, so the Quantocks very much resonate with me, yet the irony is that I was largely cocooned within my own little world so never really got to explore them, save for the occasional trip down into the village for supplies. The boundary of the Quantocks AONB actually extends to, and includes, a short section of the coast, embracing **Kilve** and its famous fossil beach, so it's for this reason that I have included that in this chapter, as opposed to the main coast chapter (*Chapter 5*); to this end I have also outlined a fabulous little walk taking in a section of the South West Coast Path.

1 NETHER STOWEY

Lying just off the main A39 road, Nether Stowey is by far the most visited of the Quantock villages, though that's almost entirely due to the presence of **Coleridge Cottage** (35 Lime St ✐ 01278 732662 ☉ Mar–Oct, daily; National Trust), a rather plain-looking Georgian building standing at the far end of Lime Street. A place his wife Sara bemoaned as 'a miserable cottage' (the fact that they had a miserable marriage may have had something to do with that), Samuel Coleridge only lived here for three years, between 1797 and 1800, though that was long enough for the poet to produce his most enduring works. Many of the rooms have been restored to resemble how they might have looked back in Coleridge's day – the parlour, kitchen and service room for example, though the cottage was in fact substantially altered later in the 19th century when it was run as an inn for a period. The National Trust acquired the property in 1909.

Alongside first editions are many of Coleridge's personal effects: ink stand and pot, goose quill pens, a book slide culled from the wood of a beech tree under which he and Wordsworth met/would meet, locks of hair, and various items of correspondence – in one, to his brother, he expounds despairingly of his (very brief) time serving in the army. Meanwhile, listening posts dotted around the place allow you to contemplate some of the poet's work. Once done inside, take a stroll through the long garden, followed perhaps, by a cuppa and slice of farmhouse cake in the courtyard tea room. The cottage aside, the village is pretty enough, though without any other significant sights to detain you; that said, there are a couple of bustling pubs you could happily avail yourself of, and this is probably your best bet as a base if you are planning on spending a few days in the Quantocks.

COLERIDGE & THE QUANTOCKS

Born in Ottery St Mary in 1772, **Samuel Coleridge** attended Jesus College, Cambridge before enlisting in the 15th Light Dragoons, although this was a short-lived career. As a political agitator in Bristol, he preached on many subjects, though he was particularly vocal about the city's slave trade, as well as an enthusiastic supporter of the French Revolution. However, it was as one of the great Romantic poets that his reputation was sealed. Indeed, Coleridge was at the forefront of this movement, which emerged during the latter half of the 18th century. Along with **William Wordsworth**, with whom he forged a close and lasting friendship, he wrote *Lyrical Ballads* (1798), the volume generally considered to have launched the Romantic poetry movement. Not only neighbours (by this time Wordsworth had moved into nearby Alfoxton House), they were great walking buddies – Wordsworth's wife, Dorothy, frequently accompanied them – and it was trudging these hills that inspired Coleridge to write his greatest works, among them *Frost at Midnight, The Rime of the Ancient Mariner*, and *Kubla Khan*. A prodigious canon of work, Coleridge would never again be as prolific as he was during his three years here in the Quantocks.

Despite, or perhaps because of, his genius, Coleridge was a heavy drinker who became addicted to opium and generally suffered from poor health and depression. He died, aged 61, in 1834 and was buried at St Michael's Church in Highgate, north London. In 2018, the poet's well-preserved lead coffin, alongside those of four other family members, was found in the church's wine cellar, a surprising turn of events given that it was assumed he had been buried under a memorial slab in the nave above.

You can follow in the poet's footsteps, literally, by undertaking the **Coleridge Way** (⊘ coleridgeway.co.uk), a 51-mile-long path beginning in Nether Stowey and ending in Lynmouth, in north Devon. If you have the time and inclination (and a bit of good weather), this is a wonderful trek, one ideally completed over a leisurely five or six days.

FOOD & DRINK

Ancient Mariner 42 Lime St, TA5 1NG ✆ 01278 733544 ⌨ marinernetherstowey.co.uk
Of course there had to be a pub named after one of Coleridge's works in his home village, and so it is here with this 16th-century inn, located directly opposite the cottage and which the author himself no doubt frequented. The food is steady rather than spectacular, but this is compensated for by a creditable selection of ales, including a selection from the nearby Quantock Brewery and a warm, inviting atmosphere.

2 KILVE BEACH

A unique fossil-rich slate shore, Kilve Beach – which I've included here (as opposed to *Chapter 5*) because it lies within the Quantocks AONB – is Somerset's equivalent of Dorset's more famous Jurassic Coast, albeit on a much smaller scale. But, like Dorset's Jurassic Coast, Kilve is a classic ammonite-rich locality, its slate and shingle foreshore and lias (limestone) cliffs concealing all manner of ammonites, marine reptiles, belemnites (squid-like creatures) and shells – it's a fossicking destination *par excellence*. Access to the beach is easy enough (it's just a short walk from the car park by the ruins of Chantry Manor), though you could take it in as part of the walk outlined in the box on page 136. Do take sturdy footwear, however, as it can be tough going over this rugged, rocky shore. Don't forget, too, to keep an eye out for tide times; one good website is ⌨ tideschart.com.

FOOD & DRINK

Chantry Tea Gardens Sea Ln, Kilve TA5 1EG ✆ 01278 74145. This privately run teahouse, abutting the ruins of Chantry Manor, makes for a welcome sight after completing the walk on page 136. As the name suggests, it's outdoor seating only (there is some cover), and very pleasant it is too, with nicely prepared tea, coffee and homemade cake, as well as light lunches. If you're feeling particularly indulgent, get your chops around a calorific cream tea.

3 QUANTOCK COMMON & DEAD WOMAN'S DITCH

From Nether Stowey, it's around half a mile across high ground to **Quantock Common**, a mixed area of open heathland and dense woodland grazed by sheep, cows and ponies. Smack bang in the centre of the common, next to the car park, is the sinister-sounding **Dead Woman's Ditch**, a distinctive earthwork running along one side of the car park that is suggestive of some kind of Iron Age territorial boundary. According to local folklore, this place takes its name from a particularly

Kilve & East Quantoxhead

✤ OS Explorer Map 140; start: pay & display car park by Chantry Manor on Sea Ln, just off the A39 ♀ ST149434; 3 miles; easy to moderate

This is an undemanding but varied and immensely enjoyable walk through wheat fields to the hamlet of East Quantoxhead. More fields and a narrow country lane beckon before you come to the best bit of the walk – a clifftop trek along a section of the South West Coast Path with glorious views. It's mostly flat with just a few moderate climbs.

1 From the car park, walk across the courtyard of the 13th-century **Chantry Manor** (with the church on your left), through a gate before shortly crossing a ford. Here you proceed along a gravel track through three wheat fields before the path bends slightly to the right and between hedges. Some 100yds later, go through another gate with **East Wood** on your left.

2 At the end of the field, cross the stream, at which point you'll see a path to your right with a sign pointing to the beach; ignore this and continue straight on following the sign to **East Quantoxhead**; to your right you can just about glimpse the pretty gardens of medieval **Court House**. Emerging on to an asphalt road, turn right by the large duck pond towards Court House, then take an immediate left through the car park (before the stone gate entrance). Follow the path (with the wall and **St Mary's Church** on your right) and go through the kissing gate. Here, take a sharpish left, go through the field and another gate, and walk through the wide open field until you hit the lane; note that there are often quite a few cows here.

grisly murder that occurred hereabouts in 1789, when local charcoal burner John Walford reputedly slit his wife's throat (they'd only been married three weeks) and dumped her body here. Walford was found guilty and hanged at nearby Doddington Green, where his body was left to rot from a gibbet for a year. If that hasn't spooked you too much, this is a lovely spot for a long picnic.

4 CROWCOMBE & COMBE FLOREY

Beyond a viewing point at Withyman's Pool (1,175ft), a little further on from Dead Woman's Ditch, the road descends to **Crowcombe**, which merits a brief stop on account of its 15th-century **Church of the Holy Ghost**. As is standard in these parts, the exterior, now heavily weathered, is all red sandstone, though the tower is of a notably darker hue than

3 Turn right along the lane and continue until you get to a left-hand bend; go straight ahead up the narrow, high-hedged track (Underway Lane). After about 600yds, you arrive at a crossing; turn right through the metal gate on to the permissive footpath, walking straight ahead. Slowly but surely the sea hoves into view, as does Exmoor away to the left and Wales straight ahead in the distance.

4 Reaching the clifftop, take a right through the gate; you are now on the **South West Coast Path** (part of the England Coast Path). Soak up the fantastic views as you walk along the perimeter of successive undulating fields; after around 800yds you come to a narrow inlet; don't take the path that continues inland (which leads back down to East Quantoxhead) but instead continue around what are the ruins of an old lime kiln and along the clifftop. The path gradually descends to the shore before a path on your right returns to the Chantry Tea Gardens (page 135) for some well-earned refreshment.

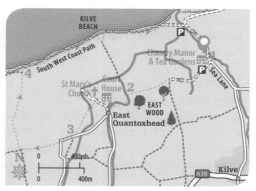

the body of the church. Inside, it's a riot of resplendent wood and stone carving, from the elegantly sculpted arcades to the medieval bench ends etched in a variety of floral, geometric and pagan designs (look out for the three Green men spouting foliage) – surely the finest in all of Somerset. The pulpit, rood screen and font, too, are all exuberantly carved; you can even detect traces of the original paintwork on the font. From Triscombe, two miles south of Crowcombe, it's a short drive up to Triscombe Stone car park, from where you can walk the one mile to **Will's Neck** (1,260ft), the highest point on the Quantocks; hence the views from the top are among the best in the area.

Three miles south of Crowcombe, **Combe Florey** is another comely Quantock village with a fine church that's not dissimilar to the Church of the Holy Ghost, though it predates it by a couple of centuries.

Constructed from the local deep red sandstone (which is characteristic of the village as a whole), the 13th-century **Church of St Peter and St Paul** also harbours some sublimely carved bench ends (note how the pews themselves are ever so slightly angled), in addition to a splendid white-painted barrel-vaulted ceiling and, in the north aisle, a trio of stone effigies belonging to the locally renowned de Meriet's, including that of Sir John de Meriet (d 1327) and his two wives; what is particularly interesting about Sir John's effigy are the 'ailettes' (little shields) upon each shoulder, which are so unusual that it's believed there are only four such examples in the country. Most visitors to the church, however, come seeking the grave of **Evelyn Waugh** (author of *Brideshead Revisited*, among other books) who is buried here alongside his wife Laura, though their own little fenced-in plot is looking decidedly worse for wear these days. Waugh lived in the village for ten years until his death in 1966.

¶¶ FOOD & DRINK

Carew Arms Crowcombe TA4 4AD ✆ 01984 618631 ⏚ thecarewarms.co.uk. Named after the one-time lords of the manor here, the warren of rooms in this bustling hostelry have remained pretty much as they have done for the past 400 years, save for the old stables, which have been converted into a skittle alley. You can tuck into no-fuss pub grub, and beer from the nearby Quantock Brewery, in the bar – its walls plastered with stags' heads – or there's marginally more upscale fare in the adjoining restaurant.

5 BISHOPS LYDEARD & THE WEST SOMERSET RAILWAY

The last village along this stretch of the A358 is Bishops Lydeard, though most people completely ignore the village itself and make an immediate beeline for the West Somerset Railway on the other side of the main road. This is a shame as it's an attractive spot, its main street lined with a uniform row of red sandstone cottages. At the southern end of the High Street, on a tidy patch of green, stands the **Church of St Mary the Virgin**, its magnificent pinnacled tower typical of so many in Somerset. Even if you are all churched out by this point, do spare a moment to have a look inside. Top billing here goes to the medieval fan-vaulted rood screen, distinguished by a richly carved cornice running along the top, and lower panels boasting some exquisite tracery; the red, blue and gold painted bits on one side of the screen were the result of restoration by the great Gothic Revival architect Sir Ninian Comper in the 1940s. As at Crowcombe and Combe Florey, the bench ends are beautifully carved; these ones, dating from 1540, are the work of nomadic Flemish artists. Moreover, and of great historical importance, it was here, in 1291, that a charter granting the Bishop of Bath and Wells the right to hold a weekly fair in Bishops Lydeard was signed by Edward I – and so it is on display here.

While here, it's worth popping your head into the **Quantock Brewery** (✆ 01823 662669 ◊ quantockbrewery.co.uk), located in the business park just 200yds from the train station; another Somerset micro-brewery doing great things, you can sample a few of their ales (bearing cool names like Ralehead and Plastered Pheasant) in their brilliant tap room before arming yourself with a few bottles to take away.

The West Somerset Railway
Bishops Lydeard TA24 5BG ✆ 01823 704996 ◊ west-somerset-railway.co.uk ⊙ Apr–Oct, check website for running dates & times

Bishops Lydeard is the southern terminus for the wonderful West Somerset Railway, which wends its way through rolling hills along the western flank of the Quantocks and a short stretch of coast before terminating at Minehead, some 21 miles distant – this makes it the longest heritage railway in the country. Trains run most days between April and October, sometimes using diesel engines as opposed to steam. In addition, there are all kinds of special event days and themed runnings, including festive trains throughout December, the details of which can be found on the website. Bikes and dogs are welcome too.

Overseen by James Burke, an assistant of Isambard Kingdom Brunel, the West Somerset Railway was founded in 1862 as a branch line of the Great Western Railway, originally running between Taunton and Watchet, before it was extended to Minehead in 1874, primarily to serve the needs of holidaymakers. The WSR survived Beeching's initial cuts before finally succumbing in 1971, though it was only five years later before it reopened as the heritage line it is today.

"It wends its way through rolling hills along the western flank of the Quantocks and a short stretch of coast."

Before boarding, do allow yourself time to visit the **Gauge Museum**, located on the other side of the platform. It's a marvellous affair holding one of the Great Western Railway's original (but since renovated) sleeping cars, built in 1897 to carry first-class passengers between London Paddington and the port of Fishguard on the Welsh coast; with its smooth wood-panelling, tip-down wash basins and underbed heating, this was very much the height of luxury back in the day. Elsewhere, wallow in nostalgia perusing old plates and signs, uniforms, photos and posters evoking a bygone era: 'Minehead, the Gateway to Exmoor', proclaims one in typically jolly fashion.

ᵞᵞ FOOD & DRINK

The Quantock Belle ⬦ west-somerset-railway.co.uk. This is food on the move! The West Somerset Railway periodically runs a special dining train that oozes nostalgia for anyone who remembers the 'Good Old Days' when meals on wheels meant being called for the first sitting. It is extremely popular so book well in advance (through the WSR website).

6 FYNE COURT

Broomfield TA5 2EQ ⬦ 01823 451587 ◴ dawn–dusk daily; National Trust

Tucked away in the tiny village of Broomfield in the southwestern corner of the Quantocks, the precise date of Fyne Court's construction is, oddly, not known. What is known is that its most famous resident was electrical scientist, philosopher and poet **Andrew Crosse**, by all accounts an eccentric chap who enjoyed stringing lines of wire among the trees to study storm effects – hence his moniker 'The Thunder and Lightning Man'. It's been suggested, erroneously in all probability, that Crosse's work may have provided the inspiration for Shelley's *Frankenstein*, the author allegedly having attended one of Crosse's lectures in London. What is also known is that the house itself burnt down in 1894 (nothing to do with Crosse or any of his experiments – he was long dead by this stage), hence there's actually very little to see at all here now. What few extant buildings that do remain now accommodate offices (including that of the Quantocks AONB, whose staff are only too willing to oblige with information), a small visitor centre and the obligatory tea shop.

As a result, it's the leisure grounds, conceived in the mid 18th century, that ultimately make a diversion here worthwhile. To this end there are a trio of short trails you can partake in, with one or two interesting features along the way, including a folly, boathouse, and a rather forlorn-looking walled garden, which is in fact now only partially walled, much of it having crumbled away over time. If it's a warm day, pack a picnic.

BLAKE OF BRIDGWATER

Although much less feted than the celebrated mariner and explorer Sir Francis Drake, **Robert Blake** was no less a distinguished naval hero. Born in Bridgwater in 1598, Blake schooled in the town before a career in politics beckoned, albeit a short-lived one, as Member of Parliament for Bridgwater, though he did return for a second stint some years later. It was, however, as a military man that Blake excelled. As an ardent Parliamentarian during the English Civil War, he commanded troops in successful campaigns at Bristol, Lyme Regis and Taunton, among other places. Appointed Cromwell's General-at-Sea in 1649, Blake set about rebuilding a credible naval force, and among his many initiatives was the introduction of welfare for sailors. Blake was quite the fighting machine too, chalking up a number of noteworthy successes, including victories against the Dutch and Spanish navies, and the routing of a fleet of Barbary pirates at Porto Farina in the Gulf of Tunis. Blake died at battle in Santa Cruz, Tenerife in 1657, though such was his status that he was afforded a state funeral and buried at Westminster Abbey.

ⵌ FOOD & DRINK

Clavelshay Barn Lower Clavelshay Farm, North Petherton TA6 6PJ ℘ 01278 662669 ⌀ clavelshaybarn.co.uk ⏲ 18.30–22.00 Thu–Sat, noon–14.00 Sun. Located on a working dairy farm three miles east of Fyne Court, hence its relative isolation, this sympathetically converted, two-floored stone barn has become one of Somerset's go-to foodie destinations. It's a fairly small menu (just the way I like it) but the dishes are divine: Quantock rabbit terrine, rhubarb and sherry vinegar, and Somerset pork belly with fondant potato and sauerkraut are typically refined plates; the owners, Sue and William, also run a well-regarded cookery school here.

BRIDGWATER & AROUND

7 BRIDGWATER

⋏ Hunstile Organic (page 236)

Bridgwater generally gets a bad rap, and to be fair, it's not entirely unjustified. It wasn't so long ago that visitors to the town would be greeted by an odious stench from the local cellophane factory, which would be enough to send most people scurrying off to the nearby Quantock Hills quicker than the time it takes to pronounce them. And, on the face of it, Bridgwater ('the kind of place the M5 was designed to pass by' is often one of the kinder comments thrown at it) doesn't appear to have much going for it. Dig a little deeper, however, and you'll find the occasional gem.

One of these is the rather delightful **Brick and Tile Museum** (East Quay ✆ 01278 426088 ⏣ swheritage.org.uk/our-sites/brick-and-tile-museum/ ◷ 10.00–16.00 Tue & Thu), located a ten-minute walk north of the town centre. Easily identifiable by its now truncated brick kiln, the only bottle kiln still remaining in the South West and one of six that once stood on this site, its position on the banks of the Parrett can be explained by the fact that the thick alluvial deposits from the river provided a ready-made material for the manufacture of red bricks, roof tiles, ornamental gable ends and more. One of its best-known products was the Bath Brick cleaning pad, which was typically used for cleaning and polishing metalwork, a sort of prototype for the scouring pad.

The brick industry peaked in Bridgwater during the mid 19th century, when there were no fewer than 16 brickyards (the one at this museum owned by the Barham Brothers) operating along this stretch of the river, exporting goods as far away as the Americas and North Africa; over half the town's male workforce was employed in the industry at this time. Decline set in during the 1960s, and this particular kiln, thought to date from around 1855, was last fired in 1965. Alongside the kiln is a fine display of bricks, tiles, moulds and plaques, alongside informative panels explaining some of the methods employed in their production.

"The brick industry peaked in Bridgwater during the mid 19th century, when there were no fewer than 16 brickyards."

In the town centre itself there are further exhibits pertaining to the brick and tile industry in the similarly illuminating **Blake Museum** (Blake St ✆ 01278 456127 ⏣ bridgwatermuseum.org.uk), though the greater part of this lovingly curated collection is given over to the deeds of local naval hero Robert Blake (see box, page 141), who was born here in 1598, or so it's thought. Otherwise, the rooms are themed, for example the Battle Room, Transport Room, Bridgwater Room and so on – suffice to say that after surveying this little lot there's not much you won't know about the town.

The streets themselves hold a smattering of Georgian architecture, the most impressive of which is the **Corn Exchange** and market hall on Cornhill, the town's historic centre. Built in 1834, the handsome Grade I-listed Exchange building sports a fine shallow-domed circular portico with a protruding lantern; these days it's home, rather prosaically, to a branch of Prezzo, though there are worse places to munch on pizza. In

CARNIVAL CAPERS

Carnival is as much a part of the Somerset landscape as cider and cheese. Processions take place in a dozen or so towns throughout the county during October and November, among them Chard, Ilminster, Glastonbury, Wells and Shepton Mallet, though the daddy of them all is **Bridgwater Carnival** (bridgwatercarnival.org.uk), which claims to be the largest illuminated carnival in Europe. Taking place each year on the first Saturday of November and attended by an estimated 150,000 people (there are even grandstands), more than 50 carts (don't dare call them floats round these parts), accompanied by various bands and foot parties, proceed along a 2½-mile course around town. The carnival's origins can be traced way back to 1605 and specifically Guy Fawkes's (and his Catholic co-conspirators) failed attempt to blow up the Houses of Parliament, an event that occasioned much celebration throughout town among the local Protestant population. The first local carnival committee was formed in 1881, since which time carnival has become quite the industry here, with scores of clubs in towns and villages across the region competing to design the biggest, best, or just downright wackiest cart for the night. The evening concludes with a uniquely Bridgy event, namely 'squibbing', which involves the simultaneous firing of 'squibs' (large fireworks) along High Street – there's a statue of a 'squibber' along here. It's great fun, and if you are anywhere near the area around this time, this is one event worth sticking around for.

front of the Exchange, facing down pedestrianised Fore Street, stands a prominent statue of Blake, right arm outstretched. Across the way stands **St Mary's Church**, whose magnificent red-sandstone steeple is ever so slightly askew; the church's oldest parts date back to the early 13th century, although it's now mostly of Victorian orientation. Among its many distinguishing features is the hammer-beam roof, oak pulpit and dazzling Italian altarpiece; here too is the font where Robert Blake was baptised.

8 THE BRIDGWATER & TAUNTON CANAL
 canalrivertrust.org.uk

Although no longer linked to any other waterway, the Bridgwater and Taunton Canal, which extends for 14 miles between the River Parrett in Bridgwater and the River Tone in Taunton, was built in 1827 as part of a more ambitious scheme to link Bristol with south Devon. Although it was never in the same league as the powerhouse canals of the Midlands and the north, the B&T Canal was, nevertheless, an important artery for the transportation of goods, in particular, coal and iron from south Wales. Taken over by the Great Western Railway, the canal's importance dwindled (ironically, it was the railways that ultimately did for it) to the extent that commercial traffic ceased in 1907; thereafter it was used solely as a freshwater course and drainage channel before gradually falling into disrepair and becoming unnavigable – which it remained until 1994.

"The B&T Canal was an important artery for the transportation of goods, in particular, coal and iron from south Wales."

These days, the towpath makes for excellent walking and cycling (it's part of both the River Parrett Trail and National Cycle Route 3), with numerous access points along its length – useful if you don't fancy starting in either Taunton or Bridgwater Docks. Somewhat randomly, the towpath is intermittently lined with scale models of the solar system, an installation entitled the **Somerset Space Walk**; the sun lies at the halfway point, **Maunsel Lock**, itself a convenient spot to pause for some refreshment at the visitor centre and tea room, housed inside the old lock keepers' cottage; kids in particular will have fun identifying the various planets. There's plentiful wildlife here too – if your luck's in, you may even spot herons or kingfishers.

Along the canal, you won't fail to notice the occasional pill box; these were part of the so-called **Taunton Stop Line**, a World War II defensive frontier that ran from an area just north of Bridgwater to Seaton in south Devon – some 50 miles in total. Poignant reminders of a more brutal period in recent history, over 300 of these concrete structures were built in the days after Dunkirk, of which around two-thirds remain. Designed to contain, as opposed to stop, enemy troops advancing from the west, they remain an integral, if not altogether graceful, part of the Somerset landscape. Countrywide, there were more than 18,000, though the vast majority of these have long since disappeared.

9 HESTERCOMBE GARDENS
Cheddon Fitzpaine TA2 8LG ℰ 01823 413923 ᚼ hestercombe.com

I must admit that I wasn't aware of Hestercombe prior to embarking upon this book, which was rather remiss of me because of all the gardens I visited during the course of my research – and there were quite a few – I found these to be the most rewarding. Conceived in the 1750s by landowner and amateur landscape painter Coplestone

Warre Bampfylde – a finer name you won't find anywhere in this book – Hestercombe boasts quite some history. The **house** itself, the earliest parts of which date back to 1280 (believe it or not), has had an interesting life. Remodelled on several occasions, most extensively in the 1720s by Bampfylde's father, the Parliamentarian John Bampfylde, its last inhabitants were the Portmans who, by the time they'd departed in 1951, had given it a typically thorough Victorian overhaul. The house then served as the headquarters of the Somerset Fire Brigade, whose base it remained until 2006, though the call centre stayed open until 2012 – there are still reminders though, such as the utilitarian lighting, and the occasional 'Emergency 999' sign still knocking about. Now in the hands of the Hestercombe Gardens Trust, the first floor of the house has been given over to an accomplished modern art gallery; make sure you check out the views over the formal gardens and, in the distance, the Vale of Taunton and the Blackdown Hills. Downstairs, you'll find an excellent secondhand bookshop and a fine restaurant.

Two of Britain's most distinguished architects – **Edwin Lutyens** (of Whitehall's Cenotaph) and the renowned horticulturist and garden designer **Gertrude Jekyll** – were also involved in Hestercombe's overall development, joining forces to create the marvellous **Edwardian Formal Garden**, completed in 1908. Lutyens, incidentally, also designed the so-called Daisy Steps (it's obvious why when you see them) down to the gravel pathway in front of the house. The most impressive element of the formal garden is the fragrant-smelling Orangery, its bright, yellow/gold façade instantly recognisable as Ham Hill stone (see box, page 193). Throughout, the garden bears Lutyens's unmistakeable stamp, particularly in his recurring use of layered slate, for example on the Pergola, an elegant structure crawling with vines and honeysuckle that extends the entire width of the garden.

"Edwin Lutyens and Gertrude Jekyll joined forces to create the marvellous Edwardian Formal Garden, completed in 1908."

As lovely as these gardens are, I was more enamoured with the **Georgian Landscaped Garden**, a sprawling, quite hilly, valley walk with follies hidden away at every turn. Starting out by the 17th-century watermill – once powered by water from the nearby Pear Pond – take the path leading uphill to the right. One after another a different folly reveals itself: the Trophy Seat, Temple Arbour and the Witch House to name but three – from the last of these there are glorious head-on views of the Great Cascade, an impressively sized waterfall that tumbles theatrically into the wooded combe below. One of these follies, the Rustic Seat, was only uncovered in 2011 after a ten-year search for its whereabouts, having been concealed for more than 250 years.

⊞ FOOD & DRINK

Column Room Restaurant and Stables Café Hestercombe House ✆ 01823 410112 🖉 hestercombe.com ☉ restaurant Wed–Sun, café daily. Grandly set within the Portmans' original sitting room, and offering lovely views over the formal gardens, the Column Room restaurant serves scrumptious lunches (such as pork tenderloin with cauliflower purée and apple cider sauce) alongside a selection of traditional afternoon teas – expect the full sandwiches and scones experience. If you don't want to go all out though, the Stables Café offers lighter bites alongside coffee, cake and the like.

TAUNTON & AROUND

10 TAUNTON

Few would be daft enough to pretend that Taunton – the county town – is an especially exciting destination, but its setting astride the River Tone (together with some verdant green spaces) partly makes up for that. So too do its two big-hitting attractions – the superb Museum of Somerset and Somerset County Cricket Club, a source of much local pride. Throw in some ecclesiastical interest, and a decent selection of places to eat and drink, and you've potentially got yourself a very rewarding day out – and, if you fancy watching a bit of cricket, quite a long one. Thursday is a good day to be here on account of the weekly farmers' market, which consumes much of the pedestrianised High Street.

Taunton Castle & Museum of Somerset

Castle Green, TA1 4AA ✆ 01823 255088 🖉 swheritage.org.uk ☉ Tue–Sun

Since its original Saxon incarnation in the early 12th century, **Taunton Castle** has assumed several identities, mostly recently towards the end of the 18th century when it was rebuilt in largely Georgian fashion after falling into a parlous state. The castle has seen its fair share of drama over the years; in 1497 it held the trial of the infamous charlatan Perkin Warbeck (another splendid name), who for six years masqueraded as Richard, Duke of York, though it was actually his plot to overthrow

Henry VII that eventually did for him. Then, in 1685, the castle's Great Hall was the principal court setting for Judge Jeffreys' notorious Bloody Assizes, resulting in 514 prisoners being tried for treason, 144 of whom were sentenced to death – little wonder he was nicknamed 'The Hanging Judge'.

"In 1685, the castle's Great Hall was the principal court setting for Judge Jeffreys' notorious Bloody Assizes."

The castle is now the venue for the compelling **Museum of Somerset**, which brings together the county's most valuable treasures all under one roof. There are so many memorable exhibits spread over the museum's three floors that it makes it impossible to single any one out. That said, the Roman (and pre-Roman) displays take some beating, not least the Low Ham mosaic from the village of that name near Langport; depicting the lovers Dido and Aeneas, as portrayed in Virgil's poems from around 25BC, it is stunning in its completeness – and, incidentally, best viewed from the balcony above. Both the Frome Hoard and the Shapwick Hoard, two substantial caches of Roman coins, also merit closer inspection, the former unearthed by a local metal detectorist as recently as 2010 (page 55).

Further items of prestige include a grouping of exquisite bronze figurines of Roman gods from Lamyatt Beacon near Bruton, and the South Cadbury Shield, a wafer-thin metal plate decorated with more than 6,000 individually stamped bosses. And you can't really miss the Shapwick Canoe suspended from the ceiling; culled from a single piece of oak some time around AD350, it was recovered from a deep peat bog on Shapwick Heath in 1906. Taking pride of place up on the third floor is the Wellington Reredos, a superbly carved limestone panel from St John's Church in Wellington that dates from 1540 and which, despite being badly defaced during the Reformation, still bears traces of its original medieval paintwork. Here, too, is what is thought to be the first complete skeleton of a Plesiosaur found in Britain, discovered in 2003.

Somerset County Cricket Club

Priory Av ✆ 01823 425301 ⬚ somersetcountycc.co.uk

Set against a lovely backdrop of the River Tone and the Church of St James, the **County Ground** has been home to **Somerset County Cricket Club** since 1882, though the club itself was formed in 1875. It may be one of the smallest cricket grounds in the country (its capacity is just

8,500), but it has hosted a number of international matches, mostly of the One Day and T20 variety, including World Cup matches – in any case, size isn't everything.

Although Somerset has never won the County Championship, the club has had some wonderful players over the years, its heyday in the late 1970s and early 1980s coinciding with the arrival of three world-class players, namely Viv Richards and Joel 'Big Bird' Garner from the West Indies, and local boy, Ian 'Beefy' Botham – more recent stars include Andy Caddick and Marcus Trescothick, both of whom have a pavilion named after them. To my mind there are few greater pleasures in life than kicking back with beer in hand on a warm summer's day listening to the sound of leather on willow – Slow doesn't get much better than this.

You can learn more about the exploits of these fantastic players in the splendid little **museum** (7 Priory Av ✆ 01823 275893 ⊙ somersetcricketmuseum.co.uk ⊙ Apr–Oct, Tue–Fri non-match days only), housed within the Grade II-listed Old Priory Barn, which is all that remains of the priory demolished in 1537. For your £1 entry, you get to see portraits, photos and trophies, and cabinets stuffed with all kinds of memorabilia: test caps belonging to Viv Richards and Ian Botham; the bat used by Botham during the famous 1981 Ashes series win against Australia; Joel Garner's enormous size 13 boots; and the bat and gloves that Marcus Trescothick used during his highest test match innings score of 219 against South Africa in 2003; there's also a leather wallet belonging to arguably the most famous cricketer of them all, W G Grace. Refreshingly, the museum also dips into the history of women's cricket, which is apt as The County Ground is the home of the England Women's cricket team.

"The club has had some wonderful players over the years, its heyday in the late 1970s and early 1980s."

Churches of St Mary Magdalene & St James

Lying in wait at the end of Georgian-era Hammet Street, just off the main thoroughfare, is the **Church of St Mary Magdalene**, which could well be the largest parish church in the county – for sure its magnificent tower, a dazzling combination of old red sandstone and Ham Hill stone, is, at 163ft, the highest in Somerset; its construction was overseen by

Sir Giles Gilbert Scott. Completed in the early 16th century on the site of an old Saxon church (and a subsequent 13th-century edition), the church interior is unique for having double side aisles (one of just five such churches in England constructed this way); it was designed this way to allow for more processional space. Up above, a flourish of gilded angels adorns the dark wood ceiling, as do dozens of decorated shields and bosses carved with medieval masks. The church is actually quite a sociable little spot on account of its busy coffee shop, which makes for a welcome change from the panoply of humdrum cafés along the neighbouring streets.

Towering over the County Ground, but otherwise of more modest persuasion than St Mary Magdalene, **St James's Church** retains some interesting features, most notably a gorgeous 15th-century stone font with carved panels bearing images of Christ on the cross and the 12 disciples, each one bearing an item of some description. At 120ft, the tower is considerably shorter than the one at St Mary Magadalene, but its bells still make quite the din if you're seated close by watching the cricket.

₩ FOOD & DRINK

Augustus 3 The Courtyard, TA1 1JR ✐ 01823 342354 ☖ augustustaunton.co.uk ◷ 10.00–21.30 Tue–Sat, noon–14.30 Sun. Headed up by former Michelin-starred chef Richard Guest, this intimate bistro, tucked away in a small brick courtyard, is currently serving up the most original food in town; expect the likes of rabbit faggots with creamed potatoes, and duck rillette with cornichons and sourdough – and while not especially cheap, it matters not when the food is this good.

Mint and Mustard 10 Station Rd, TA1 1NH ✐ 01823 330770 ☖ mintandmustard.com ◷ 17.00–23.00 Tue–Sat, noon–21.00 Sun. One of a small chain (the other three are in Wales), this upscale Indian restaurant offers a menu as brilliant as it is bold; try the pan-fried sea bass on a bed of curry mashed potato or one of the many sensational veggie dishes – the melt-in-the-mouth Bombay chaat is sensational.

The Wickets 51a St James St, TA1 1SF ✐ 01823 324412 ◷ 08.00–15.00 Mon–Sat. Within a six of the County Ground, this cheerful and popular caff serves up freshly prepared hot and cold sarnies, soups and salads, and the best coffee in town. Happy, smiley staff to boot.

11 WELLINGTON

Located seven miles southwest of Taunton, it comes as little surprise to learn that well-heeled Wellington makes great play of its association (albeit a rather tenuous one) with the eponymous military commander, who apparently took his title from this small Somerset market town because it sounded much like the family name – the Duke of Wellington having been born Arthur Wellesley. As an interesting aside, the capital of New Zealand is named after the Duke, so by that very association one could reasonably suggest that, ultimately, the Kiwi capital takes its name from little old Wellington here in Somerset. Not a bad claim all told. It's debatable as to whether Wellington ever actually visited the town, though some sources suggest that he may have done so on one occasion.

"The eponymous military commander apparently took his title from this small Somerset market town."

Wellington was once an important staging post on the Bristol to Exeter trade route, thanks to the Grand Western Canal (1835) and the Bristol and Exeter Railway (1843), the latter closing in 1964. The museum aside, there's not an awful lot to see or do here, but a browse around the town's many independent shops is a pleasurable way to pass an hour or two. You can learn more about the town's not insignificant history in the pleasingly old-fashioned town **museum** (28 Fire St ✐ 07971 242904 ✆ wellingtonmuseum.org.uk ☻ Easter–Nov), occupying the old Squirrel Inn dating from the late 17th century. Everything and anything is on display in its one room, from items pertaining to 19th-century domestic life through to Wellington's deeds, the two World Wars, and a model of the Wellesley cinema; there's even coverage of two, somewhat obscure, world championships that have been held here: ploughing and snuff-taking – make of that what you will. Otherwise, Wellington is further recalled in the 1930s Art Deco **Wellesley Cinema** on Mantle Street, and the Iron Duke pub on the corner of Cornhill and North Street, which, if you can get past the fact that it's a Wetherspoons, is worth a look inside for its superb architectural detail.

Wellington Monument

The Duke of Wellington's reputation was sealed following his victory over Napoleon at Waterloo, a victory commemorated by an ostentatious, 175ft-high **monument** 2½ miles south of town on the edge of the Blackdown Hills – which, apparently, makes it the tallest three-sided obelisk in the world. Mind you, it took some time to erect, given that the first stone was laid in 1817 and the last one in 1854, two years after the Iron Duke's death – a 'shambolic construction' is how it has frequently been described. The monument, now under the care of the National Trust, has been closed to the public since 2005 pending extensive renovation, particularly to its upper reaches, parts of which have crumbled away substantially. Repair work began in 2019, though the ongoing quest for funds means that it's likely to remain in a state of limbo for a while yet – and whether or not the viewing platform ever opens again is anyone's guess. Although it's not currently possible to enter the monument, it's an impressive specimen when observed close up, and the elevated views from here are tremendous. From town (it's fairly well signposted), head down South Street past Wellington School, go over the M5 and then up some steep windy lanes to the NT car park; from here, it's a 30-minute walk through woodland to the monument.

▌ FOOD & DRINK

Cheese and Wine Shop 11 South St ✆ 01823 662899 ⬦ thecheeseandwineshop.co.uk ◔ café 09.00–16.30 Tue–Sat, shop 09.00–17.30 Mon–Sat. Hidden away at the back of this fabulous food shop you'll find a top-drawer café whose lunchtime light bites (Somerset rarebit, blue cheese risotto) are complemented by a selection of more sophisticated dishes such as roast duck leg on gratin potato; alternatively, you can pop in for coffee and cake. On your way out, it'd be remiss not to stock up with the odd goody or two, perhaps a wedge of local cheddar or a slab of chocolate.

12 THE BLACKDOWN HILLS

⬦ blackdownhillsaonb.org.uk

If you thought that the Quantocks were quiet, then a short period of time spent here in the Blackdown Hills might force you to reassess that opinion. Straddling the Somerset/Devon border (about a third is contained within Somerset), these little-frequented hills embrace steeply wooded scarp, deep valleys covered in oak, beech and ash, medieval fields and high hedgerowed country lanes connecting villages and hamlets. There

"Somerset has the lion's share of the upland area, including Blackdown's highest point, Staple Hill."

are remnants, too, of lowland heath, common and scrub. Somerset has the lion's share of the upland area, including Blackdown's highest point, **Staple Hill** (1,033ft), before the landscape plateaus towards the Devon side. All of this makes for wonderful walking country. If walking here in springtime, there's some wonderful flora to observe, including many wildflowers, in particular bluebell and purple orchid. Wildlife is flourishing here too, the hills being home to several nationally scarce species like nightjars, Bechstein bats and hazel dormice.

While Somerset can boast the Blackdowns' most dramatic scenery, Devon has the monopoly on historic sites. The only major site of note on the Somerset side (over in the northeast) is **Castle Neroche**, a late Iron Age hillfort that was later converted to a military outpost, and whose vast earthen ramparts are now covered in oak and beech, thus largely obscuring whatever view there may once have been, though there are a couple of breaks in the treeline.

Also worth targeting, especially if time is limited, are the **Otterhead Lakes**, nestled just inside the Somerset bit of the Blackdowns. These two sinuous bodies of water (there were originally seven lakes) were once part of the Otterhead House estate, which was demolished in 1952, leaving the remainder of the grounds to fall into disrepair; the walled gardens remain closed. Otherwise, the lakes and surrounding area have been reinvigorated as a nature reserve supporting a number of semi-natural habitats: alder and willow, deciduous woodland and freshwater ditches.

☍ FOOD & DRINK

Greyhound Inn Staple Hill, Staple Fitzpaine TA3 5SP ✆ 01823 480227
⌂ thegreyhoundinntaunton.co.uk. A handsome-looking 16th-century Grade II-listed building concealing several flagstone-floored rooms sporting inglenook fires, squishy chairs and sofas, and an array of knick-knacks splayed across the walls – all very cosy. Good food – which includes some lovely local dishes such as Somerset lamb's liver with bacon, and a cracking Ploughman's with local smoked cheddar – good beer and good cheer.

FOLLOW US

Tag us in your posts and share your adventures using this guide with us – we'd love to hear from you.

f BradtTravelGuides
@bradtguides
bradtguides

@BradtGuides & @normlongley
bradtguides

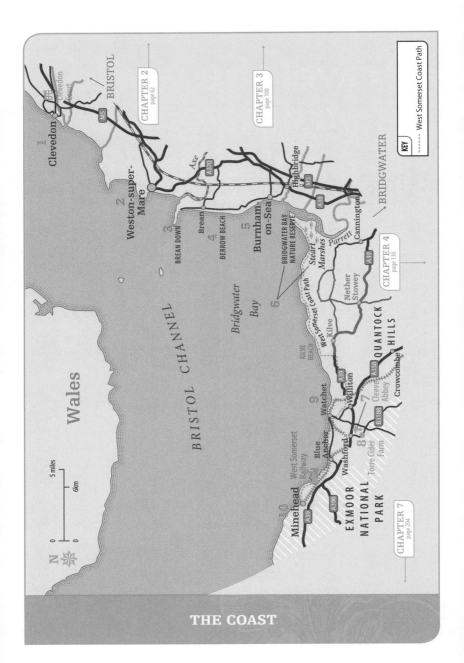

THE COAST

5
THE COAST

With so much to detain visitors inland, Somerset's coastline often gets bypassed, which is a shame as there's lots to get excited about here. The coast's two major resorts, **Weston-super-Mare** and **Burnham-on-Sea**, are typically gutsy seaside towns with all that entails, yet beyond the usual timeworn pleasures there is cultural provision too: Weston has its museums and art, Burnham its lighthouses.

If you like your **piers**, this short stretch of coast has them in (buckets and) spades; historic beauties they are too, especially Clevedon's – the country's only surviving Grade I-listed pier – and Birnbeck in Weston, although sadly this remains in a terrible state. **Clevedon** itself couldn't be further removed from Weston or Burnham, offering a gentler pace of life than either of the aforementioned seaside towns. **Watchet**, too, with its enjoyably disparate sights clustered around a large, circular harbour, is similarly worth taking time to get to know. **Minehead**, the last destination covered in this coast chapter, is the last (or first) stop on the West Somerset Railway, so you may find yourself winding up here, which is no bad thing as it has a lovely little museum and some pleasant walks to go alongside the traditional seaside pursuits.

The Bristol Channel's high tidal range – the second highest in the world after Fundy Bay in Canada – means that parts of the coast can seem like one endless expanse of mud. That said, at the right times there are some wonderful belts of sand, especially between Burnham and **Brean Down**, an epic, dune-backed stretch of shore that's perfect for lengthy strolls under blue summer skies. Although Porlock, and the area west of here up to the border with Devon, is on the Somerset coast, I have included it in the Exmoor chapter (*Chapter 7*) as this area is technically part of that National Park – and it just seemed like a better fit. The fossil beach at Kilve, meanwhile, is included in *Chapter 4*, owing to its location within the Quantocks AONB.

GETTING THERE & AROUND

Road access to the main seaside resorts of Weston-super-Mare and Burnham is excellent thanks to the M5, while Minehead and Watchet are reached by the A39 (from Bridgwater) or the A358 (from Taunton). Weston-super-Mare is on the main Bristol to Taunton **railway** line, with half-hourly services to both (in addition to several daily services straight through to London Paddington). This line also serves Burnham-on-Sea, albeit the station (Highbridge and Burnham) lies two miles south of town, with a bus transfer. Minehead is the northern terminus of the **West Somerset Railway** (page 139), which runs down to Bishops Lydeard near Taunton, calling in at Watchet, Washford and Blue Anchor along the way.

BUSES

In terms of reaching the coast by bus, Weston-super-Mare is the main hub, with bus 126 linking the town with Wells, via Axbridge and Cheddar. Otherwise, both Weston and Burnham are served by bus 21 from Bridgwater. Minehead can be reached via buses 16 and 24 along the A39 from Bridgwater, though a better option is the number 28 from Taunton, along the Quantocks' western flank. Between April and October, two open-top Coaster buses operate from Weston: bus 1 runs up to Sand Bay via Worlebury Hill, while number 20 shuttles between Weston-super-Mare and Burnham-on-Sea, stopping at Brean and Berrow along the way.

WALKING & CYCLING

There are wonderful possibilities for long coastal walks, especially since the inauguration of the **West Somerset Coast Path** in 2016. At 58 miles long, the path stretches from Brean Down to Minehead, whereupon it continues as the **South West Coast Path** all the way round to Poole in Dorset – at 630 miles, it is the UK's longest national trail. Eventually these paths will form part of the England Coast Path, which is expected

---

ℹ TOURIST INFORMATION

Minehead The Beach Hotel, The Avenue, TA24 5AY ✆ 01643 702624 🖉 mineheadbay.co.uk
Watchet The Boat Museum, Harbour Rd, TA23 0AQ ✆ 01984 632101 🖉 lovewatchet.co.uk
Weston-super-Mare Tropicana, Marine Parade, BS23 1BE ✆ 01934 888877 🖉 visit-westonsupermare.com

to be complete in 2020 and will then be the longest waymarked coastal path in the world. More manageable is the eight-mile-long **Brean Down Way**, a shared-use, traffic-free path between Weston-super-Mare and Brean Down.

Brean Bike Hire has an excellent selection of bikes available for one, three or seven days (⌔ 07798 930345 ⌔ breanbikehire.co.uk).

FROM CLEVEDON TO BRIDGWATER BAY

The northern portion of the Somerset coast embraces the area's two largest seaside resorts in **Weston-super-Mare** and **Burnham-on-Sea**, and while neither is particularly attractive on the eye, delve a little deeper and you'll find some cultural gems in among the typical pleasure-seeking pursuits. Far lovelier is **Clevedon** with its magnificent Grade I-listed pier, reason alone to visit this spruce little seaside town. In any case, you don't have to go far to escape the hurly-burly of these (relatively) large centres and slow things down. **Brean Down** offers a spectacular walk overlooking the Bristol Channel, while further solitude can be had by roaming **Berrow Beach** in your own good time. On the other side of the River Parrett lurks **Bridgwater Bay**, at the heart of which is the newly formed **Steart Marshes** wetlands. Apart from Steart, access to all these places is fairly simple, with the Great Western Railway serving both Weston and Burnham, and buses zipping up and down this stretch of the coast.

1 CLEVEDON

More refined than most places along the Somerset coast, the dignified clifftop town of Clevedon never fails to enamour. In fact, it was the highlight of this chapter for me. The shoreline is too pebbly and muddy for beachbound activities – rather the town's charms manifest themselves in other ways: a flurry of independent shops and restaurants, some exciting architecture and an invigorating headland walk. But overwhelmingly the main reason to come here is the pier, one of Britain's finest. Otherwise, the promenade is a lovely place for a stroll, not least because it's largely devoid of all the usual seaside clutter. The most enjoyable spot south of the pier is **Marine Lake** (built 1929), an enclosed body of seawater that's long been a popular training ground for long-distance and endurance swimmers. It is open to all-comers though: swimmers, paddlers, canoeists, sailors and even model-boat enthusiasts share this chilly space.

Indeed, sea swimming has quite a tradition here in Clevedon, reflected in a number of annual events, though the big one is August's **Clevedon Long Swim**, which has taken place every year (except during World War II) since 1928. The mile-long race starts at Ladye Bay under the pier and finishes on Clevedon Beach; even if you don't fancy it yourself, it's worth coming along to watch – it's great fun. You may, in fact, have seen a group of hardy Clevedon sea swimmers feature as one of the BBC's most recent idents (those images you see between programmes), which first aired in January 2017.

Marine Lake is also the starting point for the **Poet's Walk**, which takes its name from the many poets, Tennyson and Coleridge among them, who sought inspiration on their strolls around this breeze-bashed headland – in fact, both Coleridge and J R R Tolkien honeymooned in Clevedon. A mile or so in total, the path loops around Wain's Hill, taking in a short stretch of coast path, bits of woodland and St Andrew's Church, all the while delivering gorgeous views.

Heading inland from the pier, it's a short walk uphill past neat rows of handsome villas to the main drag, Hill Road, itself lined with a decent smattering of shops, cafés and restaurants. Running parallel to Hill Road, Alexandra Road is similarly endowed with lots of places to spend your money. There are buildings of further interest south of here, starting in the very centre of town with the old **clock tower**, a superbly preserved specimen from 1898 plastered with Eltonware pottery tiles (page 160). A short walk from here, on Old Church Road, stands the Art Deco-tinged **Curzon Community Cinema**, reputedly the oldest continuously operating picture house in the country. Its brick and stonework exterior stretches over six shop fronts, and visitors are greeted with an Art Deco sunrise embracing the venue's name in neon lights over the entrance – like the Roxy Cinema in Axbridge (page 81), it's a rare opportunity to catch a movie in an authentic picture house.

Clevedon Pier

The Beach, BS21 7QU ☎ 01275 878846 🖉 clevedonpier.co.uk

'Graceful as a spider's web, elegant as a piece of lace, simple in design, endearingly secure for over a hundred years, Clevedon Pier has added grandeur to our environment.' So recalled Sir Arthur Elton, an early pioneer in the field of documentary film-making and one of the town's great champions. And indeed, England's only intact Grade I-listed pier is truly a thing of great beauty and, for my money, the most outstanding architectural legacy of this coastline. Clevedon Pier was built in 1869 to a design by John William Grover and Richard Ward of Hamilton's Windsor Ironworks in Liverpool, ostensibly to receive paddle steamers from south Wales and Devon.

"The pier was constructed from discarded railway lines used by Isambard Kingdom Brunel on the Great Western Railway."

Constructed from discarded railway lines used by Isambard Kingdom Brunel on the Great Western Railway, the wrought-iron was fashioned into eight graceful 100ft arched spans either side of a wooden boardwalk; this has since been adorned with over 10,000 brass plaques bearing the names of all those people who have contributed to its upkeep. Closed in 1970 following its partial collapse, the pier reopened in 1989 with further restorative work in 1998, since which time it has looked better than ever. The end of the pier is crowned by an elegant Edwardian-style pagoda, which now houses a café (☺ Apr–Oct) that must surely possess one of the best views from any pier in the country.

Back at the other end, the former **toll house** – where you're still obliged to pay a fee to enter the pier – is now home to a superb visitor centre with an illuminating exhibition on the pier's history. The toll house was formerly the Pier Master's dwelling, who variously served between two and 28 years in the job, though it should be pointed out that the last person to hold the post was a woman, Linda Strong, who served between 2005 and 2015. There is still one, of sorts, though the title is now known somewhat more prosaically as 'Pier Business Manager'.

Clevedon Court

Tickenham Rd, BS21 6QU ☏ 01275 872257 ☺ Apr–Oct, 14.00–17.00 Wed, Thu & Sun; National Trust

Marred only by the persistent roar of traffic from the nearby M5, Clevedon Court, a mile east of town, is neatly concealed behind a thick bank of trees just below steeply wooded Court Hill. Originally constructed over 700 years ago, Clevedon Court has been the Elton family home ever since Abraham Elton moved in here in 1709.

Its present incumbent is Julia Elton, who can often be seen wandering about the place and is only too happy to chat to any visitors seeking extra nuggets of information, though the volunteer guides stationed in each room do a fine job of that themselves.

It's by no means a big place, and it won't take you very long to poke around, but that doesn't make it any less enjoyable. The house is entered via the narrow Screen's Passage, off which lies the Great Hall, a room of immense height and eclectic furnishings. Upstairs, and just off the state bedroom, is an exquisite little chapel, whose most distinguishing feature is the reticulated tracery on the windows; it was variously used as a boudoir and writing room before being restored to its original function in 1882 following a fire though, interestingly, it isn't actually consecrated.

"Pore over cabinets crammed with 'Eltonware', the distinctive style of glazed art pottery fashioned by Sir Edmund Elton."

Finish your tour of the house with a quick nose around the museum, quartered in the old kitchen, where you can pore over cabinets crammed with 'Eltonware', the name assigned to the distinctive style of glazed art pottery fashioned by Sir Edmund Elton. A man of industrious nature, Edmund was also the founder, as well as first captain of, the Clevedon Fire Brigade; his gleaming silver helmet hangs on one wall. After exploring the house, take a walk around the well-tended grounds, an alluring mix of parkland, ornamental woodland and extensively terraced gardens rising high above the building.

FOOD & DRINK

Puro 32–34 Hill Rd, BS21 7PH ✆ 01275 217373 ⬡ purorestaurant.co.uk ◷ 17.00–23.00 Wed & Thu, noon–15.00 & 17.00–midnight Fri & Sat, noon–22.00 Sun. This elegant, contemporary dining space is a great place to tuck into outstanding modern British food made with fresh farm and sea produce. The intriguing menu lists dishes such as megrim sole with foraged sea vegetables and charred spring onion, and Cornish Porthilly mussels in Somerset cider.

Tiffin @ The Pier Clevedon Pier, BS21 7QR ✆ 01275 872425 ⬡ tiffingroup.com. Classy outfit whose floor-to-ceiling glass windows offer unencumbered views all the way down to the Pagoda Café at the far end of the pier – views really don't get much better than this. The food concept is nice and simple, with two menus: a lunchtime 'picnic menu' (a fish finger sandwich has rarely tasted so good) and a dinner menu, with mouth-watering dishes such as Cornish scallops with spring onion mash. Very nice indeed.

ICONIC VIEWS

Whether it's the climb up to Dunkery Beacon, looking out across the Bristol Channel from Hurlstone Point, or standing atop Glastonbury Tor, there are superb views from just about every corner of the county.

1 A misty morning across the Levels over Glastonbury towards its eponymous tor.
2 Walkers on the South West Coast Path, near Bossington.

SOMERSET DAYS OUT

Seeking a fun and inspirational day out? Look no further than the likes of Hestercombe Gardens or Montacute House, though younger ones will love the fantastic Haynes International Motor Museum and the Fleet Air Arm Museum.

1 The West Somerset Railway runs from Bishops Lydeard to Minehead. **2** Willing volunteers at the Exmoor Pony Centre. **3** Foraging and nature walks are just some of the Valleyfest activities on offer. **4** Car fanatics should head straight to the Haynes International Motor Museum. **5** The Exmoor Owl & Hawk Centre, Allerford. **6** Hestercombe Gardens.

ADAM GASSON

EXMOOR PONY CENTRE

EXMOOR OWL & HAWK CENTRE

THE HAYNES INTERNATIONAL MOTOR MUSEUM

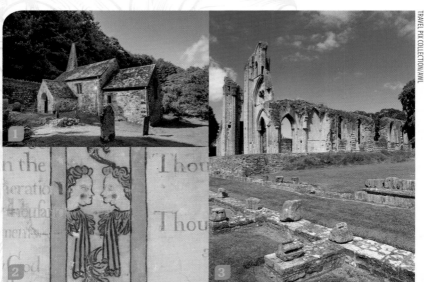

SACRED SOMERSET

Beyond Somerset's twin ecclesiastical glories of Wells Cathedral and Glastonbury Abbey are dozens of splendid castellated churches, such as St Mary's in Bishops Lydeard and St James's in Cameley.

1 The diminutive Culbone Church, Exmoor. 2 St James's Church, Cameley, dates from the 12th century. 3 Glastonbury Abbey. 4 The breathtaking Wells Cathedral.

2 WESTON-SUPER-MARE

⌂ Church House (page 236)

Compared with Clevedon's sedate charm, Weston-super-Mare – an amalgamation of 'West Tun' (meaning settlement) and 'above the sea' (*super mare* in Latin) – is a much more brash place altogether. That said, there's much to enjoy about Somerset's premier seaside resort, which still pulls in the punters. Initially an unimportant fishing village, it was the coming of the railway in 1841 that set in train (excuse the pun) Weston's development as a resort town, a process accelerated by the Victorians. Like most resorts since those days, the town's fortunes have waxed and waned, and today it remains a resolutely old-fashioned place, albeit one spruced up here and there. Best of all, the views across to Steep Holm, and beyond to south Wales, are superb, and the sunsets can be spectacular.

Set a few streets back from the seafront, the town centre is best avoided (unless you want to visit the excellent museum, that is – page 162),

A TALE OF TWO PIERS

Dominating Weston's seafront is the Edwardian, Grade II-listed **Grand Pier** (⌂ grandpier.co.uk), rebuilt in 2010 after its pavilion burnt down two years earlier; it had previously been destroyed by fire in 1930 having originally been built in 1904. Wrapped in stainless steel and shiny glass, the Grand Pier is, to all intents and purposes, an indoor mini theme park with rollercoaster, laser maze, go-kart track and so on – you get the idea.

North of the Grand Pier, on Anchor Head, are the dilapidated ruins of **Birnbeck Pier**, whose history is infinitely more interesting than its near neighbour. Dating from 1867 and, uniquely, the only seaside pier in Britain that links the mainland with an island, it variously functioned as a lifeboat station and amusement park before the admiralty

appropriated it during World War II and the island became HMS Birnbeck, operating as a secret facility for weapons testing. Its principal post-war role was as a calling point for paddle steamers arriving from across the water in south Wales, along with Minehead and Ilfracombe a wee bit further along the coast. However, the construction of the Severn Bridge, together with the growth of the motorcar, resulted in the pier's inevitable, terminal decline. These days it stands forlornly awaiting its fate, looking for all the world as if it's about to crumble into the water, though the Birnbeck Regeneration Trust is doing its very best to raise funds for its conservation. In the meantime, do go and take a look – who knows how long this special piece of history may, or may not, be here for.

but in any case you're more likely to want to spend your time taking in the bracing sea air along the wide, two-mile-long promenade, which largely eschews the tackier elements of your average prom. Otherwise, all the traditional seaside pursuits are here in abundance: a spanking new pleasure pier, amusement arcades, Ferris wheel, donkey rides, and fish and chip shops, though the beach itself is more mud-fest than sand-fest at low tide owing to the Severn's notorious tidal range.

Despite appearances to the contrary, the town does offer a few concessions to culture, reflected in a couple of eminently enjoyable museums and a brilliant **street art trail** courtesy of local graffiti artist Jamie Scanlon (aka JPS). While not in the same league as Banksy (a native of nearby Bristol and whose infamous Dismaland theme park here in 2015 made national headlines), these 21 pieces, scattered around town, are nevertheless of high quality – nor do they take themselves too seriously. I stumbled across half a dozen pieces, though two that I particularly enjoyed were *Dark Knight* and *Girl Having a Strop*. I won't reveal their whereabouts, because you can go and seek them out yourself (with the help of a map available from the visitor centre, page 156) but suffice to say that they are guaranteed to raise a wry smile.

Weston Museum

Burlington St, BS23 1PR ✐ 01934 621028 ⊘ westonmuseum.org ⊙ mid-Feb–Oct, daily; Nov–mid-Feb, Tue–Sun

If you want to delve deeper into Weston's long and colourful history, get yourself along to the marvellous Weston Museum. Occupying the old Weston Gas Light Company building, the galleries have been recently refurbished and look so much the better for it. Presented chronologically, it begins with the arrival of the Romans around AD43; among the many remarkable finds is a stash of grave goods (bone, ivory and jet pins, brooches) and some exquisite gaming counters. Next up, in the medieval gallery, is a fabulous display of church woodcarvings.

"Among the many remarkable finds is a stash of grave goods and some exquisite gaming counters."

Unsurprisingly though, the greater part of the museum is devoted to Weston's development as a holiday resort, and to this end there are some wonderfully nostalgic items on show: a donkey chair, a 1930s ice-cream

SAND SCULPTURE FESTIVAL

Each year, between April and September, Weston-super-Mare hosts the Sand Sculpture Festival (westonsandsculpture.co.uk), which attracts master sand sculptors from all over the world. The result is a stupendous array of larger-than-life sculptures based upon a particular theme, which in the past has included 'Under the Sea', 'Fairy Tales', 'Circus' and, in 2019, 'What If?' Technically, the sculptures – which take on average nine or ten days to craft – are made solely from sand and water and, despite whatever the weather may throw at them (the sculptures are kept permanently outdoors), are remarkably robust. At the end of the festival, the sculptures are ceremoniously bulldozed and the sand returned from whence it came (er, the beach) for sunbathers to enjoy once again.

sales tricycle and, inevitably, Punch & Judy puppets. But it's the many images that best capture the resort's glory days, including a fabulous wall-length print of the railway in 1895, and a photo of local-born actor John Cleese taken in 1972. Seek out, too, the evocative little exhibition on the Women's League of Health and Beauty, a nationwide charity set up in 1930 to promote outdoor activity – largely in the form of big group physical training-style drills – but which was particularly popular in Weston thanks to the town's big open spaces, such as the prom; these days it's known somewhat more prosaically as the Fitness League.

What I didn't expect to find here was such a prestigious art collection, but there is, and it stars two paintings by Gainsborough (including one of the Reverend Wadham Pigott, who did as much as anyone to promote Weston's charms back in the mid 19th century) and a selection of works by the renowned graphic artist Alfred Leete, who studied the subject in this town. There's a good on-site café, too.

Helicopter Museum

Locking Moor Rd, BS24 8PP 01934 635227 helicoptermuseum.co.uk Wed–Sun

Just outside of town, on the A371 road out towards the M5 (bus 126 from Weston to Wells stops outside), Weston's Helicopter Museum claims to hold the world's largest collection of rotorcraft. An impressive boast for sure and one that, having spent a good hour or so admiring the many aircraft, I've no doubt has substance – though to be fair there can't be that many museums of this kind, can there? One thing is undeniable though: along with the Fleet Air Arm Museum and the Haynes International Motor Museum (both covered in *Chapter 6*), the Helicopter Museum completes a wonderful triumvirate of top-class transport museums in Somerset.

The museum occupies one of the original hangars on the site of Weston-super-Mare's old airport, whose history is as long and illustrious as it is unfamiliar to most people. Opened in 1936, it initially served civilian aircraft (mainly operating flights to Cardiff just across the Bristol Channel), before the outbreak of war saw the transfer of operations to the RAF. Civilian flights resumed after the war, alongside helicopter flight testing, and continued to do so for another 50 years or so (the old runway is now the main road that runs parallel to the present-day airfield).

The fleet here extends to some 50 aircraft, many truly outstanding, among them a US Army Bell UH-1H shot down in Vietnam, a Russian Hind attack helicopter (one of several fearsome-looking Soviet models on display), and the iconic Wasp, this one having plied its trade on the Leander-class frigate HMS *Galatea*, aboard which my father once served. Here too is the G-Lynx, officially the world's fastest helicopter, having clocked an impressive average speed of 400km/h over a 15km (or 248mph over a nine-mile) stretch of the Somerset Levels in 1986 – a record it still holds to this day. No mention of the museum would be complete without reference (or indeed deference) to Westland Helicopters (now Leonardo's) in Yeovil (page 189), as this is where the G-Lynx, as well as many other aircraft on display here, was manufactured.

"The G-Lynx, officially the world's fastest helicopter, clocked an impressive average speed of 400km/h."

Don't leave without popping your head into the **aviation exhibition**, housed inside the former pilots' block (next to the refurbished control tower), a few paces away from the hangar near the old taxiway. Small it may be, but it sheds fascinating light on the airport's history, as well as that of the now-defunct RAF Locking a mile or so down the road. Visitors can get their aviation thrills courtesy of the **Weston Air Show** in mid-June, a rare free event along the seafront.

⛏ FOOD & DRINK

The Blitz Tearoom 22 Waterloo St, BS23 1LN ☎ 01934 709475. Wonderful 1940s-themed tea room with photos, Union Jack flags and bunting, and all manner of World War II paraphernalia – even the waiting staff are suitably attired. Tea is served in old-fashioned teapots complete with knitted cosies, while three-tiered tea stands come stacked with elegantly cut sandwiches, cakes and pastries. Great fun.

Meze Mazi 45 Oxford St, BS23 1TN ℰ 01934 626363 ⬦ mezemaziweston.co.uk. Weston may not be the Med, but this terrific Greek/Cypriot establishment is about as authentic as you can get. Hefty plates of *souvlaki* (grilled meat and veg on a skewer), *kleftiko* (marinated lamb with herbs) and *gigantes* (white beans baked in a tomato sauce) are all on the menu, while salads and sides are equally tasty. There's a decent selection of native beers and wines too.

3 BREAN DOWN

A towering, blade-shaped peninsula nosing out into the Bristol Channel, Brean Down is essentially the last remnant of the Mendip Hills escarpment. A Site of Special Scientific Interest (SSSI) and now owned by the National Trust, the walk up to and around the headland, which rises to a height of 318ft, should take no more than 90 minutes, notwithstanding time spent admiring the views, and perhaps a stop for a picnic lunch; either way, this is one exhilarating jaunt. Beginning at the Brean Down Café, head up the steep set of steps to the top of the down. Here, take the path to the left, which shadows the southern slopes and continue across the clifftop meadow, brushed with hawthorn trees and, in summer, clumps of purple heather over which butterflies

BREAN DOWN WAY

Inaugurated in 2017, the Brean Down Way is an eight-mile mixed-use path between Weston-super-Mare and Brean Down. Now part of **National Cycle Route 33**, the traffic-free route is mostly level, and there is also the option of walking (and cycling) a couple of beach-bound sections, though obviously only at low tide. Beyond the suburb of Uphill, 2½ miles south of Weston and a nature reserve at Walborough (roughly the four-mile mark), you come to the River Axe and the **Brean Cross sluice bridge**, across which a wooden bird screen has been built in order to prevent neighbouring wildlife from being disturbed. Soon, a sharp right takes you towards **Brean Beach** which, depending upon the tide, can be accessed as part of the route; otherwise, use the path running parallel to the beach. At this point you've almost reached your final destination, save for the small matter of Brean Down itself (see above), looming menacingly high above the beach. There are a few refreshment stops en route, but Brean Down Café, overlooking the beach, has the bonus of a lovely terrace with expansive sea views (page 166). Note that cars are allowed on the beach outside the summer season.

skim and dart. There's abundant wildlife up here, and you'll likely spot stonechats and skylarks, and maybe the occasional peregrine falcon – keep an eye out too for the rare white rock rose flower, which is partial to the thin limestone soil prevalent here and is usually present between May and July.

The peninsula culminates in the substantial ruins of a **Victorian fort**, one of a series of so-called Palmerston Forts constructed throughout coastal areas in the 1860s (and named after the prime minister at the time) to counter the threat of French invasion, though in the event this one never saw action. It did, though, serve as an artillery battery during World War II, then later as a testing site for rockets. Widely dispersed across the tip of Brean Down, the many structures that comprise the fort include the old barracks, officer's mess, magazine and observation post, and the rusting supports of two massive gun emplacements.

The views are of course sensational: south Wales, Exmoor, the Quantocks, the Mendips and the Somerset Levels – and directly in front of you, Steep Holm, which is about as close as you are going to get to the island without actually being on it. From the fort, you can return the way you came, or you can head back along the other (northern) path, following it around to the right before arriving back at the steps. Note that, although dogs are permitted up here, they must be kept under close control (preferably on a lead), lest your pooch decides to venture seawards.

¶¶ FOOD & DRINK

Brean Down Café 2 Brean Down Rd, TA8 2RS. After a breezy walk up on Brean Down, you'll find plenty of restorative refreshments at this National Trust-run beachfront café. Refuel with soups, sandwiches and salads, or treat yourself to some delicious homemade cake, washed down with a cuppa.

4 BERROW BEACH

For a fantastic Slow stroll along the coastline, head north from the Low Lighthouse (see box, page 168) towards Berrow Beach, the midway point of a largely unbroken expanse of sand extending between Burnham and Brean Down, several miles distant. Backed by the largest remaining area of sand dunes along the Somerset coast, Berrow is as tranquil a spot as you could wish for. Part of the area forms the **Berrow Dunes Local Nature Reserve**, which supports in excess of 250 species of wildflower, including sea milkwort and common sea lavender. Like Bridgwater Bay as a whole, the beach is also an important habitat for wintering wading birds, among them dunlin, oystercatcher and curlew.

At low tide, the skeletal remains of SS *Nornen*, a Norwegian barque that ran aground here in 1897, slowly reveal themselves. In attempting to navigate the notoriously treacherous Bristol Channel, the ship got into difficulties during one particularly brutal storm and drifted ashore, though fortunately all ten crew members were saved. Despite threatening to have the wreck removed, the council relented and so today anyone is free to probe among its algae-riddled hull – keep an eye on that tide, however, as it comes in fast here.

"At low tide, the remains of SS Nornen, *a Norwegian barque that ran aground here in 1897, slowly reveal themselves."*

If driving, the best place to access Berrow Beach is the (free) car park at the nature reserve just north of St Mary's Church, near the village of Berrow itself – and not the car park some 400m further on from here, which is expensive, though it does permit access to the beach. From the nature reserve car park, follow your nose through the dunes until you find yourself on the sand.

5 BURNHAM-ON-SEA

Smaller and less obviously in your face than Weston, Burnham-on-Sea doesn't, on the surface at least, appear to offer very much; yet there are things here that will surprise you. At just 121ft long, Burnham's stubby little **pier**, built in 1914, is reckoned to be the shortest in the country, which, in the absence of any kind of aesthetic quality, at least gives it some kind of kudos. Consisting of little more than a big white pavilion plonked on top of concrete pylons – the first in Europe to use the material for pier construction – it's said to share many of the design features Brunel used in his construction of Bristol Temple Meads station, though I can't quite see it myself.

Much like Weston, the slightly scruffy town centre, set back a street or two from the main promenade, has little to commend it, but you don't have to walk far to find the 14th-century **St Andrew's Church** on Victoria Street. Here, your eyes will immediately be drawn to its wonderfully wonky tower, which leans, rather disconcertingly, at a 15° angle – that's about 3ft from top to bottom; while comparisons with the leaning tower of Pisa are inevitable (and a little far-fetched),

LOVELY LIGHTHOUSES

It may seem a little indulgent to have three lighthouses in one place, but that's exactly what Burnham has. How did this come about? One story has it that, in 1750, or thereabouts, a fisherman's wife, anxious for the safe return of her husband, lit a candle and waited at the window to guide him home. From then on, a light was placed at the top of St Andrew's church tower – until the **Round Tower Lighthouse** was erected close by around 1800. Decommissioned in 1832, and reduced from four storeys to two, it is now a guesthouse.

The most instantly recognisable of Burnham's three lighthouses is the **Low Lighthouse**, an elegant box-shaped structure standing sentry in the middle of the beach, as if casually washed up by the tide. Built in 1829, atop nine spindly legs (hence its moniker, the Lighthouse on Legs), with a flash of red paint through its otherwise whitewashed exterior, this is the only one of the three lights still in active service. Although you can't go inside, the Low Lighthouse affords fabulous close-up photo opportunities.

Heading in the direction of Berrow, you can't fail to notice the slender, cylindrical tower protruding above the surrounding houses and trees. Built the same year as the Low Lighthouse, the **High (or Pillar) Lighthouse** is an eight-floored granite structure that was once equipped with a paraffin-fired lamp. Deactivated as recently as 1990, it's now a private residence and so can't be visited.

it's still a startling sight. Entering the church via a massive, beautiful oak door, you're confronted by a capacious nave. St Andrew's single most important feature is the **Gibbons sculpture**, actually a series of superbly carved marble pieces dispersed around the church; commissioned by James II, and completed by Grinling Gibbon, the sculptures have enjoyed a nomadic existence, variously residing in Westminster Abbey (as part of an altarpiece by Christopher Wren) and Whitehall Palace before being brought here by one Walter King, Bishop of Rochester and, by happy coincidence, the Vicar of Burnham.

ᵀ⊺ FOOD & DRINK

The Front Parlour 6 The Esplanade, TA8 1BB ✆ 01278 787383 ⊙ noon–19.00 Wed–Sat, 11.00–18.00 Sun. Burnham doesn't lack for cafés, though few warrant a visit. One that does, however, is the mint-green Front Parlour on the seafront, which feels a bit like stepping into someone's living room, with its happily cluttered interior and inviting welcome. There are treats galore here, including roast dinners, though most people swing by for one of their awesome cream teas.

6 BRIDGWATER BAY NATIONAL NATURE RESERVE & STEART MARSHES

Stretching all the way from Minehead to Brean Down, and including the yawning mouth of the River Parrett, **Bridgwater Bay National Nature Reserve** is an extraordinarily diverse landscape of intertidal mudflats and river estuaries, sand flats and shingle ridges – as well as being a wetland habitat of international importance. At the heart of the Bay is **Steart Marshes**, the country's largest new wetland reserve, a tidal area measuring some 1.8 miles long and 0.6 miles wide. Managed by the Wildfowl and Wetlands Trust, this so-called working wetland was created to counter the effects of rising sea levels – it's anticipated that the River Severn will rise by 1m within the next century – and comprises three types of wetland habitat: brackish lagoons, freshwater marsh and saltwater marsh, the last grazed by sheep during summer months. It takes about an hour to walk from the main car park to Breach Point, where a channel of the Parrett has been diverted to create a vast area of coastal marsh, across which a series of artificial creeks have been established, the whole shaped like a curved herringbone; the breach is best visited during a big spring tide when water surges through.

These low-lying marshes are as important a wildlife habitat as the Somerset Levels, a popular haven for wintering waterfowl and waders, especially teal, widgeon and golden plover, which, in summer, give way to lapwing, little egret and skylark, as well as one of the largest gatherings of shelduck anywhere in Europe. There are permissive footpaths throughout the reserve, with plenty of opportunities to observe birds from several beautifully constructed hides. The whole site has been sensitively managed by the Wildfowl and Wetlands Trust since its inception, who are keen to ensure that it doesn't get overrun, though such is its isolation that it receives relatively few visitors.

FROM CLEEVE ABBEY TO MINEHEAD

The stretch of Somerset coast extending west from Bridgwater Bay provides a selection of somewhat lower-key charms when compared with the coast's northern reaches. For starters there's **Cleeve Abbey** and **Torre Cider Farm** which, when done together, makes for a most satisfying day trip. Heading further west still, a Slow day spent in and around the pretty harbour village of **Watchet** – with its many quaint pubs – is immensely rewarding. This portion of the coast winds up at **Minehead**, which, despite its detractors, retains a busy vibe; moreover, it is the terminus for the fabulous **West Somerset Railway** and starting point for the 630-mile-long South West Coast Path. Note, though, that the remainder of the Somerset coast – from Porlock to the Devon border – is covered in the Exmoor chapter, as it falls within that national park's boundary. The descriptions of Cleeve Abbey, Torre Cider Farm, Watchet and some of Minehead are taken from *Slow Travel North Devon & Exmoor* by Hilary Bradt.

7 CLEEVE ABBEY

🏠 **Railway Cottage** (page 236)

Washford TA23 0PS 🖉 0870 333 1181 ⊙ Apr–Oct; English Heritage

Dissolved by Henry VIII in 1536, much of the 800-year-old Cistercian Cleeve Abbey is too ruined to be of great interest, but the refectory is absolutely splendid. Here is a Great Hall, remodelled in the 15th century by the increasingly prosperous community. It imitated the Great Halls found in manor houses, and has a wonderful wagon roof.

Another marvel is the refectory floor, now housed in a purpose-built building, which shows it off to perfection. The beautiful glazed tiles, in subtle earth colours – ochre, terracotta and black – decorated with heraldic designs including two-headed eagles and coats of arms, were made in the late 13th century. The explanation board says that the subject matter 'hints at the relationship between the monks of Cleeve and their patrons, some of the greatest noblemen of their age'. Though each title is painted in great detail, together they make a harmonious whole. When the abbey was destroyed, the floor, or pavement, was covered in earth and thus protected until it was excavated in 1876.

"There's also an excellent Monk's Trail, where signs describe how the monks lived and worked in the abbey."

Other rooms of particular interest are the Painted Chamber, off a passageway leading from the refectory, showing 16th-century wall paintings, and the Dormitory with some decorative tiles on the windowsills, making each personal area a little bit more special for the monks. There's also an excellent Monk's Trail, where signs describe, in simple language, how the monks lived and worked in the abbey. All this, plus spacious grounds where children can play or picnic, means that visiting Cleeve Abbey is well worth the effort. To walk there from Washford, avoiding the main road, turn left out of the station and walk to the bus shelter. From there follow the signs to the abbey.

8 TORRE CIDER FARM

Washford TA23 0LA ℘ 01984 640004 ⌘ torrecider.co.uk ⊘ 10.00–16.00 daily

Just half a mile down the road from Cleeve Abbey is this 6½-acre cider-producing farm that has diversified into a family-friendly attraction with a few rare-breed animals (kunekune pigs, sheep and unusual chickens) and a large adventure playground for kids.

Three types of cider are made here: Bee's Knees (sweet), farmhouse (medium) and Sheep's Stagger (dry), all of which are flat ciders, since the fizzy variety is much more complicated to make, and this is a relatively small farm by Somerset standards. And that is the attraction. You can wander round the orchard and well-labelled Cider Press Room, or take a tour (phone ahead to book) where you can learn all abut the business of producing cider – and there's no charge for any of this. They use 20 varieties of cider apple, all grown here and harvested by hand – a good old-fashioned shake of the trees and the apples are then gathered from the ground. West Country cider apples (there are at least 150 varieties) have some lovely names, such as the brilliant Slack Me Girder. The tour ends in a tasting (of course) but you can also taste before you buy in the shop. There's also a good café and well-stocked shop selling a variety of goodies including 'sheep poo' (actually chocolate-covered raisins) which will delight children.

9 WATCHET

Whether or not it's true that Watchet was the inspiration for *The Ancient Mariner* – or at least matched the harbour of Coleridge's imagination where 'merrily did we drop/Below the kirk, below the hill, below the lighthouse top' – the poem has certainly stood this delightful little town in good stead. On the seafront stands a fine statue of the mariner with the albatross round his neck, and the commercial implications are not lost on the town's business community. Coleridge supposedly stayed in The Bell Inn, penning the first few lines of his poem there.

Watchet is satisfactory in so many ways: small enough to walk around, with two museums, a Wednesday market, a good (and level) ramble along a disused railway line, and an interesting church (though some way from the town). It is also the most arty place in the region, with several galleries and the imaginatively used shipping containers at the eastern end of the Esplanade that comprise **Contains Art** (⊘ containsart. co.uk ⊙ Easter–Oct, 11.00–16.00 Wed–Sun) – studio/exhibition spaces for a variety of artists. At this end of the Esplanade is another, more permanent work of art, the **St Decuman pebble mosaic**, depicting scenes from the life of this colourful saint including a suitably gruesome severed head.

The **Market House Museum** (⊘ 01984 632266 ⊘ watchetmuseum. co.uk ⊙ Easter–end Oct, 10.30–16.30 daily), housed in the old market by the harbour, is particularly interesting, with a fine 'Chronicles of Watchet' at the back of the building where you can trace the history of the town from prehistoric times to the present day through illustrations and photos. Watchet was the terminus of the **Mineral Railway**, built in the mid 19th century to carry iron ore from the Brendon Hills to Watchet harbour; the museum has photos and explanations and a portion of the railway has been exposed at the West Quay. Some of the old railway track is now a popular two-mile walk to Washford.

"Watchet was the terminus of the Mineral Railway, built in the mid 19th century to carry iron ore from the Brendon Hills to Watchet harbour."

Watchet's second museum is part of the Visitor Centre on Harbour Road (page 156), by the railway station. Housed in the old railway goods shed, designed in 1862 by Isambard Kingdom Brunel as the terminus of the Bristol and Exeter Railway, the **Boat Museum** (4 Swain St ⊘ 01984 634242 ⊙ 10.30–17.00 Tue–Sun) displays a fantastic collection of Watchet boats. Mostly designed for the shallow water of the estuary, these include a Flatner, a keel-less, double-ended boat, and the Mud Horse, a sort of sledge, used by a fisherman to tend his nets on the mud flats.

Finally, it's worth keeping one eye on the town calendar as it's packed with events; the big one is the **Watchet Music Festival** at the end of August, which attracts some surprisingly big names.

▌▌ FOOD & DRINK

The Bell Inn 3 Market St, TA23 0AN ⊘ 01984 631279 ⊘ the-bell-inn.co.uk. A historic, 16th-century, family-run pub, oft frequented by Coleridge himself, serving good food and a wide range of local beers in pleasant surroundings, plus open fires in winter. Quiz nights, open mic and live music evenings complete the package. Dog-friendly too.

Pebbles Tavern 24 Market St, TA23 0AN ✐ 01984 634737 ☌ pebblestavern.co.uk. Not a restaurant but a bar specialising in cider – around 30 draught varieties – along with ales and spirits. They've won the Cider Pub of the Year five times, so you can expect knowledgeable service; you can taste before ordering. Regular music nights. No food but you can bring a take-away.

Star Inn Mill Ln, TA23 0BZ ✐ 01984 631367 ☌ starinnwatchet.co.uk. A quiet pub tucked behind a traffic-free street, with a wonderfully convivial beer garden. A varied menu, well cooked, along with a wide selection of real ales from all over Somerset.

10 MINEHEAD

🏠 **The Old Ship Aground** (page 236) ⚊ **Minehead Camping and Caravanning Club** (page 236)

Butlin's or the start of the South West Coast Path, amusement arcades or a network of leafy foot and cycle paths high above the town – Minehead has something for everyone, but the Slow traveller will be drawn to the western and upper parts of the town where history and rural pursuits take precedence. Minehead is also the start/finish point (and the headquarters) of the **West Somerset Railway**, though this is covered in greater detail in *Chapter 4*.

A few paces from the station, inside the Beach Hotel, is the TIC (page 156), which can provide you with plenty of inspiration to keep you busy for a few hours. You can begin your explorations, however, in the very same building, with a gander around the sweet little **Minehead Museum** (✐ 01643 702624 ☌ mineheadmuseum.co.uk ☉ mid-Mar– Oct, 10.00–16.00 Tue–Sun, plus Mon in Aug), which dotes on the town's surprisingly colourful history, chunks of which, sadly, have long since disappeared – for example, the Gaiety Theatre, torn down in 1979 to

"The Slow traveller will be drawn to the western and upper parts of the town where history and rural pursuits take precedence."

make way for an amusement arcade, and the Olympic-sized lido, which was flattened in 1990. Look out too for a photo of the Beatles shooting *A Hard Day's Night* here in 1964, and a cabinet of objects devoted to the achievements of science-fiction author Arthur C Clarke. Born in Minehead in 1917, Clarke grew up in Bishops Lydeard and Taunton before a career in the RAF beckoned; he spent the last 50 years or so

MINEHEAD'S HOBBY HORSE
Hilary Bradt

Whereas Padstow's Hobby Horse gets national media coverage, Minehead's, which is just as old and weird, is known only to locals. Like Padstow's, the origin of this festival is lost in the mists of time, but it's certainly being going on for a long time. The earliest recorded mention of the event in Minehead is in 1792 but it's likely to have been taking place for centuries before that. The hobby horse comes out of hiding on the evening of 30 April at the Old Ship Aground (see opposite), and starts its parade at dawn on 1 May when it twirls, sways and gambols around the area including a trip to Dunster Castle, accompanied by men playing drums and an accordion. This goes on for three days.

Very little of the hobby horse resembles a horse – it's much more like a boat, reinforced by the fact that 'Sailors Horse' is painted on its sides, amid decorative rings. It has a tail, however, with which it chastises onlookers who fail to make a donation (which go to charity). On the last day it might be confronted by the Town Horse with a fight ensuing. All in all, it's a weird and wonderful spectacle and one not to be missed if you're around at the time.

of his life in Sri Lanka, during which time he wrote the majority of his books, most famously *2001: A Space Odyssey*, which was also adapted into a film by Stanley Kubrick.

Most shops and restaurants are on The Avenue, while the posh hotels and B&Bs are up the steep hills that lead to **Higher Town**, with its large, elegant houses. Among the shops that draw locals to Minehead is the excellent **Toucan Wholefoods** (3 The Parade), which has a vegetarian restaurant upstairs. Continuing the food theme, Minehead has one of the longest-running **farmers' markets** in the area; it's held every Friday from March to December. For lovers of fresh produce, **Exmoor Food & Crafts** (4 The Avenue) is a co-operative of food producers and craftspeople. The **Courtyard Gallery** on Friday Street has a sizeable collection of artwork and prints, plus ceramics, jewellery and the like – it also has an excellent sister gallery, the Churchgate Gallery, in Porlock.

Walkers, meanwhile, will drift along to the western part of the seafront since, even if you're planning to do no more than walk the seven or so miles into Porlock, it's more or less mandatory to have your photo taken next to the **sculpture** that marks the start of the 630-mile **South West Coast Path**, which depicts a pair of hands holding an Ordnance

Survey map. If you are in Minehead for the May bank holiday you're in for a treat: the **Hobby Horse Festival** is one of only two in the country (see box, opposite).

¶¶ FOOD & DRINK

Cream 20A The Avenue, TA24 5AZ ✆ 01643 708022 ⬡ cafecream.co.uk ⊙ 09.00–17.00 Mon–Sat, 10.00–16.00 Sun with slightly longer opening hours in summer. A crisp, modern – and licensed – place serving excellent breakfasts, light lunches and, in the summer, dinners, with good coffee and cakes at any time. Popular with locals.

Old Ship Aground Harbourside, Quay St, TA24 5UL ✆ 01643 703516 ⬡ theoldshipaground. com. A beautiful traditional pub in a lovely location on the harbour, close to the start of the South West Coast Path. Open fires in the winter, outdoor seating in the summer, and excellent food.

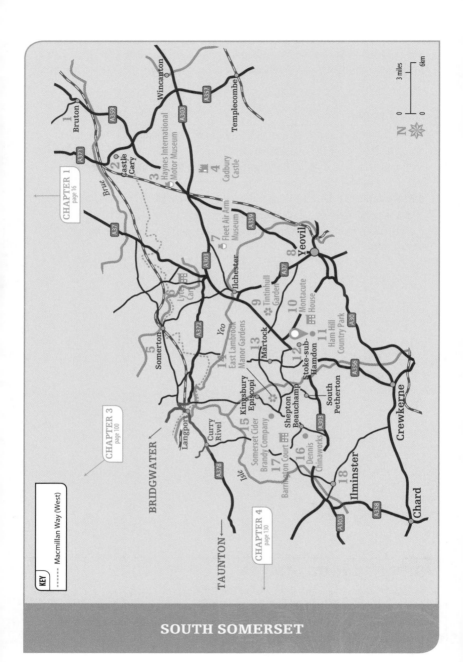

SOUTH SOMERSET

6
SOUTH SOMERSET

Don't expect to move particularly fast around these parts. This is real backcountry lanes territory, which means overhanging branches, tall hedgerows, and tractors of course – Slow Somerset at its very best. South Somerset is defined, above all, by its hamstone villages, whose golden-toned buildings are at their glorious best in Martock, Montacute and Stoke-sub-Hamdon. The source of all this gorgeous masonry – once described by the author and editor Simon Jenkins as 'the loveliest stone in England' – is Ham Hill, where it has been quarried for centuries. Not far from Ham Hill, and south Somerset's most prominent town, is **Yeovil**, though with all due respect it's not a place to linger, unlike **Bruton** or **Castle Cary**, two small towns oozing charisma. The former, in particular, has become something of a must-visit destination since the arrival of a world-class gallery, unlikely as that may sound.

The area is run through with historic properties, so you may need to be selective if time is an issue. One hopes it won't be though, in which case you can slowly work your way around the likes of **Barrington Court, Lytes Cary** and **Tintinhull** – enchanting places all – though none can rival **Montacute,** for my money *the* grandest of all Somerset's houses. All these places boast triumphant gardens too, though there are minor delights elsewhere in this department, not least **East Lambrook Manor Gardens**, one of my favourite visits in this entire chapter. I very much enjoyed too, the **Fleet Air Arm Museum** and the **Haynes International Motor Museum**, two world-class transport exhibitions one could happily spend hours poring over.

Last but by no means least, south Somerset is hardcore cider territory (where isn't in Somerset, I hear you ask) with orchards everywhere. With one or two exceptions, such as the innovative **Somerset Cider Brandy Company**, it's largely the preserve of smaller-scale producers, most of whom are happy for visitors to drop by as and when. In fact, come along at harvesting time and get picking – they'll be pleased to see you.

GETTING THERE & AROUND

By **road**, the main entry point into south Somerset – if coming from the east or the west – is the fast A303; mostly dual carriageway, it bypasses Ilminster before continuing as the A30 beyond the Blackdown Hills and into Devon. Tom Fort's highly entertaining *The A303: Highway to the Sun* is worth reading, whether you're travelling the road or not. Coming from a northerly direction, the main road is the A37, which continues beyond Yeovil down towards the Dorset coast; many of the attractions in this chapter lie within a stone's throw of both the A303 and A37.

TRAINS

Surprisingly for such a rural corner of the county, this part of Somerset is well served by **rail**: Castle Cary is on the Reading to Taunton line (with several daily trains direct from London Paddington) as well as the slow Weymouth to Bristol line (which includes stops at Yeovil Pen Mill to the south and Bruton, Frome and Bath to the north, these last two destinations covered in *Chapter 1*). Yeovil has two stations: Yeovil Junction, on the main London Waterloo to Exeter line, and Yeovil Pen Mill.

BUSES

With a smattering of decently sized (for Somerset) towns in this part of the county, bus services offer a feasible way of getting around. A number of services emanate from Yeovil, the main provider being South West Coaches (⟡ southwestcoaches.co.uk). Among the most useful are route 1 to Castle Cary and Shepton Mallet (the latter in *Chapter 1*); 52 to Tintinhull and Martock; 81 to South Petherton via Montacute, Stoke-sub-Hamdon and Norton-sub-Hamdon; and 96 to Chard via Crewkerne. Note that few, if any, buses run on Sundays.

WALKING & CYCLING

The landscape of south Somerset is predominantly flat, though that's not to say there aren't enticing **walks** to be had. The one long-distance trail of relevance here is the **Macmillan Way (West)**, named after the eponymous founder of the Macmillan Cancer Research Trust, who was

> **i TOURIST INFORMATION**
>
> **Bruton** 26 High St, BA10 0AA ✐ 01749 812851
> **Castle Cary** The Market House, BA7 7AH ✐ 01963 351763
> **Ilminster** Arts Centre, East St, TA19 0AN ✐ 01460 57294
> **Martock** The Market House, Church St, TA12 6JL ✐ 01935 310040
> **Yeovil** Petters Hse, Petters Way, BA20 1AS ✐ 01935 462781 ◈ discoversouthsomerset.com

born in Castle Cary and where the trail begins; from there it continues westwards to Somerton and the Levels before traversing a section of both the Quantocks and Exmoor en route to Barnstaple. Elsewhere in this chapter I've outlined one fabulous walk we did around Ham Hill (page 194), though you could quite happily wander from village to village without too much bother, as you could by **bike**, so cyclists needn't feel short-changed either.

BRUTON TO CADBURY CASTLE

Bruton was always one of Somerset's most enjoyable destinations, but its popularity has grown tenfold in recent times thanks to the arrival of one of the world's great art galleries. No less deserving of a day's exploration is Castle Cary, a thriving community town packed with some excellent independent shops. Further south, Cadbury Castle provides historical excitement and wonderful views, while, close by, motorcar buffs will love the brilliant Haynes Motor Museum, one of the finest of its kind anywhere in the world.

1 BRUTON

🏠 **At the Chapel** (page 236), **High House** (page 236) 🏡 **Durslade Farmhouse** (page 236) ⛺ **Batcombe Vale** (page 237)

Bruton had always been a fairly well-heeled place, thanks partly to the presence of several top-rated public schools, albeit one that few outside Somerset really knew much about. That all changed in 2014 with the arrival of Hauser & Wirth, one of the world's most influential art galleries – an event, it's no exaggeration to say, that transformed this small, unassuming town's fortunes overnight. Factor in a smattering of independent shops and a coterie of outstanding restaurants, and it's not difficult to see why Bruton has become such a hot destination.

The gallery aside, there's plenty to keep you entertained here for a few hours, starting with a little trot along the High Street and the sweet little **museum** (✆ 01749 813014 ⌖ brutonmuseum.org.uk ◷ 11.00–13.00 Mon–Fri, 11.00–15.00 Sat), which offers a decent overview of the town's history. One delightful little feature of the museum is its monthly Casespace exhibition, whereby local artists get to showcase their work. Crossing Church Bridge from the museum, have a quick peek inside **St Mary the Virgin Church**, which, in the first instance, is unusual for its little and large twin towers built roughly 100 years apart. Inside, make a beeline for the chancel, a riot of rococo, especially its dazzling reredos.

From town, a couple of footpaths wend their way up to Abbey Park – formerly the deer park of the long since vanished Bruton Abbey – site of Bruton's roofless 16th-century **dovecote**, though it most likely served as a watchtower for the abbey before its conversion; inside are six tiers of nest boxes with some 200 pigeon holes. The dovecote is also just a short walk from Hauser & Wirth, and if driving, there's a car park close by. Heading out of town on Station Road, you'll likely find it hard to resist popping into the **Godminster Shop** (⌖ godminster.com), one of the area's finest cheese outlets, its counters groaning with a mouth-watering array of cheddars.

Hauser & Wirth

Durslade Farm, Dropping Ln, BA10 0NL ✆ 01749 814060 ⌖ hauserwirthsomerset.com
◷ Tue–Sun

When you consider that Iwan Hauser and Manuela Wirth's five other locations are London, Hong Kong, New York, Los Angeles and Zurich, it makes it even more astonishing that they should have chosen this sleepy little Somerset town as another (it was the fourth location) for one of the world's most prestigious contemporary art galleries. But they did and it's stunning. Out on the edge of town, just beyond the train station, the site occupies the formerly derelict Durslade Farm and its cluster of outbuildings (stables, cow shed and piggery among them), augmented by two new wings. The couple themselves were so enamoured with the area that they decided to move here.

All exhibitions are temporary and, as you'd expect, consistently of the highest order; in the past these have included the likes of Phyllida Barlow (large-scale sculptural installations), Matthew Day Jackson (collages, paintings and sculptures), Turner Prize-winning artist Susan Philipsz (sound installations), and the celebrated photojournalist Don McCullin, who just happens to be a local resident. But what is as impressive as the quality of the art is the space, or rather, spaces. Sequenced around a cloister courtyard, there are no fewer than five separate galleries, the most spectacular occupying the old threshing barn, which revels in light flooding in from the massive glass doors.

Outside, the **Oudolf Field**, created by revered Dutch landscape designer Piet Oudolf (the man responsible for New York's acclaimed High Line), is a long, sweeping meadow packed with thousands of perennials, culminating in the monolithic-like Radić Pavilion by the eponymous Chilean architect. Supported by enormous quarry stones, it previously stood by the Serpentine Lake in London's Hyde Park before being dismantled and reinstalled here. There is of course a cool-as-hell restaurant located here, too.

A recent addition to the Hauser & Wirth portfolio is a new two-room gallery at 13 High Street (⊙ 10.00–13.00 & 14.00–16.00 Wed–Sat), which showcases specially curated exhibitions; to coincide with these, they also have workshops, talks and other community-related events.

¶¶ FOOD & DRINK

At the Chapel 28 High St, BA10 0AE ✆ 01749 814070 ⌕ atthechapel.co.uk ⊙ 08.00– 21.30 daily. This much-lauded restaurant, deli, wine merchant and baker has been reviewed – and praised – to death in the national press, but don't let that put you off. Both the venue – a commodious, all-white space with a cocktail bar where the altar once was – and the food are top drawer; the pizzas are fab, but there's also more sophisticated fare available, for example wild mushroom polenta with garlic and sage, and hake with chilli aioli and lentils.

Matt's Kitchen 51 High St, BA10 0AW ✆ 01749 812027 ⌕ mattskitchen.co.uk ⊙ 18.30–22.30 Wed–Fri. From decorator to self-taught cook, Matt Watson opened his restaurant – which is essentially the front room of his small terraced house – in 2011. The format is refreshingly simple: at each sitting, a single main dish is bookended by a choice of three starters and three desserts – one week's menu might feature, for example, shin of beef, pancetta and roast shallots or poached chicken with lemon thyme and duck aioli, all of which is beautifully cooked and presented. BYO (£3 corkage) too, but note that it's cash only. You'll need to book well in advance.

Roth Bar & Grill Hauser & Wirth, Durslade Farm, Dropping Ln, BA10 0NL ✆ 01749 814700 ⌕ rothbarandgrill.co.uk ⊙ 09.00–16.00 Tue–Thu & Sun, 09.00–22.00 Fri & Sat. Almost an art installation in itself, the on-site restaurant is as classy as the gallery it's housed in. More importantly, the menu lives up to expectations; local meats (beef, lamb) are cured in-house and fruit and veg are picked fresh from the farm; the Kitchen Salad menu is especially worth a punt. If you don't have the time or the means for a full-blown meal, just swing by for a coffee after viewing the galleries.

2 CASTLE CARY

Despite the name, there is no castle here – and hasn't been since about 1153. It's hard to believe today that Castle Cary was once one of the largest fortifications in Britain, after Colchester, Dover, the Tower of London and Middleham in North Yorkshire. The castle survives as nothing more than earthworks up on **Lodge Hill**, but it's a pleasant stroll up there all the same, and the views, especially the higher up you go towards the ridge, are lovely; to get there head up Paddock Lane next to the George Inn. The railway has undoubtedly attracted the commuting class to Castle Cary in recent years, yet the town remains a determinedly down-to-earth kind of place and folk here are tremendously welcoming, which counts for much these days.

The main, gently curving High Street is delightful, with tightly packed ranks of Crunchie-coloured buildings fielding a plethora of independent shops (clothes, hardware, food), cafés and pubs, and even the occasional gallery. My favourite is **Bailey Hill Bookshop** on Fore Street (leading away from the High Street) – that there is a bookshop at all in a town as small as this is unusual, but that this one is so exceptional is even more reason to celebrate.

"It's hard to believe today that Castle Cary was once one of the largest fortifications in Britain."

The town's most conspicuous building is the magnificent, Flemish-style **Market House**, which today functions more or less as it did when it was built in 1855 – these days the market takes place on Tuesdays (09.00–14.00), which makes it the best time to visit the town, if you can. Conversely, one time you may not want to be here is during Glastonbury Festival (see box, page 109), when the town's train station (otherwise very handy) becomes the official festival station.

But back to the Market House; inside, on the ground floor, you'll find the tourist information centre and exhibition space, and upstairs, the **Castle Cary & District Museum** (✆ 01963 350680 ◊ castlecarymuseum. org.uk ◔ Apr–Oct 10.30–12.30 & 14.00–16.00 Mon–Fri, 10.30–12.30 Sat), which offers a wonderfully haphazard evocation of the town's history. The core of the exhibition dwells on local industry, the town traditionally having lived off farming and weaving. At one time there were several horsehair weavers in the area, but now there is just one, **John Boyd Textiles**, which has been in operation since 1837. In fact, it's now Britain's sole remaining horsehair weavers, with a roll call of prestigious clients that has included the Bath Pump Rooms, Charles Rennie Mackintosh and Amsterdam's Concertgebouw. The town's most famous resident was **Douglas Macmillan**, founder of the eponymous cancer research charity, who was born here in 1884. Macmillan is duly honoured with his own display case of personal effects, including the MBE awarded to him in 1911 for his work in the field; what is less well known is that Macmillan enjoyed writing poetry (often written in the Somerset dialect), samples of which are here. For all that though, there's one item that stands out: a pair of underdrawers (knickers to you and I) belonging to Queen Victoria, as the 'VR' insignia on the waistband reveals, though why or how they ended up here is anyone's guess.

Up behind the Market House is the **round house**, colloquially known as the pepper pot, for reasons that are pretty obvious once you clap eyes on it. Dating from 1779 – and reputedly one of just half a dozen in the country – it served as a temporary lock-up for miscreants and drunkards. Beyond the chunky double doors (the keys are available from the tourist information centre, page 179), there's little to it, save for a stone seat and two small grilles for ventilation. Close by, note the post office and library, occupying two more distinguished-looking buildings – this town is well served for sure. At the bottom of Fore Street (itself flush with some fine buildings), the **Horse Pond** is actually a remnant of the old moat, but even more incongruous is the war memorial (1920), plonked right in the middle.

FOOD & DRINK

The Bakehouse High St, BA7 7AW ☏ 01963 350067 ◈ castlecarybakehouse.co.uk ◷ 09.30–16.00 Tue–Sat. Coffee shop and Thai restaurant may not seem the likeliest of bedfellows, but that's what this popular daytime-only establishment does, and does very well. *Pad ka-ree* (noodles), sticky roast duck and spicy Thai fishcakes are just a few of the mouth-watering lunchtime offerings.

The Deli/The Somerset Wine Company Market Pl, BA7 7AL ☏ 01963 548228 ◈ somersetwinecompany.com ◷ 10.00–18.00 Mon–Fri, 10.00–17.00 Sat. Both the coffee and hot chocolate are worth savouring in this tiny bolthole, with its two tables overlooking the Market House. Sharing the premises is the Somerset Wine Company, offering a top-drawer selection of wines from around the world, mostly France and Italy, but also from some less heralded wine countries such as Greece and Hungary – it's good to see a selection from Somerset, too. Otherwise, make a beeline for the shelf with wines costing less than a tenner. Supper club evenings and wine tasting events are also held here.

The Gallery Bar & Kitchen High St, BA7 7AW ℰ 07901 671495 ⊘ thegallerybar.co.uk ⊙ 18.30–23.00 Fri & Sat. Secreted away in the stunning vaulted basement of this well-respected local gallery, this rambling bar doles out scrumptious wood-fired sourdough pizzas (each named after an artist, naturally) and handcrafted burgers, often to the soundtrack of live music. Grab a cocktail while you're at it.

3 HAYNES INTERNATIONAL MOTOR MUSEUM

Sparkford BA22 7LH ℰ 01963 440804 ⊘ himm.co.uk

A sleek, glass-fronted building welcomes motorcar fans to the Haynes International Motor Museum, named after its founder and publisher of the iconic workshop manuals, John Haynes, who died in 2019. It is without doubt the most impressive assemblage of vintage and classic cars and bikes in the UK, and ranks among the top tier of motoring exhibits anywhere in the world, though you really don't have to be a car nut to enjoy this. I'm not, but I spent hours engrossed in this marvellous haul of over 400 road vehicles, based around Haynes's original, private collection of 30-odd cars. That Somerset should have two such outstanding transport museums at all, let alone two in such close proximity to each other (they're just four miles apart), is quite something, though I wouldn't advise visiting both this and the Fleet Air Arm in one day.

Multiple, themed halls are jammed solid with vehicles – and what a line up it is! Starting in the Veteran and Vintage hall, you're immediately confronted with some beauties, including a Daimler Phaeton from 1919 and Rolls Royce Phantom Sedanca (1930). Nearby, and many people's favourite, the dazzling Red Room speaks for itself: an Alfa Romeo Spider Veloce, Pontiac Trans Am Firebird, Triumph Spitfire and MG Midget all vie for attention among dozens of other spectacular scarlet models. The American Dream hall features some rare monsters, among them an Auburn Speedster, Lincoln Zephyr, Ford Fairlane Skyliner and a 1965 Cadillac de Ville. And if you've seen the film *Back to the Future*, you'll instantly recognise the DeLorean sports car, from the infamously defunct factory. One Russian riposte to the giant US manufacturers was the formidable GAZ M13 Chaika (1959), as preferred by the KGB and on display here – it's quite the beast. For those of us of a certain age, the **Memory Lane** hall will induce a real sense of nostalgia: among the vehicles here you'll find a Ford Anglia, Cortina and Capri, and a 1930 Morris Oxford Saloon, Haynes's first purchase and the one that kickstarted this whole project.

Visiting with family in tow, we each had our favourite, and for me it was a gorgeous navy-blue E-Type Jaguar, that most iconic of 1960s sports cars, in the **Great British Marques** hall, which is otherwise dominated by famous names such as Aston Martin, Jensen and Lotus. Formula One fans, meanwhile, will enjoy the small exhibition devoted to Mark Webber; centre stage is the Red Bull he drove during the 2010 season, during which he won four races and finished third in the drivers championship. If all of this has got you in the mood (and it probably will), there's a neighbouring karting track where you can unleash your inner racer.

4 CADBURY CASTLE

Rising up within earshot of the A303, the site of Cadbury Castle may well have been occupied as long ago as the Neolithic period, as suggested by pottery finds dating from around that time. What is more certain is that there was an Iron Age hillfort town here from around 500BC onwards, before that was cleared out and taken over by the Romans around AD70. For reasons unknown, it then remained deserted for several hundred years, only to be rebuilt around AD500 – this likely included a sizeable timber hall, nothing of which remains. Incidentally, Cadbury is yet another in a long list of sites to be associated with King Arthur's Camelot (see box, page 105), though it has no stronger claim than anywhere else.

The site is easy enough to reach: from the car park at the southern end of South Cadbury village, follow the signpost to the start of a stony track, which climbs steeply through woods to an enclosure at the top. There's nothing of substance there these days, just a vast mound and a series of concentric rings of bank and ditch ramparts. But don't let that disappoint you – a complete circular walk around its uppermost, ridge-like ring affords peerless views, as good as any in Somerset. Surveying the surrounding countryside, it's not difficult to see why this was such a formidable arena.

SOMERTON & AROUND

One of Somerset's more low-key villages, Somerton – the former county town no less – merits a visit on account of a clutch of architectural gems; better still, it possesses one of the county's finest pubs. It also makes a good base for a couple of standout attractions: Lytes Cary Manor, with its marvellous Gertrude Jekyll-designed gardens, and the enduringly popular Fleet Air Arm Museum, which is more than a match for the Haynes Motor Museum just up the road.

5 SOMERTON

The White Hart (page 236)

Originally named 'Summer tun' by the Saxons, sedate Somerton once held the status of county town, taking over from Ilchester in the 13th century, before Taunton assumed the mantle around 1370 – a title that that town retains to this day. Somerton's position on the London to the Exeter trade route ensured that it became a major coaching stage, prompting huge business for hotels and inns. This partly explains the proliferation of historic buildings clustered in and around Market Place, and is as good a reason as any to pay a visit – OK, there's a cracking pub here too.

"The old octagonal Buttercross was used to keep cheese, butter, milk and other dairy products cool on a hot day."

Your best bet is to start on West Street, where you'll find both the Old Grammar School and Red Lion Court, the latter just one of the town's former coaching inns. From here it's a short hop to Market Place and the old octagonal **Buttercross** (1673), which acquired its name for the very good reason that it was used to keep cheese, butter, milk and other dairy products cool on a hot day – and, conversely, to protect those same goods on a soggy day. Not exactly rocket science, but it was effective all the same.

Across the road, beyond the sympathetic-looking **War Memorial** erected in 1921 from Portland Stone, a neat row of clipped hedges leads to **St Michael and All Angels Church**, whose crowning glory is its richly carved oak roof, divided into 700 square panels, and reputedly the handiwork of the monks at Muchelney Abbey. Look hard enough and you'll spot, among other things, a greyhound, an eel, a devil with a pig's snout, and two cider barrels, one in full relief, the other in half relief; somewhat easier to identify are the several pairs of dragons – the symbol of Somerset – at each spandrel. To save you from straining too much, use the mirrored trolley available in the aisle. While much of the rest of the church pales in comparison, the splendid Jacobean altar table provides close competition to the roof. Heading towards the bottom of West Street, near the railway track (Somerton's station closed in 1962), are the Grade II-listed **Hext Almshouses**, a row of Elizabethan terraced cottages built in 1626.

FOOD & DRINK

The White Hart Market Pl, TA11 7LX ☏ 01458 272273 ⌖ whitehartsomerton.com. One of the town's few surviving coaching inns, the popular and stylish White Hart has been trading since the 16th century. Its cheery bar, frequented by locals (always a good sign that) manifests all kinds of mismatched furnishings – a suede banquette here, an old trunk there – beyond which is the thoughtfully designed restaurant fronted by an open-plan kitchen. The food is imaginative though not especially cheap, but if you're counting the pennies, wood-fired pizzas are also in the offing.

6 LYTES CARY

Charlton Mackrell TA11 7HU ☏ 01458 224471 ⊙ Mar–Oct, daily; National Trust

Five miles southeast of Somerton, Lytes Cary is invariably overlooked in favour of the more celebrated stately homes in this part of Somerset – in particular Montacute and Barrington Court. Yet it is as lovely as any of those and, unlike many National Trust properties, actually feels lived in (though it no longer is). Originally built for William le Lyte in 1286, the house developed piecemeal over the centuries before its completion in the 16th century, by which time it had become home to the medieval herbalist Henry Lytes. With financial pressures mounting, the family relinquished their interest in the manor in 1755. Thereafter it lay more or less derelict, until the intervention of Sir Walter Jenner and his wife Flora, who bought the property in 1907 and promptly set about reviving its fortunes.

The centrepiece of the two-storey house is the 15th-century Great Hall, a slight misnomer for what is actually a rather modest room, but one that sports a fine collar-beam ceiling. Also kept here is the house's single most important item, a first edition of Lytes's *Nieuwe Herball*; a hefty tome on the history of herbs and plants, published in 1578, it is an updated translation of a Flemish title by Rembert Dodoens. Here and elsewhere, the splendid Jacobean wood-panelled rooms are crammed with ceramics, paintings and tapestries, and Jenner's copious knick-knacks. The west wing of the house has been given over to rented accommodation, so if you fancy living like a lord for a night or two, and assuming you can stump up the not insignificant funds required, it's all yours. The gardens were conceived by Jenner but heavily influenced by the style and colour schemes devised by the prolific garden designer Gertrude Jekyll, who also had a major hand in the development of Hestercombe Gardens and Barrington Court.

ⓘ FOOD & DRINK

The Red Lion North St, Babcary TA11 7ED ℘ 01458 223220 ⌂ redlionbabcary.co.uk. A pretty pub in a pretty village, just five miles from Lytes Cary, the thatched Lion is up there with the White Hart in Somerton (page 187) and the Halfway House in Pitney (page 122) as one of the most satisfying hostelries in the area. Although very much a drinker's pub, the food is top-notch (Cornish mussels in cider, salt beef fritters) and, in summer, there's also a wood-burning stove in 'The Den', which opens up to a flower-filled garden, a perfect spot to kick back with a pint of cold, crisp cider on a warm day.

7 FLEET AIR ARM MUSEUM

RNAS Yeovilton, Ilchester BA22 8HT ℘ 01935 840565 ⌂ fleetairarm.com ⊙ Apr–Oct, daily; Nov–Mar, Wed–Sun & bank holidays

I must confess to a personal interest here, for it was some years ago (quite a few in fact) that I undertook a couple of weeks' work experience at the Fleet Air Arm Museum. Moreover, RNAS Yeovilton, home of the Fleet Air Arm Museum, is also where my father was stationed for eight years while serving in the Royal Navy.

The museum is much changed since I was first here, but overall does a brilliant job of retelling the history of naval aviation, from the earliest pioneering aviators like Samuel Cody, whose remarkable man-lifting kite you'll find in Hall 1, and Francis McClean, who, among his many deeds, flew a biplane along the course of the Nile, and on another occasion flew a Short Brothers plane through Tower Bridge in London – a replica of which is on display here. Among the many other magnificent aircraft on show is a Sea Fury, a de Havilland Sea Vampire Mk1, and a Sea Harrier which flew to the Falklands in 1982 as part of the British military Task Force. There are plenty of aircraft you can clamber aboard, including a Wessex Sea King helicopter, and – the highlight for many – Concorde 002, the first British prototype to be flown (001 was the

French equivalent), though you'll be surprised at just how cramped it is. There are reminders, too, of the vital role that the Royal Navy has played in search and rescue operations; here is the Sea King pressed into action during the 2004 Boscastle floods and the 1979 Fastnet disaster off the Irish coast, which claimed the lives of 15 men, including three rescuers. Static aircraft aside, there's loads of interactive stuff including a simulated Phantom fighter preparing for takeoff, though the replica HMS *Ark Royal* experience, while cleverly done, now feels a little dated.

Of greater interest to me was the exhibition on the Falklands War, in large part because my father saw action in this conflict; among the many sobering exhibits are land missiles, wreckage of a McDonnell Douglas, and a nose cone and ejection seat from an Argentine Skyhawk. Somewhat randomly, there's a chunk of the Berlin Wall here too. If you can navigate the (admittedly very good) souvenir shop without your wallet taking too much of a bashing, more power to you. Once through there, take to the Swordfish Café (or at least bring a picnic) and let the kids loose in the superbly designed play area. Yeovilton's big day out though is **Air Day** in July when the Royal Navy's finest take to the skies; there are good savings to be made if purchasing tickets early.

YEOVIL & AROUND

If Yeovil itself has little to commend it, you don't have to go far to find some wonderful Slow adventures, and in particular south Somerset's glorious hamstone villages: Montacute, dominated by its magnificent Elizabethan house, Stoke-sub-Hamdon and Martock, among them. All of these were built using the distinctive stone quarried at nearby Ham Hill, itself a wonderful spot for walks, one of which I have described here. Also close by are the understated but very lovely Tintinhull Gardens.

8 YEOVIL

🏠 **Little Barwick House** (page 236)

I won't even try and pretend that Yeovil, by some distance the largest town in south Somerset, is an appealing place, because it's not really. But it's where I grew up, and still have family, so perhaps I should cut it some slack. In actual fact, Yeovil has long been an important centre of industry, thanks mainly to Leonardo's (formerly and better known as Westland's), Britain's largest helicopter manufacturers – thus you'll likely see lots of sky-bound activity hereabouts. Established in the 1950s, and the town's biggest employers by far, the Italian-owned company produces helicopters for military and commercial markets all over the globe.

"Yeovil was a major centre of the gloving industry hence the football team's nickname 'The Glovers'."

Yeovil was also a major centre of the gloving industry during the late 18th and early 19th centuries – hence the football team's nickname 'The Glovers'; Pittards, established in 1826, remains one of the country's foremost leather manufacturers; in 2015 it even managed to buy back its original, purpose-built tannery on Sherborne Road to the east of town. In truth though, there's little in Yeovil to detain you, but it does make a useful base if you're intending to spend any length of time exploring the many nearby attractions, such as Ham Hill, Montacute, Stoke-sub-Hamdon and Tintinhull. If you do happen to find yourself in town, pop your head into the 14th-century **Church of the St John the Baptist**. An imposing limestone edifice with dressed hamstone, it's a particularly fine example of the Perpendicular style; it's also known as the 'Lantern of the West' owing to the prolific number, and size, of windows present – though the stained glass itself is far from being of vintage persuasion.

To be fair, Yeovil does have some pedigree when it comes to its railways – there are two stations here – so for the steam buffs among you, it's worth calling in at **Yeovil Junction**, two miles south of town in Stoford. Here, at the **railway centre** (✆ 01935 410420 ⌨ yeovilrailway. freeservers.com) there's a fully working turntable, engine shed and workshop, and a visitor centre housed inside an old transfer shed built in 1864 for the Great Western Railway. Best, though, to come on a steam train day (selected dates), when a mainline steam (occasionally diesel) train and miniature railway run, among many other fun activities. Buses run every 30 minutes (Mon–Sat) from the town bus station to the Junction.

9   TINTINHULL GARDEN

Farm St, Tintinhull BA22 8PZ ✆ 01458 224471 ☉ Apr–Sep, daily; National Trust

Set around a handsome 17th-century Grade I-listed house, Tintinhull was designed by Phyllis Reiss following her move to the property in 1933, before it was passed over to the National Trust in 1961. What is perhaps less well known is that Penelope Hobhouse, the renowned garden historian, lived and worked here between 1980 and 1993.

Much smaller and more intimate than most, the gardens comprise a sequence of compartments, or 'rooms', partitioned from each other by a wall or a hedge. All in all, it's a delightful synthesis of perfectly clipped lawns, well-tended flowerbeds and soothing pools; there's also an abundant kitchen garden, an orchard and a woodland walk. Any of the seven gardens make for an ideal reading spot, so you'd do well to bring a book, perhaps a flask of tea too, and take your time.

Originally a farmhouse owned by the Napper family, **Tintinhull House** passed through the hands of several different families in quick succession. A modest, two-storeyed construction of hamstone ashlar, it is best viewed from the western forecourt, aka Eagle Court, itself presaged by a pair of square piers surmounted by two ferocious-looking stone-carved eagles, but otherwise enclosed by high red-brick walls. Sadly though, it's no longer possible to venture inside because, like an increasing number of National Trust properties, it's now used as a holiday let.

10 MONTACUTE HOUSE

Montacute TA15 6XP ✆ 01935 823289; National Trust

Dominating this diminutive hamstone village, where the golden glow of the buildings somehow always seems more lustrous than elsewhere, is Montacute House, one of England's great Elizabethan Renaissance masterpieces. Completed in 1601 by Edward Phelips, erstwhile Speaker of the House of Commons and one of the prosecuting lawyers in the trial of Guy Fawkes, the house remained within the same family until 1915, before it was briefly owned by Lord Curzon, former Viceroy of India, and then Ernest Cook, grandson of the travel entrepreneur Thomas. Unsurprisingly, it has served as the backdrop to many a television and film production: *Sense and Sensibility*, *The Libertine* and *Wolf Hall* to name but three.

Visits to the house are self-guided, allowing you to wander freely and at your own pace. Each room (within the house) has its own special detail. The Great Hall boasts a wonderful plasterwork frieze entitled *The Skimmington Ride* – a form of public shaming in medieval times, in the scene here an adulterous husband is carried aloft a pole (a skimmington) while being mocked by a group of villagers; look out too for another scene depicting a man being chastised by his wife for drinking as he minds the baby. The library has its vibrant stained-glass windows and intricate wood-carved bookcases, and the Crimson Bedroom boasts an ostentatious four-poster oak bed.

Above all, the house is known for its collection of portraits, which cover almost every conceivable bit of wall space. There are more than a hundred paintings alone in the top-floor Long Gallery (at 170ft the longest of its type in the country), run in conjunction with the National Portrait Gallery in London. Although many of these paintings – overwhelmingly royal subjects such as Queen Elizabeth I and Henry VIII – are by unknown artists, this doesn't diminish their appeal. There are fabulous views from here too; of the sweeping West Drive on one side, and of the perfectly manicured lawns of East Court, which fronts the house, on the other.

As an overall ensemble, the formal gardens are as neat and as lovely as anything you'll come across: south of East Court, the silky-smooth Cedar Lawn is bordered by some wonderful wibbly-wobbly hedges, while the other side is consumed by the North Garden, where gravelled walkways converge on a central fountain. A circuit of this garden will eventually bring you to a glasshouse orangery bursting with lush ferns, just as it would have done under the Victorians, who had a peculiar obsession with this group of plants.

11 HAM HILL COUNTRY PARK

Ringed by three miles of defensive ramparts, Ham Hill, or Hamdon Hill to give it its proper title, has been a source of building stone ever since quarrying began here in Roman times. By the early 19th century there were 24 quarries here employing some 200 men working a landscape that would have been run through with cranes and tramways. Although commercial quarrying still takes place today, it's much scaled down, with just two companies presently operating. Centuries of workings have left a distinctive landscape pockmarked with hilly mounds and dips, one that has made it such a popular recreational spot. I used to love coming here as a child and to this day it remains one of my favourite walking spots. There are a couple of geology trails you can do (pick up the leaflet outside the Ranger's Centre by the car park), which incorporate the park's key sights, including the Millennium Stone Circle and the Time Stones (both modern constructs), a limekiln

HAMSTONE

Throughout south Somerset you'll find entire villages hewn from the soft, golden-coloured stone quarried at Ham Hill, including them Montacute, Martock, South Petherton, Stoke-sub-Hamdon and Norton-sub-Hamdon – in many ways it's what makes this whole area so distinctive. Moreover, hundreds of other buildings, including a good number of manor houses and church towers, across Somerset – and indeed neighbouring Dorset – bear some sort of hamstone embellishment, typically a dressing around the doors or in the window tracery; the stone's decorative nature also makes it suitable for use on pillars, memorials and monuments.

Geologically speaking, hamstone is a medium- to coarse-grained limestone composed of crushed-up fragments of shells and crystals; having sunk to the sea floor, it slowly mixed with sand and clay before eventually drying out and hardening. Its wonderful, honey-gold hue, meanwhile, is largely the result of iron compounds present within the rock.

furnace, and the War Memorial, but if you fancy a more challenging and wide-ranging walk, then have a go at the one I've outlined in the box on page 194.

¶ FOOD & DRINK

Prince of Wales Ham Hill, Stoke-sub-Hamdon, TA14 6RW ✆ 01935 822848
⬦ princeofwaleshamhill.co.uk. Retire to the warmth (or indeed the outside terrace) of this convivial walker-, welly- and dog-friendly pub located in the heart of the park and soak up the glorious, elevated views of the surrounding countryside. On summer Sundays there's live music, a pizza oven and bar outside. And if you fancy a dawn walk, it's open for breakfast from 09.00.

12 STOKE-SUB-HAMDON

Nestling at the foot of Ham Hill, it's little surprise that Stoke-sub-Hamdon (literally Stoke under Ham) rates as one of Somerset's classic hamstone villages. Its one sight of note is **Stoke-sub-Hamdon Priory** (✆ 01935 823289 ☉ Apr–Oct, 14.00–17.00 Sun & Mon; National Trust), as low-key a National Trust property as you could imagine – hence it receives barely a handful of visitors on those days it is open. Indeed it's quite easy to miss it altogether (not least because of the absence of any signage), which is a surprise, because once inside, the grounds are quite extensive. Granted, it's looking a little dishevelled these days, but I liked it and there are few such places still in existence. The term priory is somewhat

Ham Hill

✳ OS Explorer Map 129; start: car park at Ham Hill; ♀ ST476170; 2½ miles; an easy to moderate walk along well-defined paths, & across fields & meadows

This is a wonderfully varied walk that begins with glorious views across the Somerset countryside before dipping down into woods and a picturesque valley that was formerly the site of a medieval hamlet. The second half of the walk looks down over Montacute village, before more woods beckon and then finally an easy stroll across some meadows. For the most part it's fairly flat walking, with just the occasional, mildly strenuous ascent. It can get quite muddy underfoot in winter.

1 From the **Ranger's Office**, turn right towards the road and a viewing point offering glorious vistas of Norton-sub-Hamdon below, with the Blackdown Hills and Somerset Levels in the distance. Continue along the road, ignoring the narrow road that veers off to the right (signposted Norton-sub-Hamdon) and instead take the track some 164yds further along (signposted Norton-sub-Hamdon and Little Norton; marked Monarch's Way); the track then bears left along an undulating ridge. After about 300yds the path splits – here, take the flatter, right path (still Monarch's Way) and continue, with barbed-wire fencing on your left. About 100yds after passing a gate on your left, the Monarch's Way bears right but you should continue straight for just over 200yds until reaching another split in the path; one bears immediately left, while another dips down a little before then also bearing left – take this latter one. Follow this wooded track, with the woods on your right, until you reach a gate some 400yds further on.

2 Go through the gate (you should now be able to see the open valley to your left) and descend a narrow, tunnel-like track with overhanging trees and ferns, and chunky boulders underfoot. At the bottom, take a sharp left through the gate into **Witcombe Valley**, a picturesque, flat-bottomed hollow with sheep-speckled slopes rising gently from the valley floor. You'll pass a series of hummocks that denote the site of a former **medieval hamlet**, believed to have last been populated in the mid 16th century, alongside a sequence of recently restored streams and tear-shaped ponds; previously below ground, these now provide habitats for local wildlife. As you start to walk uphill, look back down the valley for fabulous views.

3 At the gate at the top (aim for the row of trees to the right of Batemoor Farm), cross the road and turn left into Hollow Lane. Go through the metal farm gate and walk along the fenced-in path

misleading, because it was in fact set up as a chantry college by the Beauchamp family in 1304 to serve the requirements of four local priests and a provost – the nearby chapel in which they served has

– which runs parallel to Hollow Lane just below on your right – 100yds further on, go through the wooden gate and take a sharp left, following the grassy path with the fence on your left. As the path snakes around the ridge, pause for a moment and take in the wonderful views over Forester's Gully and Montacute House; continue through more gates as the path descends to the field.

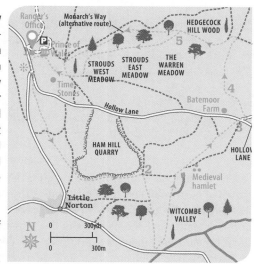

4 Walk through the lower part of the field, with the wall on your right, towards **Hedgecock Hill Wood** (roughly 200yds distant). At the gate, take a sharp left, go over the sty, and walk up through the woods; the field is now on your left. Nearing the top, the path splits, at which point there are two possibilities: either take the right-hand path and continue through the woods (along the Monarch's Way) for some half a mile before eventually emerging into the park; or, and this is the more appealing option, take the track bearing left; reaching the gate you emerge into an open meadow packed with wildflowers in summer.

5 Walk across this first meadow (The Warren), with the fence and woods on your right, towards the dry-stone wall and a gate that denotes the second meadow (Strouds East); walk through Strouds East until you reach a section of partially demolished wall and a third meadow (Strouds West). At the end of this meadow, go through the gate on your right and you're back in the park. Take a quick look at the collection of stone sculptures known as the **Time Stones** before working your way round to the Prince of Wales pub (page 193) for a well-earned pint and yet more superb views.

long since gone. The chantry, meanwhile, was abolished in 1548 and the buildings sold, thereafter remaining in private hands until the Trust took over in 1961.

DRINK UP THY ZIDER

As well as your big guns like Thatchers, there are a host of smaller producers doing great things in the world of cider, many of them based in south Somerset. One worth seeking out is **Ham Hill Cider** (⟁ hamhillcider.co.uk), based at North Down Farm near Haselbury Plucknett. Run by four local lads, Ham Hill's half-a-dozen varieties – including Early Drop, Long Barrel (sparkling), and the fruity (and rather brilliantly titled) Bop Drop, all around 6% ABV – are made from 100% fresh pressed cider apples grown in their own orchards. Visitors are always welcome to pop along (though it might be wise to give them a call first as they all have other jobs), especially during picking season (early autumn) when extra pairs of hands are always welcome – who knows, you may even get a sample or two out of it.

With most of the outbuildings (including the stables and a magnificent thatched barn) well and truly off-limits – though the dovecote is about to be restored – there's little to see save for the crumbling main hall and two featureless rooms upstairs in the main building; one was the bedroom and the other, I was told, a chapel. Like the Treasurer's House in Martock (see opposite), the remainder of the building is tenanted. Still, it's nice to nose around for a while and enjoy the solitude.

13 MARTOCK

Just off the A303 and larger than most villages hereabouts, attractive Martock was, alongside Yeovil, at the heart of the local glove-making trade (the area once counted 38 glovers), though sadly the industry became unsustainable, limping on until 2016 when the last of the factories, Burfield & Co, finally closed its doors.

At the heart of the village stands the imposing 13th-century **All Saints' Church**, the second largest in the county. Entering the vast, six-bay nave, your eyes will immediately be drawn upwards to the magnificent, carved oak ceiling (aka Angel Roof), dating from 1513 and one of the finest anywhere, and not just in Somerset. In terms of standout smaller detail, look no further than the niche paintings above the arches; depicting the 12 apostles, these are remarkably vivid given their age (17th century). Like many other churches, All Saints' suffered at the hands of Cromwell and his Parliamentarian troops, who sought to destroy the heraldic glass in the clerestory, among other elements. Curiously, the church tower – as fine as any in Somerset –

was moved from its central crossing to its present position owing to reasons of safety.

The perfect foil to the church, the **Treasurer's House** (℘ 01935 825015 ☉ Apr–Oct, 14.00–17.00 Sun & Mon; National Trust) across the road was originally built as a parsonage before its purchase by the Treasurer of Wells Cathedral – hence its name. Now a National Trust property, it makes for a fascinating, if short, visit. One of the oldest occupied dwellings in Somerset, the house was constructed in three distinct stages: first up was the manor house itself, dating from the mid 13th century, though only one

"The Treasurer's House was originally built as a parsonage before its purchase by the Treasurer of Wells Cathedral."

room, the Treasurer's private solar block, is viewable – the remainder of the house is now tenanted. Above the window is the house's most prized aspect, a largely effaced 13th-century wall painting depicting the Crucifixion, illustrating Christ and either side of him St Mary and St John – given its age, and the fact that it should have been painted in a domestic house at all, this renders it a quite remarkable specimen.

Next was the Great Hall, built later that century at a right angle to the house, hence its unusual T shape; save for a smattering of furniture it's otherwise bare, but does still retain its original ceiling timber frames. After the last treasurer left, it was variously used as a schoolroom and a cooper's workshop. The third and final appendage was the kitchen, added some time in the 15th century, its only feature of note a wide and low hamstone fireplace.

Just up the road from the Treasurer's House, the 18th-century **Market House** has variously functioned as a site for the village stocks, a market shelter and fire engine house, though today it houses the local information centre.

FROM EAST LAMBROOK TO ILMINSTER

This last little corner of south Somerset boasts a wonderfully disparate range of things to see and do, with pretty much something for everyone. The gardens at East Lambrook Manor are possibly my favourite, though you'll likely enjoy a visit to the unique Somerset Cider Brandy Company just as much. If you can manage to prise yourself away from there, then pop along to the nearby Dennis Chinaworks, a fabulous little setup with a perky café and walled kitchen garden. Finally, there's Ilminster with its imposing minster church, and Barrington Court, home to more stunning Jekyll-inspired gardens.

14 EAST LAMBROOK MANOR GARDENS

Silver St, East Lambrook TA13 5HH ✆ 01460 240328 ✎ eastlambrook.com ◷ Feb–Oct, Tue–Sat, plus Sun in Feb, May, Jun & Jul

Of all the many gardens I visited during the course of writing this book, I'd venture to suggest that East Lambrook Manor Gardens were the most satisfying. Not that they are necessarily the biggest (in fact, they were probably the smallest), or indeed the best, but rather there is just something wonderfully endearing about them; one thing is for sure, there is little attempt at contrived formality here.

East Lambrook's renown spreads far beyond Somerset, for this is a cottage garden *par excellence*, and for that it has to thank the influential gardener, and gardening writer, **Margery Fish** (1888–1969) who moved to East Lambrook in 1937 with her husband Walter Fish, one-time editor of the *Daily Mail*. Not that it was all plain sailing for Fish, whose desire for simple garden plants was severely at odds with her husband's preference for tidy lawns and formal beds; Fish once commented 'Walter would not tolerate any unhealthy or badly grown plant. Often I would go out and find a row of sick looking plants lined up like a row of dead rats'. It was only upon his death in 1947 that Fish was able to fashion the gardens in the manner she'd always craved.

> *"East Lambrook's renown spreads far beyond Somerset, for this is a cottage garden par excellence."*

There's seemingly very little order to the gardens, with ambling paths snaking between beds and borders, and plants of every description jostling for space. In true cottage-garden style, there is an emphasis on perennials: columbines, lungwort, hellebores, geraniums and primroses were especially beloved of Fish. Elsewhere, native styles and exotics rub shoulders with herbs, bulbs, shrubs, grasses and ferns; in late winter the snowdrops here are a real joy. The only concession to any kind of structure are some pollarded willows and neatly clipped shrubs.

The gardens went to rack and ruin in the two decades following Fish's death, but through a succession of owners were slowly revived.

The current custodians, Mike and Gail Werkmeister, took up residence at East Lambrook in 2008, upping sticks from London in search of a somewhat slower pace of life, though by his own admission Mike knew very little about the world of gardening. They've certainly done a wonderful job, yet there's no doubt that East Lambrook continues to reflect the indelible spirit of its creator. At the heart of the gardens stands a grand Elizabethan manor, now accommodating an upstairs gallery and the downstairs Malthouse Café, so once you've had a good nose around, treat yourself to a cuppa and a slice of homemade cake.

15 SOMERSET CIDER BRANDY COMPANY

Burrow Hill B&B (page 236)

Pass Vale Farm, Burrow Hill TA12 6BU 🔖 01460 240782 🖉 somersetciderbrandy.com
🕘 09.00–17.00 Mon–Sat

The country's only apple distillery, the Somerset Cider Brandy Company has been pressing cider in some form or other here at Burrow Hill for the best part of 200 years. But it was only in 1989, some three centuries after it was outlawed by William of Orange (the first written records of cider brandy date back to 1678), that the production of cider brandy was resurrected, thanks to Julian Temperley. However, cider brandy only received protected status – more specifically Protected Geographical Indication (PGI) – in 2011, meaning that at least one stage of production processing or preparation must take place in one particular area. This places cider brandy alongside the likes of Dorset Blue Vinney cheese and the Cornish pasty, esteemed company indeed.

An indefatigable character, on my visit Julian lent me a good two hours of his time (he's not one to rush) showing me the workings of the farm, including some massive, centuries-old wooden vats each holding around 10,000 gallons, the bonded warehouse brimful with oak sherry barrels, and the distillery itself, harbouring two beautiful copper stills (Josephine and Fifi) that Julian purchased in northern France; a third still should be *in situ* by the time you read this. The stills start working their magic at 06.00 each morning (weekdays only) and continue non-stop until 18.00, in the process converting 7% cider into 70% spirit.

Somerset Cider Brandy is bottled at three, five, ten, 15 and 20 years, though their repertoire extends far beyond this core range, for example, liqueurs (Apple Eau de Vie), a couple of aperitifs (Kingston Black and Pomona, which I loved owing to their sweetness), a delicious ice cider, and a more conventional full-bodied draught cider. Visitors are free to wander the farm and orchards, covering some 180 acres and with at least 40 varieties of apples, but if you'd like a tour, which may be led by Julian, his daughter Matilda (a renowned photographer in her own right) or one of the other members of the dedicated team here, this should be arranged beforehand – and be prepared for a serious bout of tasting.

Unbeknown to Julian at the time, their ten-year-old cider brandy featured on Prince Harry and Meghan Markle's wedding dinner menu in 2018 – something he's quite rightly keen to (excuse the pun) dine out on for many more years to come. Once done, take a walk up **Burrow Hill** itself, topped with a lonesome sycamore tree and with yet more far-reaching views of the Somerset countryside.

16 DENNIS CHINAWORKS

The New Chapel, Shepton Beauchamp TA19 0JT ✐ 01460 240622 ✐ dennischinaworks.com
☺ 10.00–16.00 Tue–Sat

Located within the converted stables of a Victorian Gothic rectory in the neat little hamstone village of **Shepton Beauchamp**, Dennis Chinaworks is one of the country's leading pottery-making centres. Sally Dennis was one half of the influential design duo Foale and Tuffin, who blazed quite the fashion trail in the 1960s (Carnaby Street and all that). With her design background, it felt like a natural transition into the world of ceramics for Sally, so she went to work for the Moorcroft Pottery Studio in Stoke-on-Trent before decamping to Somerset in 1993 with her husband Richard and establishing the studio here. It's now very much a family-oriented concern, with their son Buchan on board as one of the other designers, and his wife Jess running the fabulous tea room. Richard, meanwhile, has his own little on-site publishing enterprise, producing specialist fine art books for collectors. Completing the small team here are two more decorators (Theresa and Vanessa) and the thrower, Rory.

The wares produced here are almost exclusively vases, the richly coloured decorative pieces largely the domain of Sally, whose designs – animal, floral and figurative among them – are clearly influenced by the late 19th-/early 20th-century Arts and Crafts movement, while Buchan's pieces are of a more contemporary bent; I particularly loved his striped bottles and vases. While their vases are stocked in various outlets all over the country, they've also had work commissioned for exhibitions at some of the country's most prestigious galleries and museums, including the V&A, the Courtauld Gallery and the Royal Academy of Arts.

You can always pop your head into the studio, but in any case they do have open days when you can get all messy at the wheel. There is a shop too, though the pieces don't come cheap. While you're here, take a wander around the walled garden, the results of which sustain the Pottery Kitchen.

¶¶ FOOD & DRINK

The Pottery Kitchen Shepton House, Shepton Beauchamp TA19 0JT ⌀ 07875 315218 ⌀ dennischinaworks.com ⊙ 10.00–16.00 Wed–Sat. Across the grassy courtyard from the studio is the delightful Pottery Kitchen, whose menu basically comprises whatever Jess can source from the garden at the time, so you may find yourself faced with the tricky decision of whether to plump for an asparagus, chive and cheddar tart, or a spinach, feta and pine nut filo pie, for example; and it'd be remiss to leave without sampling a piece of lemon and almond cake with crème fraîche and rhubarb compote, washed down with a mug of ground coffee.

17 BARRINGTON COURT

Barrington TA19 0NQ ⌀ 01460 241938 ⊙ Mar–Oct, daily; Nov–Feb, Fri–Mon; National Trust

Originally of 16th-century origin, Barrington Court was the first house to be acquired by the National Trust in 1907, though at that stage it was quite the mess, its buildings used as a farmhouse and cider store with animals roaming the courtyard. In 1920 it was leased to Colonel Abram Arthur Lyle, the director of Abraham Lyle & Sons, which later merged to become the famous sugar company, Tate & Lyle. Lyle proceeded to renovate the entire premises, and it went on to serve as the family home until 1991, when its last owner, Andrew Lyle, upped sticks and took most of the contents with him.

Now almost totally stripped bare, the Tudor house itself is of little interest, save for the beautiful wood-carved panelled rooms throughout, some outstanding stonemasonry, and the occasional hamstone fireplace, such as those in the master bedroom and the old kitchen. The library – similarly emptied of its contents – was used as the council chamber in the 2015 BBC drama *Wolf Hall*. The gloomy Long Gallery on the top floor is also devoid of furnishings or ornamentation, but does afford far-reaching views of the wider estate, comprising pleasure grounds, parkland and formal gardens. And it's these that make a visit here truly worthwhile, especially the trio of Gertrude Jekyll-designed **gardens** abutting the red-brick Strode House, a grand 17th-century pile that was originally the stables before being transformed into a domestic residence; the building now accommodates a tea room. Jekyll's smashingly colourful gardens here at Barrington – White, Lily, and Iris and Rose – rank among her finest work, including those at Hestercombe (page 144). Seek out, too, the abundant kitchen garden and orchards.

18 ILMINSTER

🏠 **Lord Poulett Arms** (page 236) 🏕 **Holly Farm Holidays** (page 237)

Ilminster was first mentioned in written records in the 8th century, around the same time that a Saxon church was erected here, though the town didn't really establish itself until the 13th century (which still makes it jolly old) when it was granted the right to hold a weekly market. Overall, it's an eminently likeable place with enough to detain you for a few hours, especially when combined with a visit to nearby Barrington Court (page 201).

The town's busy east–west thoroughfare, well populated with a mix of High Street and independent shops, is centred on the colonnaded **Market House**, which isn't a house at all, but rather a freestanding, solidly square structure comprising Tuscan-style pillars and piers and a very grand central supporting column (with a circular stone seat). Much like the Buttercross in Somerton (page 186), the Market House was used to sell perishable goods (cheese, butter and the like), in addition to being a popular gathering spot for locals.

Bookending the Market House is the dynamic little **Arts Centre** (⬧ themeetinghouse.org.uk) at the top end of East Street, housing a gallery, café, performance space and the tourist information office. At the opposite end, on Silver Street, is the stately looking **Minster Church of St Mary the Virgin**. Sited atop a pronounced rise, the earliest references to the Minster (as it's generally known) go as far back as the 8th century, though most of what you see today dates from the late 15th century. Of cross-plan, or cruciform, design, its interior is as fine as any church in Somerset but for me it has greater impact because of its central crossing tower – not dissimilar to that in Wells Cathedral (page 68) – which soars upwards to a fan vault with beautifully carved leaf bosses. To the left, as you face the altar, take a look in the Wadham

Chapel, so named because it holds the tomb of Sir William Wadham (d1452) and his mother – an ostentatious affair topped with a big black marble slab engraved with rare brass effigies. Here too are brass effigies of Nicholas and Dorothy Wadham, founders of the eponymous college at Oxford University. For all that though, the church's most impressive feature is the reredos behind the high altar; by no means ancient, it was sculpted from light grey Caen stone just prior to World War I, its statues – including Christ on the cross and King David with the Golden Harp – painted some time later in the 1950s; look closely (and I mean very closely) among the tracery, and you might just make out two caterpillars and two snails.

The town has an extra buzz about it at the end of May courtesy of its **literary festival** (⊘ ilminsterliteraryfestival.org), a high-class outing featuring some top-drawer speakers; in 2019, war correspondent Kate Adie and former labour MP Alan Johnson guested. When that's not on, pop into the fabulous Ilminster Bookshop on Silver Street (⊘ ciderandbooks.co.uk), which also sells wine and cider.

FOOD & DRINK

The Green House Silver St, TA13 0DH ⊘ 01460 55898 ⊝ 09.00–17.00 Mon–Sat. Secreted away inside the shop of the same name, all the food in this comfortable, cosy little establishment is gluten-free (not that you'd know it) and delicious, as is the lovingly prepared coffee. The shop itself, crammed with lots of recycled and upcycled goodies, is well worth a browse.

Lord Poulett Arms High St, Hinton St George TA17 8SE, 5½ miles southeast of Ilminster ⊘ 01460 73149 ⊘ lordpoulettarms.com. Dating from 1680, this gorgeous, thatched pub-cum-restaurant conceals a warren of interconnected bars graced by flagstone flooring, countrified furnishings and crackling log fires. This place set the benchmark for quality food and drink in this part of Somerset a long time ago, and it continues to excel; cider-battered fish and chips, stilton soufflé with cider cream, and herb-roasted Exmoor venison are the sort of scrummy dishes you can expect.

The Trading Post Farm Shop Lopenhead TA13 5JH, 4 miles east of Ilminster ⊘ 01460 241666 ⊘ tradingpostfarmshop.co.uk ⊝ 08.30–18.00 Mon–Sat, 10.00–14.00 Sun. As excellent as the shop is, the best reason to come to this quirky little venue, located just off the A303 on the site of what was once a petrol station, is the Railway Carriage Café, a late 19th-century model that makes for a novel eating spot, as does the double-decker bus on the other side. Food is mostly organic, with produce harvested in the neighbouring kitchen garden – the beetroot and goat's cheese burger is an absolute banger.

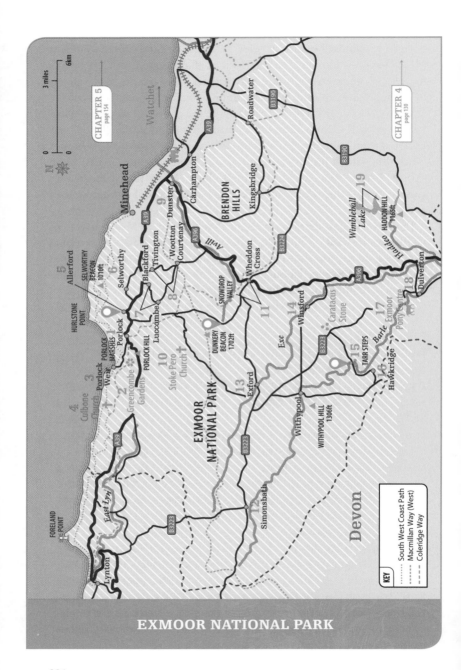

EXMOOR NATIONAL PARK

KEY
········· South West Coast Path
–––––– Macmillan Way (West)
– – – Coleridge Way

N

0   3 miles
0   6km

Devon

7
EXMOOR NATIONAL PARK

Much of the text in this chapter is reprinted, with permission, from *Slow Travel Exmoor National Park* by Hilary Bradt, with additional material by the author.

Designated a National Park in 1954, enchanting Exmoor is for many the real highlight of a visit to Somerset. It's a soft landscape of rounded hills, splashed yellow from gorse, and purple in late summer when the heather blooms, and of deep wooded valleys. It has its coast, too, adding pebble coves and sea views to its repertoire, along with the many rivers that race to the sea from the high ground, slicing into the soft sandstone; the Exmoor coast boasts the tallest sea cliffs anywhere in England. This coastal strip is by far the most touristed part of Exmoor, particularly the winsome coastal village of **Porlock**, though the nearby weir and marshes are just as worthy.

The lozenge of glorious countryside between Porlock, Minehead, the A39 and the sea offers an infinite choice of woodland trails and quiet lanes taking you through arguably the prettiest villages of Exmoor: **Luccombe**, **Allerford** and **Selworthy**, three National Trust villages that are quintessentially rural England with their thatched cottages strung along narrow lanes. There's medieval **Dunster**, too, dominated by its castle – one of just three in Somerset – though this is by far the grandest.

But, for me, it's inland Exmoor that truly excels: high heather- and bracken-clad moorland and the patchwork green fields of the lowlands. On a sunny day it's sublime, in rain it can be utterly bleak, though at least driving is easier on the high, open-view lanes. The rivers Exe and Barle, and their many tributaries, break up the 'billowy heath' in southern Exmoor with deep wooded valleys giving walkers and mountain bikers that perfect combination of high moor and sheltered combes. This consistently seductive landscape is dotted with a multiplicity of comely little villages – **Exford**, **Winsford** and **Hawkridge** among them – that offer plenty of opportunities for replenishment and respite.

There's a wonderful variety of **wildlife** too; red deer – Britain's largest native mammal – have existed here since prehistoric times and Exmoor is now one of the last remaining indigenous populations in the country. For many, the real highlight is seeing **Exmoor ponies**, which roam freely across open moorland. Elsewhere, you can seek out otters, bats and owls alongside all manner of rare bird and butterfly species. With so much of the park managed by the National Trust, clear signposting makes walking – of which there are endless possibilities – a real pleasure, though the landscape is totally geared up for a whole panoply of adventurous pursuits, organised or otherwise: cycling and mountain biking, horse- and pony riding, and even stargazing, Exmoor being a designated International Dark Sky Reserve.

GETTING THERE & AROUND

Exmoor is not the easiest destination to get to – in fact, there really is no other way than Slow. The main road route from the south is the A396 from Tiverton, which slices its way up the Exe Valley to Wheddon Cross and from there to Dunster and Minehead (the last of these is covered in *Chapter 5*). The only other main road is the A39, which runs roughly parallel to the coast, bypassing Dunster en route to Porlock before continuing to Lynton in Devon.

TRAINS & BUSES

There's not an awful lot by way of public transport, either to or within Exmoor. Unsurprisingly the park is poorly served by **rail**, the only possibility of accessing the park via train (on the Somerset side at least) being the West Somerset Railway (page 139); even then, the only station within Exmoor itself is Dunster. **Buses** are similarly thin on the ground, especially since the suspension of the Exmoor Coastal Bus and Moor Rover services in recent years. There are now less than a handful of routes servicing the park: bus 398 links Tiverton (in south Devon) with Dulverton, which is also serviced by bus 25 (from Taunton), while Dunster is served by bus 28 (also from Taunton). Marginally more useful is the 198 between Dulverton and Minehead, calling in at Winsford, Exford, Wheddon Cross and Dunster (two or three a day Mon–Sat).

WALKING & CYCLING

Walkers, of course, are spoiled for choice on Exmoor, with coastal walks and inland trails of every description. I have described three

ℹ TOURIST INFORMATION

Dulverton National Park Centre 7–9 Fore St, TA22 9EX ✆ 01398 323841
🖱 visit-exmoor.co.uk
Dunster National Park Centre Dunster Steep, TA24 6SE ✆ 01643 821835
🖱 visit-exmoor.co.uk
Porlock The Old School, West End, High St, TA24 8QD ✆ 01643 863150 🖱 porlock.co.uk

lengthy outings in this chapter: the first takes you up to Hurlstone Point overlooking the Bristol Channel and then along to Selworthy Beacon before a descent into Selworthy village; the second is a circular of Dunkery Beacon, the highest point in Somerset; and the last is a lovely walk through the Barle Valley via Withypool. But there are of course dozens more possibilities. These include several long-distance footpaths, not least the **South West Coast Path**, 35 miles of which traverse Exmoor (it starts in Minehead); the **Macmillan Way West**, which begins in Castle Cary and enters Exmoor at Withycombe before continuing to Barnstaple in north Devon; and a section of the **Coleridge Way**, originating in the Quantocks and passing through Porlock on the way to Lynmouth.

If you are planning on doing some extensive walking, then it's worth making the most of the best seasons: spring or autumn for woodland or the coast, when the landscape is at its loveliest and the crowds have thinned out, and August or early September for the moorland heather, particularly around Dunkery Beacon and Winsford Hill. Wherever you wish to walk here, it's worth picking up the OS double-sided Explorer map OL9, though it's as unwieldy as it is useful. Cicerone's guide *The South West Coast Path* is an excellent aid if you're thinking of tackling that trail, or even just part of it. All of the park's visitor centres (see above) are well equipped with the requisite books and maps.

The largely open moorland makes **cycling** a joy too, and the park is becoming an increasingly attractive destination for mountain bikers. Elsewhere, there are some lovely villages and quiet lanes to enjoy, while stronger cyclists might consider tackling Porlock Hill. But whether you're walking or cycling, be well prepared as the weather is notoriously fickle here.

One good cycle hire outfit is **Exmoor Adventures** in Porlock Weir (✆ 07976 208279 🖱 exmooradventures.co.uk.

EXMOOR FESTIVALS

Dunster by Candlelight Festival ⊘ dunsterbycandlelight.co.uk. In early December the town is plunged into darkness save for lanterns. A fabulous sight, the procession, led by stilt-walkers, wends its way through the streets, which are banned to cars, and cafés and shops that are normally closed in the winter open for business.

Dulverton by Starlight ⊘ dulvertonbystarlight.co.uk. This Sunday festival in early December sees the town celebrate in style; the entire place is decorated, the shops stay open, there's an evening fireworks display from the church tower, and other events are held to help get people into the Christmas spirit.

Exford Show ⊘ exfordshow.com. In mid-August the village bursts into life courtesy of Exmoor ponies, equestrian events and parades of hounds. There are classes for Exmoor breeds of sheep and stands selling Exmoor crafts and produce, along with the latest in agricultural machinery. Everything, in fact, to showcase the Exmoor way of life, making it a prestigious event with local farmers.

Exmoor Dark Skies Festival ⊘ exmoor-nationalpark.gov.uk/enjoying/stargazing/dark-skies-festival. In the second half of October, this tremendously popular gathering offers a fantastic programme of both daytime and nocturnal events; stargazing aside, you can participate in dusk safaris, night-time mountain biking and wild lake swims, talks and suppers, among other things.

Exmoor Pony Festival ⊘ exmoorponyfestival.com. To celebrate Exmoor's iconic animal, this week-long festival, run by the Exmoor Pony Centre, entails a variety of events and activities all around the park, including breed shows, Land Rover safaris, walks and, of course, rides.

COASTAL EXMOOR

Coastal Exmoor throws up all manner of delights. The main centre here – and a good place to base yourself – is Porlock, an enduringly charming village which is within walking distance of Porlock Weir with its cute little harbour and pebble beach; sandwiched in between these two, Porlock Marshes is now a fascinating coastal wildlife area. Further inland, but still within striking distance of the coast, the genteel villages of Allerford and Selworthy are best visited on the thrilling walk outlined in this chapter, a walk that also embraces Hurlstone Point and Bossington Hill, both of which offer tremendous views – the former out to south Wales, the latter inland to the brooding heart of Exmoor. The jewel in this area's crown though is Dunster, one of England's prettiest villages dominated by an awesome castle.

1 PORLOCK & AROUND

Once a port, this picture-book village became separated from the Bristol Channel by a huge wedge of fertile silt in the Middle Ages. Today, Porlock, along with Lynmouth and Lynton (in Devon), is one of the three most populated parishes on Exmoor. It combines its villagey feel with wonderful rural surroundings, yet provides all the amenities that visitors need: some delightful cottages and gardens, interesting shops and good restaurants, pubs and tea shops. The poet Robert Southey loved it, writing to his brother: 'If only beauty of landscape were to influence me in choice of residence, I should at once fix on Porlock.'

The town is tightly contained along its High Street – marred only by the constant flow of traffic – where almost every business provides something desirable, whether cream teas, specialist coffee or cheeses, antiquarian books, or paintings and crafts. Set back from the main street in Vale Yard is the factory and shop of **Miles** (∅ milesteaandcoffee. com), a family firm well known for their specialist teas and coffees; here the coffee is roasted, ground, blended – and sold, together with tea, chocolate and a whole lot of other temptations. They now run occasional Roastery Tours – check the website for dates. Near the church, **The Big Cheese** (∅ thebigcheeseporlock.co.uk) has a popular café as well as a wide selection of local cheeses, preserves, chutney and cider. On the High Street towards Doverhay is something completely different: **Squire** is ostensibly a pet shop, but the place is actually crammed with antler creations and vintage entertainments; try the one-armed bandit. Art is well represented too, with several art and craft galleries including the upmarket **Churchgate Gallery** (∅ churchgategallery.co.uk), which displays the work of some 30 artists from across the country and publishes its own art books.

Akin to a witch's hat, the truncated steeple of the **Church of St Dubricius** provides a handy landmark; legend has it that the top of the steeple landed up on Culbone Church (page 213), possibly with the help of a giant, but a storm in the 1700s was probably responsible. Dedicated to St Dubricius, an obscure Welsh saint who is credited with the crowning of Alfred the Great as King of England, the church is full of interest. There are two exceptional monuments, one to Lord John Harington, who fought for Henry V at the Battle of Agincourt, providing 86 archers and 29 lancers, and another to his wife Elizabeth, with her feet on a strange, cloven-hoofed animal. The other effigy is a knight, crossed-legged to show that he fought in the Crusades, dating from the end of the 13th century. What is most striking about these monuments is the quantity and age of the graffiti scratched into the soft alabaster – nothing is sacrosanct; for example, Elizabeth's face is covered in initials. The clock at the western end of the nave possibly dates from around 1450, but the oldest object in the church is the fragment of a pre-Norman cross set in the wall of the south aisle. From the church, take a stroll up Parsons Street to the area called Hawkcombe, which brings you to some attractive old cottages; carry on and you'll come to Hawkcombe Woods Nature Reserve. Here the path follows Hawkcombe Water up to Hawkcombe Head, which is open moorland with plenty of walking opportunities.

A WALK AROUND PORLOCK MARSHES

Norm Longley

One of the coast's more fascinating natural wonders is Porlock Marshes, which was created as recently as 1996 when the tail-end of Hurricane Lili smashed a hole in the shingle ridge allowing seawater to flood the land. A decision was made to let nature take its course, hence the remarkable, and constantly evolving, salt marsh environment we see today. The best way to appreciate the marshes is on a **circular walk** which, apart from the not inconsiderable shingle ridge, is all flat. From Porlock, head north along Sparkhayes Lane and when you reach the marshes, turn left (signposted Porlock Weir), at which point you are now on the South West Coast Path. Immediately to your left is a memorial commemorating the 11 men who lost their lives when the US Air Force bomber *Liberator* came down in October 1942 after clipping the top of nearby Bossington Hill. A little further on are the empty remains of an L-shaped Decoy House that was later used as a linhay, an old farm building typically used to house cattle; surrounded by the skeletal remains of bleached trees, it's an eerily atmospheric corner of the marshes.

The path then turns right, running along the western rim of the marshes towards the beach. Upon reaching the shingle ridge you can continue left to Porlock Weir or take a right walking along the ridge, which can be fairly hard going. After 15 minutes or so, you'll come to a boardwalk heading inland – this takes you back down to Sparkhayes Lane. Continuing along the ridge, in the direction of Bossington, you'll come to a couple of World War II pillboxes, as well as an old limekiln, a reminder of the time when lime was bought across the water for use on the local farms. From here you can continue to Bossington or retrace your steps back towards Porlock. Before you set out, be sure to check tide times at the visitor centre in Porlock (page 207).

The oldest secular building in Porlock is the delightful **Dovery Manor**, at the eastern end of the High Street. This small 15th-century manor is home to the local **museum** (*⊘* doverymanormuseum.org.uk ☉ May–Sep, 10.00–17.00 Mon–Fri, 10.30–16.30 Sat) and is a lovely example of the architecture of the time. Its exhibits relate mostly to Porlock and its literary connections, but there is a good display of ceramics by the highly regarded local potter, Waistel Cooper (1921–2003). Among the other curiosities

"Among the other curiosities on display is a patten, a medieval shoe designed to keep the wearer's foot out of the mud."

on display is a patten, a medieval shoe designed to keep the wearer's foot out of the mud, which was found in a chimney where it had been placed to ward off witchcraft. The museum also has a small physic garden. Admission is free, but its trustees rely entirely on donations.

2 GREENCOMBE GARDENS

West Porlock TA24 8NU *⊘* 01643 862363 *⊘* greencombe.org ☉ Apr–Jul, 14.00–18.00 daily

Hidden off the road between Porlock and West Porlock, on a steep hillside with an uninterrupted view of the sea, Greencombe is about as close to a secret garden as you can get. This was the life's work of Joan Loraine, who died in 2016, and everything you see in the garden today is there because of her vision and dedication. It is now managed with the same enthusiasm by her nephew Rob Schmidt and his wife Kim. Mossy paths wind through flowering shrubs and dark trees, with surprises around every corner.

The garden's steep slope is used to maximise enjoyment of the planting. Overhead are oaks, conifers, sweet chestnuts and hollies – one holly is said to be the largest and oldest in the country. Among the ferns below are camellias and azaleas, roses and clematis, hydrangeas and rhododendrons. Greencombe also has the country's best collection of erythroniums (part of the lily family). The hillside is quite dry, Porlock being sheltered from westerly winds by Exmoor's hills, so more than 25 tons of home-produced compost and leaf mould are needed each year to keep the soil in good condition. Ruthless pruning is needed throughout the year to stop the garden becoming a jungle. Before leaving, don't miss the chapel at the far end of the garden; a simple wooden shelter protects the most beautiful woodcarving – almost life size – of a mother and child.

3 PORLOCK WEIR

🏠 Locanda on the Weir (page 237)

The sea left Porlock's working harbour high and dry back in the Middle Ages, but at neighbouring Porlock Weir the shingle bar protected a tidal inlet and kept the harbour open – as it has been now for at least 1,000 years. In the 18th and 19th centuries, Porlock Weir was a busy little port for coasters carrying timber across to south Wales and returning with coal. There was also an oyster fleet, and these delicacies are once again being farmed here (see box, below); yachts, too, come and go from its sheltered marina while fishing boats bring in their catch. The row of thatched cottages next to the harbour provides a strand of brightness between the grey expanse of shingle and the dark woods above.

PORLOCK BAY OYSTERS

Hilary Bradt

Porlock Weir, the home of Porlock Bay Oysters, was dredged for oysters in the mid 19th century, with medieval fish ponds used as holding pools and the new railway at Minehead transporting the bivalves speedily to London. Overfishing (from outside raiders) put paid to the trade until 2012 when the parish council, concerned about the lack of jobs in Porlock, set up Porlock Futures to come up with some ideas. The consensus was oyster farming. History was on their side, the extreme tides were a help, and Porlock Weir had the cleanest water in the West Country. So, how to fund it? Oysters take three years to grow to table-ready maturity so that financial gap had to be bridged. A not-for-profit Community Interest Company was set up and some money raised from grants, but the real breakthrough came through the generosity and enthusiasm of local people. The organisers wrote to 800 households asking for a loan of up to £1,000, interest-free if they wished. £157,000 was raised in this way and Porlock Bay Oysters became a reality through the generosity of the local community.

Harvesting oysters is a complicated business though: a specialist seed company in Guernsey provide the baby oysters, which are then transferred to a nursery site in Bantham on the River Avon where the water is warmer and not as clean, allowing them to thrive. When they reach restaurant size they come to Porlock to be 'finished' in the clean water for two months – the medieval fish traps once again serving as oyster beds – before spending their last few days in special tanks where UV light kills off all bacteria, a process called depuration.

You will find Porlock Bay Oysters (🖫 porlockbayoysters.co.uk) all over the South West, and you won't do better in quality. Retailing for around £2–3 each, they have achieved top A-grade rating. Try 'em, you won't regret it.

Facing the harbour is a variety of places to eat including the **Harbour Gallery and Café** ($\oslash$ harbourgalleryandcafe.co.uk) which combines homemade cakes, good coffee, ceramics and paintings and the excellent **Ziangs** (page 214). A few paces further along, a little maritime **museum** ($\odot$ 10.00–17.00 daily) displays some interesting old photos and relics, and next door is **Exmoor Glass** ($\oslash$ exmoorglass.co.uk), where you can browse a selection of stained-glass objects and sometimes watch demonstrations of glass-blowing. Finally, the village has a large car park, with toilets and a small **natural history centre** ($\odot$ May–Sep, 13.30–17.00 Wed & Thu) at one end.

4 Culbone Church

Dwarfed by silent hills, diminutive Culbone Church (officially St Beuno's Church) is said to be the smallest in the country still in regular use. One thing is for sure: it is utterly enchanting. The only caveat is that access is on foot via the coastal path, a 2½-mile walk uphill from Porlock Weir – still, it's a lovely tramp through oak and beech forests with frequent glimpses of the sea and welcome benches. These woods

"Diminutive Culbone Church is said to be the smallest in the country still in regular use."

were one of the favourite haunts of Samuel Taylor Coleridge, who revelled in the local wildlife and views of Wales across the water. He stayed in a farmhouse nearby where he had his opium-induced vision of a 'stately pleasure dome', which became the unfinished poem *Kubla Khan*, interrupted by the arrival of a person from Porlock.

The name Culbone is a corruption of Kil Beun, or Church of St Beuno (pronounced Bayno), a Welsh missionary saint. Inside, there's no room for anything except the pews (the interior seats 33 at a pinch), including a box pew for the Lovelace family, a tiny harmonium squeezed into a corner, spattered with candle wax, and the Norman font, so roughly carved that the marks of the stonemason's chisel are still visible. One of the oldest features is the twin window on the north side of the chancel, which may be a thousand years old, with a strange face carved above it that looks more like a cat than a man. Beyond it is a window where the decorative tracery that holds in the glass is made from wood, not stone. And between the two is a 'leper squint' – a tiny window at eye level that supposedly allowed the lepers who had been banished to the surrounding woodland to get a glimpse of a church service.

¶¶ FOOD & DRINK

Lapsewood High St, Porlock TA24 8PU ℘ 01643 862288 ☺ 18.00–21.00 Tue–Sat. Porlock's most exciting dining option, Lapsewood is a small and unpretentious establishment with a menu packed with fantastic meaty treats, such as rump steak (from the local Devon red cattle) and venison casserole.

Piggy in the Middle 2 High St, Porlock TA24 8PS ℘ 01643 862647 ☺ 17.00–21.00 Tue–Sun. There's one very good reason to venture to this homely café-cum-restaurant and that's the homemade pies (steak, barbecue pork, lamb and mint), though the fish and chips aren't half bad either. Sit in or take away, though reservations are recommended in the holiday season when they may be too busy to cope with the demand.

The Ship Inn Porlock Weir TA24 8PB ℘ 01643 863288 ♂ shipinnporlockweir.co.uk. Also known as the Bottom Ship (to distinguish it from the other Ship Inn – the Top Ship – on Porlock's High St), this thatched and whitewashed harbourside inn is just the job for a reviving pint after a stroll along the pebbly beach or nearby marshes.

Whortleberry Tea Rooms High St, Porlock TA24 8PY ℘ 01643 862891 ♂ whortleberry. co.uk ☺ 09.00–16.45 Wed–Sun. You can't move for tea rooms in this part of the world, it seems, but this welcoming place is the pick of those in Porlock itself; if you want to go the whole hog, tuck into a cream tea, complete with locally produced jam – whortleberry of course.

Ziangs 6 Harbour Studios, Porlock Weir TA24 8PB ℘ 01643 863215 ♂ ziangsworkshop.com ☺ noon–22.00 Mon–Sat. Porlock isn't short of places where you can get decent fish 'n' chips, but this place beats them all hands down; even better, it serves up delicious Asian street food treats like sambal chicken rice and Malaysian curry.

5 ALLERFORD

Tiny, and very pretty, Allerford is centred on a picturesque 17th-century packhorse bridge that arches over the fast-flowing Aller Brook. Close by, the delightful **Rural Life Museum and Victorian School Room** (℘ 01643 862529 ♂ allerfordmuseum.org.uk ☺ Apr–Oct, 10.30–16.00 Tue–Fri, 13.30–16.30 Sat & Sun), housed in the old village school that ran from 1821 to 1981, has the original desks and benches, slates and textbooks, as well as a large assortment of artefacts that would have been used by our rural ancestors. Opposite is a handy car park for walkers.

Less than half a mile north of the village is the **Exmoor Owl & Hawk Centre** (West Lynch Farm, TA24 8HJ ℘ 01643 862816 ♂ exmoorfalconry.co.uk), where you can observe many different species of both owl and hawk, as well as other, more unusual birds of prey like a palm-nut vulture. In addition to the flying displays (Apr–Sep, 14.00

Wed, Thu, Sat & Sun), they offer in-depth bird-of-prey experiences, and barefoot riding. The centre also offers B&B, and serves lunches and teas.

6 SELWORTHY

🏠 **Hindon Organic Farm** (page 237)

Larger and more spread out than Allerford, Selworthy is another absurdly attractive, if overly twee, village with a spacious green and many custard-coloured thatched cottages. The village's most startling sight is the whitewashed – or rather lime-washed – **Church of All Saints**, which makes for a refreshing change to the usual grey colours that are so typical of England. Its battlemented tower, too, is quite different from others in Somerset. Before exploring inside, take in the splendid view of Dunkery Beacon. The interior is full of interest, not least three contrasting wagon roofs, the most impressive of which is the one in the south aisle with its carved angels at the bottom of each brace. Elsewhere, an hourglass by the pulpit ensures the sermons ended on time, and over the font is a rather predatory-looking wooden dove incorporated into the mechanism for raising and lowering the lid. Keep an eye out, too, for a wonderful chest, all worm-eaten wood and ancient iron, looking like something straight out of *Treasure Island*; it's thought to be over 400 years old and is now used for contributions to the church's upkeep.

Light lunches and cream teas are served in the garden of nearby **Periwinkle Cottage** (◷ 10.00–17.00 daily); the selection of cakes is terrific, as is the variety of ploughman's lunches. Above it is the **Clematis Gift Shop**, which, in addition to souvenirs, has leaflets describing various walks in Selworthy and Horner Wood.

7 LUCCOMBE & BLACKFORD

The essence of unspoiled Exmoor, **Luccombe** (not to be confused with the scatter of houses that is nearby West Luccombe) is just far enough off the beaten path to thin the influx of visitors. The one site of note in the village is the **Church of St Mary**, which is lovely both inside and out; lift the rug at the altar end of the nave to admire the 17th-century brass of William Harrison, resplendent in his ruff and gown.

An easy 20-minute walk east of Luccombe brings you to **Blackford House**, which is little more than a curious medieval **dovecote**, over 20ft high and circular in shape, with a small door to let you inside. The domed roof has an opening, an oculus, which allowed the birds to fly in

Hurlstone Point & Selworthy Beacon

Norm Longley

❋ OS Explorer Map 9; start: Allerford village car park ♀ SS904470; 5 miles; the first part of this walk is fairly steep going on the approach to Hurlstone Point, beyond which there's a tough little scramble, but thereafter it's relatively flat going

This walk takes in several outstanding viewpoints and a couple of picturesque thatched villages. Deciduous woodlands after the start soon lead to gentle grassy cliffs, then a steep, sharp haul, rewarded by the views from Hurlstone Point and Bossington Hill. The route descends gently across grassland, then more steeply down a partially wooded combe to reach Selworthy, where a road and then track leads back to the start. There is good signposting most of the way on well-defined paths and tracks.

1 Turn right out of the car park, then left after 50yds over the packhorse bridge. Follow the road uphill for 50yds then left through the gate (signposted Bossington). Bear half right and walk 150yds to a gate by the woods. Pass immediately through a second gate to enter the woods; ignore a left fork after 30yds and follow the path to the next junction. When you get to **St Agnes Fountain**, continue forward on the level path (signposted Hurlstone Point Lower Path) for 500yds to another gate.

2 Beyond the gate, at the crossroads (signposted Hurlstone Point, one mile) – you are now in **Lynch Combe**, a heavily wooded dell – go straight ahead and follow the gently rising path until it leaves the woods. The path curls around the treeline, emerging from the woods with spectacular views all round: Porlock Marshes and the coastline, south Wales, and the hills of Exmoor. Continue on up to **Hurlstone Point**, unfortunately crowned by an ugly concrete structure, but still with unbeatable views.

3 From here carry along the clifftop path, which is fairly exposed (and very windy), for more fabulous views overlooking Selworthy Sands. Shortly, the path curls around to the right and uphill slightly; continue along the path, which winds its way up the rock face via numerous switchbacks – this is the undoubted highlight of the walk, but also the toughest section. Upon reaching the summit, continue along the path you're on – narrow and stony with thick gorse all around – which runs roughly parallel to the South West Coast Path in the combe below.

4 After about 200yds the two paths meet. Continue forward, following the coast path markers. After 130yds, keep right at a T-junction of tracks and follow the coast path signs for another half a mile. Here, on **Bossington Hill**, I was fortunate enough to see a herd of Exmoor ponies, a wonderful sight set against the brooding backdrop of Dunkery Beacon in the distance. Eventually you'll reach **Selworthy Beacon** (1,010ft), a prominent cairn and the highest point

on the hill. Continue along the path from the beacon, then fork left after 250yds and follow the track downhill. Where the road comes into view just a few yards to your right, fork right on to a path leading to it.

5 Cross the road and take the track opposite, slightly to the left. After 200yds this is joined by another, wider track coming in from the left; 100yds later, turn right (signposted Selworthy). The wide track descends for a few hundred yards to the thickly wooded **Selworthy Combe** and then into Selworthy village itself. Have a peek inside the Church of All Saints (on your left; page 215) before walking down through the settlement. Take the first right near the bottom of the village (signposted Allerford), passing between barns, then follow the track between hedges. After half a mile, ignore the forest track on your right and continue down between the hedges. Continue forward at the corner of the lane, following this into Allerford and the bridge.

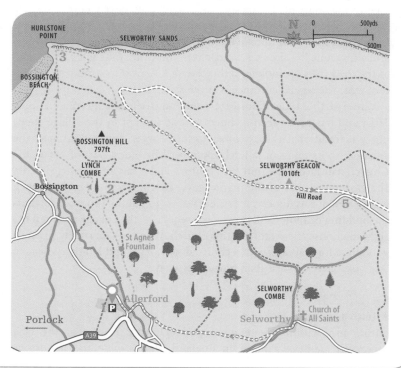

and out, and around the walls are 11 rows of nesting holes – more than 300 of them. Wealthy Normans kept domesticated pigeons to provide a luxury food, the tender meat of the young pigeons or squabs, although it was illegal for anyone except lords of the manor and parish priests to keep pigeons until the 1800s. A breeding pair produced ten to 12 young birds a year. The keeper would check the dovecote frequently and remove any squabs that were near fledging – about a month old. These birds were nearly as large as adult birds but, as their flight muscles had never been used, their meat was exceptionally tender. The dovecote can be visited at any time, free of charge.

8 TIVINGTON & WOOTTON COURTENAY

The road, or rather lane, to Wootton Courtenay from the A39 is full of interest, undulating past woodland and groups of thatched cottages. One curiosity is the unique medieval chapel of ease at **Tivington**. It adjoins the house next door, sharing a thatch, and once you've found the entrance you enter a tiny room dominated by an open fireplace. There is little else inside the simple interior save a couple of religious pictures and a tiny font, but it oozes atmosphere and history. It's not easy to find; as the road rises up, look for a thatched house next to a modern one on the right. The signed entrance is at the side.

A little further on is **Wootton Courtenay** itself, which is not National Trust and has never seen a chocolate box (except in the village shop), but is as traditional as they come. Its much larger church dominates the village with its unusual saddleback tower. The oldest part of **All Saints' Church** dates from the mid 13th century and it has an eccentric history. The Norman owner of the manor gave the church to a nearby French priory, which was dissolved by Henry VI who put the proceeds towards the building of Eton College; as a consequence, the college reserved the right to choose the rectors of this church. Wootten Courtenay makes a good base for walking, with a choice of footpaths and Dunkery Beacon (see box, page 222) less than four miles away.

9 DUNSTER

🏠 **Luttrell Arms** (page 237)

Sitting just within the national park, Dunster is one of the best-preserved medieval villages in England, with a wide and handsome main thoroughfare set against a backdrop of a splendid castle and the folly-topped mound of Conygar Wood. Moreover, the shops are tasteful, selling high-quality goods, and there are lots of quality pubs, tea shops and cafés.

It's strange to think that in the 12th century Dunster Haven was a busy port. When the shore became land during the 16th century, the town – which is around half a mile from the sea – switched its activities to the wool trade so successfully that the local cloth was known as 'Dunsters'. The octagonal **Yarn Market**, on the High Street, was built in 1609 to protect the wool traders from the Exmoor weather; it serves a similar purpose for damp tourists today.

Medieval towns like this often feel claustrophobic, but Dunster revels in open spaces and enclosed public gardens. Across one such space, the Village Garden, is the **dovecote**, which probably dates from the 14th century and still has its nest holes. It originally belonged to the priory, but after the Dissolution of the Monasteries was sold to the Luttrells (the family that lived at Dunster Castle for 18 generations).

"The octagonal Yarn Market, on the High Street, was built in 1609 to protect the wool traders from the Exmoor weather."

Near the dovecote is a lovely little garden belonging to the red sandstone **Church of St George**. First impressions are of a gloriously intricate wagon roof, some good bosses, and a font with a complicated cover. But head and shoulders above anything else here is the oak-carved rood screen stretching a full 54ft across the width of the church, which possibly makes it the longest in the country. Dating from around 1500, the screen (which would once have been painted) effectively divided the church in two, with the parish using the west chancel and the monks the east. Elsewhere, of the many tombs and effigies, it's inevitably those of the Luttrells that dominate, including an alabaster floor slab inscribed to Alys Luttrell, the last of that family to reside in the castle.

Dunster Castle
Castle Hill, TA24 6SL   01643 821314; National Trust

Spectacularly set atop the tor that dominates the town, Dunster Castle is mentioned in the Domesday Book and was home to the Luttrell family from 1405 until it was handed over to the National Trust in 1974. This unbroken span of ownership gives it a unique appeal, with features typical of each century of privileged, but usually charitable, living. The ornate plasterwork on the ceilings, the alabaster fireplaces, and the intricately carved grand-scale wooden staircase are particularly impressive, but so are the paintings and the furniture – and even the bath (installed in 1870 and one of the first cast-iron baths in England).

"Tours of the attics and kitchens give you insight into how a large house like this was run in the late 19th century."

Look too at the unique leather paintings in the Leather Room with scenes from Shakespeare's *Antony and Cleopatra*; these were done in the Netherlands in 1681 and are not to modern taste, but the technique is fascinating. Don't miss, either, the Billiards Room with its superb wall-to-wall fireplace, which was once part of the old kitchen; you can even have a bash at potting a few balls yourself on the snooker table.

Tours of the attics and kitchens (included in the price) give you added insight into how a large house like this was run in the late 19th century, through its time as a convalescent home for US soldiers in World War II to the innovations introduced for the last Luttrell, Alys, to live here, between 1920 and 1974. As you explore, remember to look at the view over the Bristol Channel from any of the eastern-facing windows: you can clearly see the distinctive islands of Steep Holm and Flat Holm, and the Welsh coast.

Buffered up against the castle, paths wind their way down through the flower-strewn South Terrace to the **River Garden**, a mixed woodland area of pine and redwood trees. Down by the River Avill is Lover's Bridge, so called because of the stone seats in the parapets, which seat two, though more impressive is the giant rhubarb flourishing by the river banks, which is at its most spectacular in summer. Beyond the gardens you'll come to the 18th-century **Dunster Watermill** (✆ 01643 821759 ⊙ 10.00–16.30 daily; entrance included with the castle), which still grinds wheat daily to produce flour for its shop and local bakeries. You can see the refurbished waterwheels (the mill is unusual in that it has a double overshot) in action periodically, and inspect a collection of agricultural implements, and there's a lovely tea room here, which makes for a nice spot to rest up by the water.

One very enjoyable way to visit Dunster Castle is to take the West Somerset Railway's Dunster Express service from Bishops Lydeard (page 139), which stops at Dunster station, whereupon you are transferred by bus to the castle; you can then make the return journey at a time of your choosing; note that the Dunster Express runs most Wednesdays and Saturdays between the beginning of April and the end of October.

🍴 FOOD & DRINK

Cobblestones 24a High St, TA24 6SD 🖉 01643 821595 👌 cobblestonesdunster.co.uk ⊙ 11.00–15.00 daily. Meals include a Sunday lunchtime roast and cream teas in comfortable surroundings. And there's a sunny walled garden for the summer. Can get busy, therefore slow, in the holiday season.

Luttrell Arms 32–36 High St, TA24 6SG 🖉 01643 821555 👌 luttrellarms.co.uk. Centuries-old, rubble-stone-built pub whose rambling interior manifests a warren of atmospheric rooms, some with open fires in winter. Alongside a bumper selection of Exmoor ales, they've got excellent bar and restaurant menus.

Reeves Restaurant 20–22 High St, TA24 6SG 🖉 01643 821414 👌 reevesrestaurantdunster. co.uk ⊙ 19.00–22.00 Tue–Sat, noon–14.00 Sun. Indisputably the best restaurant in the area, drawing clientele from Porlock and beyond for an exceptional night out; expect inventive, sophisticated food such as slow-braised beef shin with horseradish mash and a Jack Daniel's and soy reduction.

INLAND EXMOOR

As much as I love the Exmoor coast, for me nothing beats inland Exmoor. Standing atop Dunkery Beacon and being able to see three other national parks (something that makes Exmoor unique) is a great feeling. Walking here is glorious – in fact there's nowhere else quite like it in Somerset, and to this end, I have outlined two lengthy, and quite different, rambles; the first is a circular of Dunkery Beacon which showcases this wild moorland at its finest, and another combining Tarr Steps and the Barle Valley, two of the park's most important cultural and natural heritage sites.

Inland Exmoor is also where the park's most interesting festivals take place, reflecting the park's unique attributes, such as its status as an International Dark Sky Reserve (the Dark Skies Festival; see box, page 208) and its herds of wild ponies that populate this inland area (Exmoor Pony Festival; page 208). In fact, encounters with these wonderful creatures is a highlight for many to Exmoor, though if you want to get up really close, head for the Exmoor Pony Centre, near Dulverton. Astounding natural heritage aside, there are plenty of worthwhile cultural diversions, most notably the delightful Stoke Pero Church, the Simonsbath sawmill, and the bizarre Caratacus Stone.

Dunkery Beacon circular
Norm Longley

✳ OS Explorer Map 9; start: Dunkery Bridge car park ♥ SS895405; 5 miles; this is a moderate walk with a couple of steep ascents – including Somerset's highest point – but otherwise is fairly easy going across undulating fields, combes & commons

This walk begins with an immediate ascent through open moorland to Dunkery Beacon, offering some of the most rewarding views in Exmoor. Thereafter, the landscape interchanges between thickly wooded combes and undulating fields, before the final trek across further moorland back to the start point. There's good signposting most of the way on well-defined paths and tracks.

1 Turn right out of the car park and walk along the road for 100yds. Come off the road and follow the path (signposted Dunkery Beacon, half a mile), walking slowly up towards **Dunkery Beacon** (1,702ft), marked by a pronounced cairn. This really is the top of Somerset and from here, on a clear day, you can see three other national parks (Dartmoor, Brecon Beacons and Pembrokeshire); this makes Exmoor unique in that it's the only national park from where it's possible to see more than two other national parks. After savouring the views, head down the path directly opposite the one you've just come up; from here it's a steady descent beyond a crossing of paths, before the path veers slightly right towards a wall.

2 Pass through the gap in the wall (not the gate a little to the left) and dip down into the heavily wooded **Aller Combe**. Walk for about a quarter of a mile to a stream (East Water); cross this to meet the road. Turn left and walk up the road, following it around the bend and uphill to **Cloutsham Farm**. Opposite the farm, go through the gate (signposted Permitted Way); a few paces on from here, go through another metal gate and take the left path (signposted Stoke Pero, one mile).

3 Follow the line of the fence to the top left-hand corner of the field, then proceed into a second field. Walk along the track until you come to the end of this field, which then dips down into **Prickslade Combe**; go up into the next field, which has a distinctive slant, and continue all the way to the corner of the field. Enter a fourth field, initially aiming for the tree roughly in the centre and then the wall down towards the bottom; go through the gap in the wall and about 70yds beyond here through the gate, with a sign to Stoke Pero. Go down through the dell and along the path between the wall and you'll reach a farm.

10 STOKE PERO CHURCH

Exmoor's highest church, at 1,013ft, is one of the three hereabouts that were too remote to attract a parson, according to the local ditty: 'Culbone,

4 Go through the farm and, nestled atop a small rise to your left, you'll see **Stoke Pero Church** (see opposite). Stop here for a quick look before following the road for about three-quarters of a mile to another, main road (signposted Luccombe/Exford). Cross the road and go through the metal gate; follow the fairly well-worn path crossing the slanting field on a roughly diagonal trajectory, aiming for the five big gnarly trees on your left. Beyond here is Bagley Ford; cross this and take an immediate right through the gate (signposted Bridleway). With the fence on your left, walk up through **Bagley Combe** to the gate at the top.

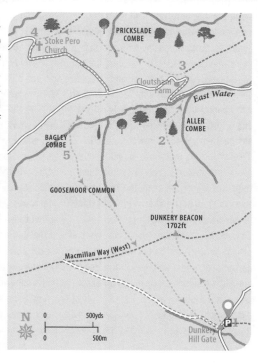

5 Emerging on to the wide open space of **Goosemoor Common**, cross the tiny brook and stay to the right of the small copse of trees, though there's no obvious path here. Follow the wide, mossy track (such as it is) before arriving at a slightly sunken trail. Cross this and keep going, following the sparse line of trees. After about 200yds, just after a tree, a bridleway crosses at a diagonal – take this (left) path uphill. Soon, Dunkery Beacon hoves back into view away to your left. Continue straight ahead at the next two crossings (the second is the Macmillan Way), and as you descend, you'll see the car park from whence you started.

Oare and Stoke Pero, Parishes three where no parson'll go.' Stoke Pero made do with a curate for much of its history. Not a lot remains of the original church; it was completely rebuilt by Sir Thomas Acland in 1897,

EXMOOR INTERNATIONAL DARK SKY RESERVE

In 2011 Exmoor was designated Europe's first **International Dark Sky Reserve**, being 'a public or private land possessing an exceptional or distinguished quality of starry nights and nocturnal environment that is specifically protected for its scientific, natural, educational, cultural, heritage and/or public enjoyment'. What makes this accolade even more impressive is that Exmoor is currently one of just three in the UK (the other two are the Brecon Beacons in Wales and Moore's Reserve on the South Downs) and 12 in the world. But it didn't come easy, requiring a combined effort between the two county councils (Somerset and Devon) and Exmoor landowners to reduce light pollution.

Although stargazing is a year-round activity, winter months offer greater absolute darkness and less chance of atmospheric humidity, resulting in clearer night skies – optimum conditions would be a hard frost, a clear night and no moon. On a clear night, it's possible to see as many as 3,000 stars in a Dark Sky Reserve with the naked eye, as opposed to fewer than 200 in an urban environment – quite the contrast.

Good Dark Sky viewing locations include Dunkery Beacon, Haddon Hill and Wimbleball Lake, but if you fancy a serious bout of stargazing, one outfit worth contacting is **West Withy Farm** (✆ 01398 371322 ⬥ exmoor-cottages. com), which has on-site telescopes for hire and whose owner (and keen astronomer), Seb, runs tours. Otherwise, you can hire high-magnification telescopes from the park's visitor centres (page 207). However you watch, and wherever you are, it goes without saying that you need to be prepared – the moorland can get darn chilly of an evening, and the weather is prone to sudden changes. So that means wrapping up warm and arming yourself with some hot drinks.

A great time to visit is during the **Exmoor Dark Skies Festival** in October; see box, page 208 for more information.

with the help of Zulu the donkey who made the journey from Porlock twice a day carrying the timbers for the roof. It's a most appealing and delightful little place, set companionably next to some farm buildings. The interior is plain (though there's an attractive barrel roof with carved floral-design bosses), candles the only lighting, and a little harmonium the only source of music. And there's a framed drawing of Zulu the donkey on the wall. You can visit the church as part of the walk outlined in the box on page 222.

11 WHEDDON CROSS & SNOWDROP VALLEY

Although there's very little to **Wheddon Cross**, the highest village in Exmoor, it's a friendly place that gained importance as a major crossroads

– so a natural travellers' rest. There's a well-used village hall, Moorland Hall, which hosts fundraising groups during the snowdrop season, when it becomes the Snowdrop Café, and an excellent supermarket/ petrol station. You can buy everything consumable here, including Porlock oysters (see box, page 212).

The village comes into its own every February when nearby North Hawkwell Wood is carpeted with snowdrops. **Snowdrop Valley** is owned by the Badgworthy Land Company and is an ESA (Environmentally Sensitive Area). From Wheddon Cross, it's a gentle 45-minute circular walk alongside the River Avill, which used to drive a sawmill, and the remains of a weir can still be seen. During the snowdrop season the narrow road leading to the valley is closed to traffic so visitors must walk there along a choice of two woodland routes or take the Park and Ride bus that runs from the Wheddon Cross car park (next to the Rest and Be Thankful Inn). A map of the walks is available from the national park visitor centre. Since February is the wettest month, be prepared for deep, glutinous mud. The area is anyway predisposed to snowdrops, and you'll see bursts of them beside the road as you drive to Wheddon Cross. Make a day of it and have a meal in the village.

12 SIMONSBATH

Despite its history of being the place where James Boevey enclosed a hundred acres of moorland for the first Exmoor farm, Simonsbath (pronounced Simmonsbath) is a relatively modern settlement that grew up at the crossroads of two tracks. That said, it's an odd place, in the sense that you could drive through it without even realising that you had. It's now popular as a walking base and for the annual **Simonsbath Festival** (simonsbathfestival.org.uk), which runs for six weeks each year in May and June and offers a daily programme of events varying from walks and music to readings by local authors.

Once a month, the water-powered **Simonsbath sawmill** is open to the public (usually the third Mon but check ✆ 01392 860895 simonsbathsawmill.org.uk). I was lucky enough to pitch up on one such day and was promptly treated to an enlightening tour of the premises, complete with the original circular saw and bandsaw. Although no longer in regular operational use – until 2010 it prepared the timber for the park's signs, gates, fence posts and so on – it is in decent working order and gets cranked into action for demonstration purposes. A fascinating – and rare – piece of industrial archaeological heritage, this 19th-century sawmill once provided power for an entire estate; here too there would also have been a carpenter's workshop, mortar mill and granary. The water wheel remains, as does the water turbine, which operated until 1952 when a diesel engine was installed, and it's this that mostly powers the saw benches today. Once you've taken a look around the sawmill, head down to the nearby River Barle, which makes for a lovely stroll. Simonsbath is also where the River Exe rises, before continuing its long journey south into Devon and onwards to the English Channel.

¶¶ FOOD & DRINK

Exmoor Forest Inn Simonsbath TA24 7SH ℘ 01643 831341 ◌ exmoorforestinn.co.uk
◌ 11.00–22.00 daily; closed Mon in winter. After a stroll along the River Barle, rest up a while here at this cosy inn with a pint from their terrific range of cask ales (Clearwater, Exmoor and Otter) and keg beers against the backdrop of all sorts of hunting paraphernalia – antlers, trophies, horse tack and the like. Children, dogs and wellies all very welcome.

13 EXFORD

🏠 **White Horse Inn** (page 237) 🏡 **Court Farm** (page 237)
⛺ **Westermill Farm** (page 237)

The Exe, a mere stream at Simonsbath, has gathered strength from two tributaries and is a proper river by the time it reaches Exford, giving the village much of its charm. It is seriously picturesque with its huge village green and 15th-century White Horse Inn dripping with Virginia creeper, and is quite a bustling village with a post office, a good range of shops and a few tea rooms. Exford is also the home of Exmoor's **blueberry farm**, **Sharcott Farm**, which offers pick-your-own **blueberries** in August and September (◌ exmoorblueberries.co.uk). It's at its liveliest, though, in mid-August when the **Exford Show** rolls into town (see box, page 208).

¶¶ FOOD & DRINK

Exford Bridge Tea Room Chapel St, TA24 7PY ℘ 01643 831304 ◌ 09.00–18.00 daily. The name is misleading – this excellent place serves breakfast and light lunches as well as yummy cream teas. It's licensed, so you can enjoy a beer or cider with your meal, whether that's sitting by a snug fire in the winter or out in the garden in the summer.
White Horse Inn Exford TA24 7PY ℘ 01643 831229 ◌ exmoor-whitehorse.co.uk. Popular with the hunting fraternity, this fine creeper-clad pub overlooking the River Exe offers superb

ales and filling meals in its warming lounge bar, as well as more upscale fare in the restaurant, including an indulgent five-course dinner. Log fires in cold weather and, they claim, the finest single malt whisky collection in the South West. Rooms available (page 237).

14 WINSFORD

Huddled beneath the rising moors, Winsford is yet another pretty Exmoor village, known chiefly for its eight bridges; it certainly needs them because not only the Exe but also the Winn flows through the village – go and see if you can find them all. The other thing you can't fail to notice here is the handsome, heavily thatched Royal Oak, a venerable inn of several centuries' standing; next door you'll find a general store and post office. Away from the triangular central green, the 14th-century **Church of St Mary Magdalene**, set above the village, is primarily of interest for its medieval stained-glass window, which occupies just one section in the otherwise clear glass eastern window; it shows a feisty boy Jesus dressed in yellow trousers, sitting astride Mary's shoulder, thrusting a bunch of flowers towards her. It's a vigorous and charming portrayal that needs binoculars or a zoom lens to be seen properly.

¶¶ FOOD & DRINK

The Royal Oak Halse Ln, TA24 7JE ✆ 01643 851455 🖥 royaloakexmoor.co.uk. Once a 12th-century farmhouse and dairy, the Oak retains its charm courtesy of big fires, comfy chairs and restful décor. There are several dining areas serving a menu of classic, and very reasonably priced, pub fare as well as food of a more sophisticated bent, for example pork loin steak with caramelised cider sauce and gratin potato.

15 TARR STEPS

🏠 **Tarr Farm Inn** (page 237)

The most famous antiquity in Exmoor, Tarr Steps is a beautifully preserved clapper bridge over the River Barle. Some say it's over a thousand years old but it's more likely to date from the 13th century – either way, the feat of building it out of giant slabs of stone, which were brought in from a considerable distance, is remarkable. Some slabs – there are 17 of them – are over 6ft long and weigh more than a ton. Despite their size, they are periodically washed away after heavy rain swells the river; all have been numbered so that the bridge can be reassembled correctly. Be cautious about sunbathing on the stones, however – that's the Devil's prerogative. Legend has it that he built the bridge,

Tarr Steps & the Barle Valley

Norm Longley

✳ OS Explorer Map 9; start: Tarr Steps Car Park, ♀ SS872323; 8½ miles; a reasonable amount of endurance is required for this walk, simply by virtue of its length, which is otherwise fairly flat with just the odd ascent

----

From Tarr Steps, this walk leads into solitary grazing land on the west side of the Barle Valley. Skirting Withypool Hill via moorland paths, the descent to Withypool village is followed by one of Somerset's most attractive river walks. Take care with field directions (the route is partly waymarked); erosion along the river path makes for rough going underfoot in places.

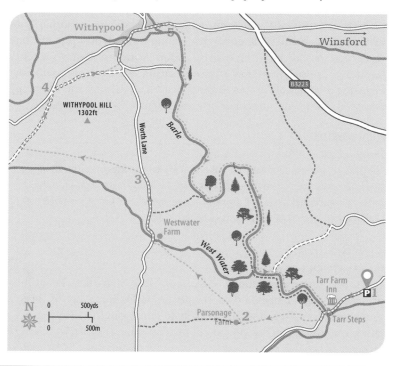

so was understandably peeved when mere mortals tried to use it. The locals asked the vicar to help; he prudently sent a cat across first to test the waters, so to speak, but it disappeared in a puff of smoke.

1 Turn left out of the car park and walk down the path past Tarr Farm Inn to **Tarr Steps**. Pick up the road on the other side of the river and take the right fork up a rising driveway signposted Tarr Steps House. Just before the house, take the right path for 400yds; go through the gate, whereupon the now slightly sunken path bends round to the right, with a field on your left; at the end of this field turn left (still inside the same field) with a hedgerow on your right. Pass through the gate into a second field and continue on the left edge alongside the hedgerow. Proceed on the left edge of the third field.

2 Turn sharp right at the end of the field, just before **Parsonage Farm**. Proceed to the top-left edge of the fourth field and then the right edge of a fifth field to a stile beside a gate; the path proceeds with a fence on your left until you enter another field by a gate. Continue down towards the bottom edge of the field (to the right of the tree), with West Water stream and **Westwater Farm** to your right. Turn right on to Worth Lane (signposted Withypool Hill) and after half a mile cross the cattle grid by the beginning of open land.

3 At the cattle grid fork left on to moorland track with a hedgerow on your left. **Withypool Hill** is now to your right. Where the hedgerow stops, continue going straight, although by now the path is far less distinct; keep forward on the level before you eventually reach a fairly obvious intersection of tracks. Turn right here, and just as you feel as if you're not really heading anywhere in particular, you'll soon see a road – use this as your marker.

4 Just as you reach the road, turn right on a rising moorland path, which soon levels (ignore a right fork) and **Withypool** village comes into view. After about 300yds you reach the road, whereupon you should turn left and head down towards the six-arched bridge at the entrance to the village. Cross the river and continue along the main village street, past the church and the (currently defunct) Royal Oak Inn. At the end of the village the road ascends.

5 After about 200yds, cross the stile on the right signed as the riverside path to Tarr Steps; from here it's an obvious route all the way back, following the **River Barle** closely – a distance of about four miles. That said, the path – which rises and dips – is not always defined and there are one or two sections where erosion has occurred and you have to pick your own way, which may include the occasional scramble over a tree trunk or two. Suitably exhausted, treat yourself to a drink and a bite to eat in the fabulous Tarr Farm Inn (page 230).

Undaunted, the reverend himself set out and after a heated argument the Devil agreed to let people use the bridge. Except when he wants to sunbathe.

On a hill some 300yds northeast of Tarr Steps, there's a large car park, though there is disabled parking down near the Tarr Farm Inn (see below), just a few paces away from the steps themselves. Tarr Steps is perfect for a family picnic, though it can get very crowded in the summer. Children and dogs love paddling in the river here, and there are several deep pools where you can get fully immersed if you wish. There's an easy circular walk up one side of the river and back the other side, and a longer, more varied one described in the box on page 228.

FOOD & DRINK

Tarr Farm Inn Tarr Steps TA22 9PY 𝒫 01643 851507 ⌂ tarrfarm.co.uk. A splendid inn serving outstanding food in an unbeatable location over the River Barle. What more could you want? Its large garden is ideal for a relaxed lunch or cream tea after a long walk, while it's more formal in the evenings for the à la carte menu. Or you can just kick back in the sociable bar. The steak here, from Red Ruby cattle raised and slaughtered on their own farm, is something else, while their menu is accompanied by a choice of over 100 different wines. Rooms available (page 237).

16 HAWKRIDGE

Hawkridge is one of those tiny, high (nearly 1,000ft) and isolated communities that still exist in Exmoor. It has a population of around 40 and there are just ten houses in the village, but the community spirit is strongly evident in the **Hawkridge Revel and Gymkhana** which has been run on the August bank holiday for nearly 75 years. They get up to all sorts of things – a dog show, mounted games, fancy dress – and stalls selling various goodies including plants 'which will probably survive anywhere in the UK'.

The village's squat **church** seems to be hunkered down against the elements, but overlooks a glorious view of the moors. Inside, the visitors' book is full of thanks from tired walkers for keeping the church open (Hawkridge lies on the Two Moors Way). There's a Norman font, but the most notable feature is the stone coffin lid, which was found in the wall behind the pulpit in 1877. It has inscriptions in Norman French and Latin, and was probably for William de Plessy, Lord of the Manor, who died in 1274. If you're planning to drive to Tarr Steps from Hawkridge, be warned: the river can be too deep for an ordinary saloon car to cross the ford, and there is no parking on the west side of the river. However, it's a lovely

"The community spirit is strongly evident in the Hawkridge Revel and Gymkhana."

walk down there from Hawkridge, and you can make it a circular walk by taking the Two Moors Way there and coming back via the lane.

17 EXMOOR PONY CENTRE

Ashwick, Dulverton TA22 9QE ✐ 01398 323093 ⚮ exmoorponycentre.org.uk ◔ mid-Feb–Oct, 10.00–16.00 Mon, Wed–Fri & Sun

About four miles west of Dulverton is the hamlet of Ashwick and the Exmoor Pony Centre, home of the Moorland Mousie Trust (named after one of the most popular pony books of all time, published in 1929). This charity was set up to give the surplus foals from moorland-bred herds a future by training them to be useful family ponies, so lovers of this distinctive native breed get a chance to meet them face to face and perhaps 'adopt' a pony to help with its upkeep. There's an informative display about the trust in the Green Room. There are various riding possibilities, from taster sessions for those with little or no experience to two- or three-hour treks on Exmoor for more competent riders; in all cases, book well in advance. They also run their own festival in August (see box, page 208).

18 DULVERTON

A busy little place, Dulverton seems to have everything going for it: lovely surroundings, plenty to see and do, yet avoiding any suggestion of being a tourist hotspot. The town's attractions include a 17th-century bridge over the River Barle, a variety of independent shops, some good restaurants, and the excellent Heritage Centre. Shops include the greengrocer H&M (1 Fore St), with a colourful display of all manner of fruit and vegetables, and a farm shop opposite the Bridge Inn, which sells fresh produce and snacks. Art lovers old and young, or anyone searching for quality crafts, should take a look at **Number Seven** (7 High St ✐ 01398 324457 ⚮ numbersevendulverton.co.uk ◔ Tue–Sun) which, as well as its cards, books and arty items, hosts the outstanding illustrator Jackie Morris and other artists. Also not to be missed is **The Tantivy** (✐ 1398 323465 ⚮ tantivyexmoor.co.uk ◔ 06.30–17.30 daily), a super café/delicatessen and general store with a large selection of local beers and ciders, and a good range of maps and books, as well as picnic supplies, so you'll be all set to head for the moor.

Across the road, and linked to the National Park Visitor Centre, is the always worthwhile **Dulverton Heritage Centre** (✐ 01398 323818

◇ dulvertonheritagecentre.org.uk ◷ Apr–Oct, 10.30–16.30 Mon–Fri, 10.30–13.00 Sat), whose fixed and shifting exhibits offer lots of variety and surprises, like Granny Baker's Kitchen where, at the touch of a button, the good lady will chat to you about her life and times. Meanwhile, the red deer exhibit tells you everything you need to know about Exmoor's iconic animal. In a separate building, a beautifully made **model railway**, correct to the last detail, shows Dulverton as it was before the line closed; the little trains purr their way through tunnels and the familiar landscape before drawing to a halt at the station.

Like so many places in Exmoor (albeit these are mostly on the Devon side) Dulverton has its **Lorna Doone** association. The hero, John Ridd met the eponymous heroine here in the book, and there's a small statue of the young woman outside Exmoor House, presented to the town in 1990 by the Anglo-American Lorna Doone Society. It's actually of Lady Lorna Dugal 'who, in the seventeenth century, was kidnapped in childhood by the outlaw Doones of Badgworthy', so probably the inspiration for the novel. If you're in the area in early December, do try and catch the wonderful **Dulverton by Starlight Festival** (page 208).

⍩ FOOD & DRINK

The Bridge Inn 20 Bridge St, TA22 9HJ ✐ 01398 324130 ◇ thebridgeinndulverton.com. Dulverton's most appealing pub is in a wonderful location with exceptionally good food, though you really should sample one of their pies, for example the Moo and Blue (beef and stilton). It also has an impressive selection of craft beers and ciders, as well as single malt whiskies.

Tongdam Thai 26 High St, TA22 9DJ ✐ 01398 323397 ◇ tongdamthai.co.uk ◷ noon–15.00 Mon & Wed–Fri, plus 18.00–22.30 Fri & Sat. It's slightly surprising perhaps to find a Thai restaurant in rural Exmoor, but locals rate this place very highly – it's especially lovely in summer when you can dine in the courtyard overgrown with grapevine and wisteria. The menu runs the full Thai gamut, from hot and sour soups and dumplings to pad Thai noodles and red and green curries.

Woods 4 Bank Sq, TA22 9BU ✐ 01398 324007 ◇ woodsdulverton.co.uk ◷ noon–14.00 & 18.00–23.00 daily. This atmospheric restaurant really does look the part, split between an intimate little pubby area with an open log fire and barrels for tables, and the rustic-heavy restaurant itself replete with deer antlers, wood-framed prints and other knick-knacks; an enticing menu features the likes of venison pastrami with globe artichoke and truffle oil, and roast loin of Northcombe lamb with salsify and confit garlic; there's an impressive wine list too.

19 WIMBLEBALL LAKE & HADDON HILL

⚑ Wimbleball Lake (page 237), **West Withy Farm** (page 237)

Wimbleball Lake Activities Centre, TA22 9NU ✆ 01398 371257 ♐ southwestlakes.co.uk

East of Dulverton, the huge expanse of water that is **Wimbleball Lake** has been developed into a country park with all sorts of water- and land-based activities in pleasant surroundings. It's the leading centre for freshwater activities in the region, and you can learn just about any water-based sport here: kayaking, canoeing, stand-up paddleboarding, sailing and windsurfing, or, if you fancy something a little gentler, you can hire a rowing boat or dinghy. There's also a fish farm so you can try angling for trout. If you don't want to go in or near the water there's archery, climbing and high ropes. A path runs right round the lake, making an eight-mile walk, but it's probably more rewarding to combine a visit to the shore with Haddon Hill and the Haddeo River. Note that dogs must be on leads by the lake and are not allowed in the water (remember, this is a reservoir).

Above the lake, networked with paths and beloved of dog walkers, is the gorse- and heather-covered **Haddon Hill** with splendid views over the reservoir and beyond. Haddon Hill has its own car park off the B3190 near the southern end of the lake; from here you can take a gentle uphill walk to the trig point at Hadborough, 1,165ft above sea level, for the view, returning along a different but parallel path. Exmoor ponies can usually be seen on Haddon Hill doing their job of keeping the heathland under control.

UPDATES WEBSITE

You can post your comments and recommendations, and read the latest feedback and updates from other readers online at ♐ bradtupdates.com/somerset.

ACCOMMODATION

Somerset has a wonderfully varied stock of accommodation, from warming, welcoming guesthouses and country inns, to remote campsites tucked away in the wilds of Exmoor. Apart from Bath, and a few spots along the coast, decent hotels are few and far between, though these tend to be overpriced anyway. Far more appealing are the plentiful and very homely B&Bs and guesthouses scattered throughout the county. To these you can add rural pubs and inns, which provide an attractive alternative overnight stay, with, in most cases, the happy prospect of a scrumptious meal to sustain you. If you're looking for a longer stay in a particular area, then you might wish to consider self-catering – try the following websites: ⌂ visitsomerset.co.uk/places-to-stay/self-catering, ⌂ thebestofexmoor.co.uk/stay-in-west-somerset and ⌂ holidaycottages. co.uk/cottages/somerset.

1 BATH & AROUND

Hotels

Bath Priory Weston Rd, Bath BA1 2XT ✆ 01225 331922 ⌂ thebathpriory.co.uk. If you fancy a little splurge, then the Georgian Priory should be your first port of call; luxurious, well-appointed rooms complemented by first-rate spa facilities.

B&Bs & guesthouses

Bistro Lotte 25 Catherine St, Frome BA11 1DB ✆ 01373 300646 ⌂ bistrolottefrome.co.uk. Above the superb restaurant of the same name, Lotte possesses half a dozen quietly stylish rooms painted in gentle pastel tones and with big rainforest showers.

Maplestone Hall Shepton Mallet BA4 5NP ✆ 01749 938356 ⌂ maplestonehall.co.uk. Nestled within its own walled garden, this one-time weaver's cottage boasts three spacious rooms with state-of-the-art amenities and garden views.

Pulteney House 14 Pulteney Rd, Bath BA2 4HA ✆ 01225 460991 ⌂ pulteneyhotel.co.uk. Classy, central Bath guesthouse offering an attractive mix of singles, doubles and family rooms; there's also a warming lounge and colourful gardens for guests to enjoy.

Camping

Greenacres Barrow Ln, North Wootton, nr Shepton Mallet BA4 4HL ✆ 01749 890497 ⌂ greenacres-camping.co.uk. Essentially one gigantic field, with 40 pitches spread around three sides of the perimeter, and a vast central swathe of green reserved for various activities, including the occasional mass football match. Perfect for young families.

2 WELLS & THE MENDIPS

Hotels

Oak House Hotel The Square, Axbridge BS26
2AP ✆ 01934 732444 ⌂ theoakhousesomerset.
com. Accomplished hotel/restaurant with
smartly decorated rooms, some of which
overlook the lovely main square.

B&Bs & guesthouses

Stoberry House Stoberry Park, Wells BA5 3LD
✆ 01749 672906 ⌂ stoberryhouse.co.uk. Five
sumptuously furnished rooms in an enviable spot
just a stone's throw from the cathedral; a sitting
room and a well-stocked pantry round things off
beautifully. Picnic hampers available upon request.

Camping

Petruth Paddocks Labourham Drove,
Cheddar BS27 3XW ✆ 07813 320870
⌂ petruthpaddocks.co.uk. Choose from the
Chillout Field or the Family Field, then kick back
and enjoy; best of all, campfires are allowed. Bell
tents and shepherd's huts available too.
Wookey Farm Campsite Monks Ford, Wookey
BA5 1DT ✆ 01749 671859 ⌂ wookeyfarm.
com. Easy-going, informally run campsite with
compost loos (no showers), campfires and swing
ropes, plus a super little honesty shop.

3 GLASTONBURY & THE SOMERSET LEVELS

B&Bs & guesthouses

Double Gate Farm Godney BA5 1RZ ✆ 01458
832217 ⌂ doublegatefarm.com. Traditional,
and very welcoming farmhouse with a selection
of cosy rooms (some river facing), a communal
lounge and a cracking breakfast.
Magdalene House Magdalene St,
Glastonbury BA6 9EJ ✆ 01458 830202
⌂ magdalenehouseglastonbury.com. Occupying
a former convent, this handsome Grade II-listed
building opposite the abbey has three beautiful,
light-filled rooms. No children under seven.

The Parsonage Muchelney TA10 0DL ✆ 01458
259058 ⌂ theparsonagesomerset.co.uk. The
three delightful rooms here are each named after
the views they afford. Guests are free to avail
themselves of the dining room and library.

Self-catering

Middlewick Holiday Cottages Wick Ln,
nr Glastonbury BA6 8JW ✆ 01458 832531
⌂ middlewickholidaycottages.co.uk. Large,
well-maintained complex of a dozen cottages,
some with wood burners, in addition to
glamping cabins and a shepherd's hut.

Camping

Thorney Lakes Caravan and Camping
Muchelney TA10 0DW ✆ 01458 250811
⌂ thorneylakes.co.uk. Pitch up wherever
you like and enjoy the freedom that this vast
campsite affords. Solar-powered showers and a
wood-pellet boiler are just a couple of its eco-
friendly features.

4 FROM THE QUANTOCK HILLS TO THE BLACKDOWN HILLS

B&Bs

The Old Cider House 25 Castle St,
Nether Stowey TA5 1LN ✆ 01278 732228
⌂ theoldciderhouse.co.uk. Sweet little four-
roomed guesthouse that's hugely popular with
walkers and cyclists, possibly because it has its
own micro-brewery.
Parsonage Farm Over Stowey TA5 1HA
✆ 01278 733237 ⌂ parsonagefarm.uk. A
traditional 17th-century farmhouse is the setting
for three cosy rooms overlooking an orchard and
walled kitchen garden.

Self-catering

The Old House St Mary's St, Nether Stowey
TA5 1LJ ✆ 01278 732392 ⌂ theoldhouse-
quantocks.co.uk. These three sweet cottages, set
within several acres of beautiful gardens, offer

the perfect retreat following a day striding out on the Quantocks. They've also got a couple of B&B rooms.

Camping

Hunstile Organic Goathurst, nr Bridgwater TA5 2DQ ☎ 01278 662358 ⌂ huntstileorganicfarm. co.uk. The couple of dozen pitches here are located in a separate field just down from the farmhouse, but you're more or less welcome to hunker down anywhere. They've also got a gypsy caravan, complete with dinky log burner and double bed, and a gorgeous, sky-blue-painted shepherd's hut trailer sleeping four.

5 THE COAST

Hotel

The Old Ship Aground Quay St, Minehead TA24 5UL ☎ 01643 703516 ⌂ theoldshipaground. com. Lovely harbourside hotel and restaurant close to the start of the South West Coast Path, and therefore a good place to break the hike. Decent food, too.

B&B

Church House 27 Kewstoke Rd, Weston-super-Mare BS22 9YD ☎ 01934 633185 ⌂ churchhousekewstoke.co.uk. A handsome old Georgian rectory that's now a welcoming guesthouse with five sparkling rooms named after islands in the Bristol Channel. Lovely sea views from most.

Self-catering

Railway Cottage Williton ☎ 01984 656622 ⌂ lavenderhillholidays.co.uk. This awesome place, an old period cottage right next to the railway, sleeps six people in four bedrooms, and also has a well-equipped kitchen and a lounge with wood burner.

Camping

Minehead Camping and Caravanning Club North Hill, TA24 5LB ☎ 01643 704138

⌂ campingandcaravanningclub.co.uk. Sited high above town, this large well-equipped site is ideally located for those hiking the SWCP.

6 SOUTH SOMERSET

B&Bs, guesthouses & inns

At the Chapel High St, Bruton BA10 0AE ☎ 1749 814070 ⌂ atthechapel.co.uk. Eight light, contemporary-styled rooms are complemented by a superb breakfast, thanks to the delicious goodies fresh from the downstairs bakery.

Burrow Hill B&B Orchard View, Burrow Hill TA12 6BU ☎ 01460 240288 ⌂ burrowhillbandb. co.uk. Right next to the Somerset Cider Brandy Company (useful that), this attractive cottage has just two rooms, and quite lovely they are, with one overlooking Burrow Hill itself.

High House 73 High St, Bruton BA10 0AL ☎ 01749 813015 ⌂ highhousebruton.co.uk. Lovely Victorian townhouse harbouring two elegantly furnished rooms, each with lots of exciting homemade treats upon arrival.

Little Barwick House Rex's Ln, nr Yeovil BA22 9TD ☎ 01935 423902 ⌂ littlebarwickhouse. co.uk. Splendid Georgian dower house possessing half a dozen countrified rooms and a sublime restaurant. No children under five.

Lord Poulett Arms High St, Hinton St George TA17 8SE ☎ 01460 73149 ⌂ lordpoulettarms. com. The five differently configured rooms variously sport exposed brick, roll-top baths and antique furnishings, while the downstairs restaurant is one of the best in the area.

The White Hart Market Pl, Somerton TA11 7LX ☎ 01458 272273 ⌂ whitehartsomerton.com. Venerable coaching inn with eight rooms oozing class and lots of lovely flourishes, one of which has a four-poster bed and cast-iron bath.

Self-catering

Durslade Farmhouse Dropping Ln, Bruton BA10 0NL ☎ 01749 814700 ⌂ durdsladefarmhouse.co.uk. Situated at Hauser & Wirth (page 180), this stunning farmhouse has six bedrooms furnished in largely antique style as well as a stylish sitting room, dining room and kitchen. Upon arrival you receive tea with freshly baked scones.

Camping

Batcombe Vale Batcombe, nr Bruton BA4 6BW ☎ 01749 372373 🖱 batcombevale.co.uk. Gorgeous, sheltered enclave offering some 30 variously sized pitches positioned on different levels, with glorious views from wherever you are. There are four small lakes – with colourful rowing boats to mess about in – from where hidden paths snake off through the valley, as well as a large grassy field for all manner of activities.

Holly Farm Holidays Peasmarsh, Ilminster TA19 0SG ☎ 07781 626117 🖱 hollyfarmholidays. co.uk. An old dairy farm offering two types of accommodation: Big Red, a former goods carriage that's been superbly converted into a comprehensively furnished abode; and a Mongolian yurt, illuminated by solar fairy lights.

7 EXMOOR NATIONAL PARK

B&Bs, guesthouses & inns

Hindon Organic Farm Nr Bratton TA24 8SH ☎ 01643 705244 🖱 hindonfarm.co.uk. This terrific 500-acre organic farm in a quiet location between Minehead and Porlock has three bedrooms and splendid home-cooked breakfasts – try Roger's homemade port sausages – with fruit from the garden.

Locanda on the Weir Porlock Weir TA24 8PB ☎ 01643 863300 🖱 locandaontheweir.co.uk. If you're not relaxing in your room enjoying the sea views, then you'll probably be in the reading room kicking back with a good novel.

Luttrell Arms 32–36 High St, Dunster TA24 6SG ☎ 01643 821555 🖱 luttrellarms.co.uk. Part of the tourist fabric of the village, this historic coaching inn has 28 rooms of considerable charm, each boasting some exquisite architectural detail or other.

Tarr Farm Inn Tarr Steps TA22 9PY ☎ 01643 851507 🖱 tarrfarm.co.uk. Superbly located just a few paces from the famous Steps, this ancient inn offers comfortable, well-furnished rooms and terrific food. No children under ten.

White Horse Inn Chapel St, Exford TA24 7PY ☎ 01643 831229 🖱 exmoor-whitehorse.co.uk. Prominent creeper-clad pub on the banks of the Exe concealing good-looking period-furnished rooms and a warm, welcoming bar that's popular with local hunters.

Self-catering

Court Farm Exford TA24 7LY ☎ 01643 831207 🖱 courtfarm.co.uk. Three well-equipped, dog-friendly cottages (with either one or two bedrooms) located in a restful spot a few minutes' walk from the village. See ad, 4th colour section.

Camping

Westermill Farm Exford TA24 7NJ ☎ 01643 831238 🖱 westermill.com. Take your pick from one of four fields picturesquely located within a lush valley, though you'd do well to try and bag one of the riverside pitches. They've also got half a dozen cottages that sleep up to eight.

West Withy Farm Upton TA4 2JH ☎ 01398 371322 🖱 exmoor-cottages.com. The place to enjoy a Dark Skies experience (see box, page 224), Ian and Lorena Mabbutt offer self-catering in their two barn conversions (one sleeping four, the other five) alongside an organic vegetable garden that produces enough, in season, for each guest to receive a veg box.

Wimbleball Lake Wimbleball TA22 9NU ☎ 01398 371460 🖱 southwestlakes.co.uk. This campsite, close to the lake and its many water activities, has three bell tents with transparent roofs so you can watch the stars in this Dark Sky Reserve. Double or twin beds, solar electricity, plus gas cookers upon request. Also two pods sleeping four, with bunk beds or a double bed, though these do not have cooking facilities.

INDEX

Entries in **bold** refer to major entries; those in *italic* refer to maps.

INDEX OF ADVERTISERS

THE BISHOP'S PALACE & GARDENS

800 years of history, 14 acres of gardens and the wells that give the city its name.

Home to the Bishops of Bath and Wells for over 800 years, this stunning medieval palace is surrounded by 14 acres of outstanding RHS Partner gardens, with diverse planting styles, a children's play area and a café with the best view in Wells.

The Bishop's Palace,
Market Place, Wells
Somerset, BA5 2PD

⊘ **www.bishopspalace.org.uk**
✎ 01749 988 111
✉ info@bishopspalace.org.uk

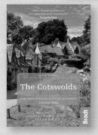
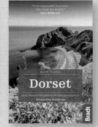
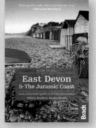
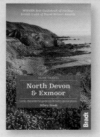
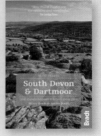